THE FORGOTTEN
TRAIL TO APPOMATTOX
Hidden Civil War Sites and Destinations
Across America

RANDY DENMON

Guilford, Connecticut

An imprint of The Rowman & Littlefield Publishing Group, Inc.
4501 Forbes Blvd., Ste. 200
Lanham, MD 20706
www.rowman.com

Distributed by NATIONAL BOOK NETWORK

British Library Cataloguing in Publication Information Available

Library of Congress Cataloging-in-Publication Data Available

ISBN 978-1-4930-3351-5 (paperback)
ISBN 978-1-4930-3352-2 (e-book)

∞™ The paper used in this publication meets the minimum requirements of American National Standard for Information Sciences—Permanence of Paper for Printed Library Materials, ANSI/NISO Z39.48-1992.

Printed in the United States of America

Contents

Introduction

When I started my hunt for the lesser-known Civil War, I wasn't exactly sure where to look. It turned out that I didn't have to dig far . . . it seemed to be everywhere I looked, the battles or important places. Most of the venues have been edged out of our collective memory by the ten or twelve battles etched in the nation's psyche that incorporate our modern history of the War.

Before I get started on this magnificent sojourn back in time, the reader needs to know that I am neither an academic nor a historian, but rather a novice Civil War fan. I stumbled and bumbled my way along. When discovering more than thirty Civil War sites, I certainly did not have time for detailed research and checking primary sources. I tend to round numbers off and generalize. Many of the facts, from events a century and a half ago, are still in dispute, but I tried to paint the most accurate picture possible. If I've made a mistake here or there, I apologize.

I am a writer though, with opinions, and hence, guilty of conveying the most colorful! I hope you enjoy this odyssey as much as I did. I would like to take some space to thank all the dedicated Civil War Preservationists who have kept the War alive and guided me along. I'm going to thank them all.

Pat Mountain, Friends of Ball's Bluff Battlefield
James Morgan, Friends of Ball's Bluff Battlefield
Sharon and Larry Laboda, Bentonville Battlefield State Historic Park
Mike Bunn, Historic Blakeley State Park
Edwina Carpenter, Mississippi Final Stands Interpretive Center
Bill Backus, Bristoe Station Battlefield
Woody Harrell, Shiloh National Military Park Superintendent, retired
Ray Flowers, Fort Fisher State Historic Site

Robby Tidwell, Fort Pillow State Park
Thomas Cartwright, The Lotz House, Carter House, retired
Dennis Frye, Harpers Ferry National Historical Park
Jack Myers, Delta Cultural Center, retired
Stephen Vaughn, Kernstown Battlefield Association
Robert Krick, Richmond National Battlefield
Michael Mumaugh, Mansfield State Historic Site
Steve Mayeux, Friends of Fort DeRussy
James Madere, Plaquemine Parish, and Plaquemine Parish Historic Society
Edward Alexander, Pamplin Historical Park
Chuck Lott, Friends of Perryville Battlefield State Historic Site
Mike Fraering, Port Hudson State Historic Site
Phillip Seyfrit, Battle of Richmond Visitor Center
Chris Calkins, Sailor's Creek Battlefield State Park, Petersburg National Battlefield, retired
Daniel Smith, Monnett Battle of Westport Fund
Arnold Schofield, Fort Scott National Historic Site, retired
Eric Petitta, Old Courthouse Civil War Museum
Terence Heder, Shenandoah Valley Battlefields National Historic District
Brian Daly, Stonewall Jackson's Headquarters Museum
Ed Wenzel, Chantilly Battlefield Association
Kevin Pawlak, Shepherdstown Battlefield Preservation Association
Steven Stotelmyer, Central Maryland Heritage League
Sarah Mink, Virginia Museum of the Civil War
Thomas Frezza, Navy Yard
Thomas Schultz, DC Military Tours

CHAPTER 1

Discovery! My Journey Begins

Port Hudson, Louisiana

This journey started one beautiful spring morning when I turned off Louisiana Highway 61, rolling over the narrow asphalt that sliced up and down through the hills and dense stand of pine, oak, and magnolia. A mile ahead sat the Port Hudson State Historic Site, run by the Louisiana Department of State Parks. In the thirty-five years that I've been driving, I've probably driven by the prominent sign, and big cannon, at the park's entrance five or six hundred times, paying little attention to what lay hidden just off the modern, four-lane highway.

Recently passing the ripe old age of fifty, my Saturdays not as busy as they once were—catching up at the office, awful yard work, or just lying around on the sofa—I decided to check out the park. I knew a Civil War battle had been fought there. But what else? I recently learned, with only a few clicks of my mouse, that the Siege of Port Hudson is one of only forty-five Civil War battles that the National Park Service considers "decisive." On these grounds, Americans fought an epic, urgent, life-and-death struggle that played a major role in the America we live in today.

In recent years, the public's interest in the Civil War has soared. In the twenty-first century, visitations to Civil War sites have tripled compared to the last few decades of the twentieth century. Why? Civil War Historian Shelby Foote put it bluntly: "Any understanding of this nation has to be based, and I mean really based, on an understanding of the Civil War. I believe that firmly. It defined us . . . It was the crossroads of our being, and it was a hell of a crossroads."

It's been said that the Civil War was fought in ten thousand places. It's all around us, everywhere, especially if you live in the south or east. I can remember being entranced by the movie *Gettysburg*. I've also consumed dozens of other movies and documentaries over the years. I've been to the Gettysburg, Manassas, and Vicksburg battlefields and even written a novel about the Civil War.

What fascinates us is that the War *is* us, what we are, and it's here, around us, everywhere. Tiny, out-of-the-way places that shouldn't be known outside the county they reside in have become sacred names in the American psyche. Chancellorsville, Gettysburg, Chickamauga, Manassas, Antietam, Spotsylvania, and Shiloh were all just corrected by my spell-checker! I live in the heart of the Deep South. I'm a Confederate, like it or not, at least four generations pure.

Shouldn't I know more about Port Hudson? Maybe it's a Louisiana thing. We're one of the few Southern states that doesn't revel in our Civil War history despite the fact that we're really the only Southern state that the Yanks made a concerted effort to conquer, and failed, except for New Orleans, and we'll get around to that later. But things got tougher for Billy Yank as he moved inland.

The moral of this story is this: There is a whole lot of the Civil War out there, among us, that few people know about. Much of it is right under our noses. We frequently drive by these sacred places, paying little mind to their significance to the nation. These are places where thousands of Americans perished in just a few days, if not hours ... 9/11s or Normandy landings in scale, measured in either carnage or importance. When it comes to the cost in blood, most are significantly bigger events proportionally when you consider the United States only had just over thirty million people in 1860, compared to over three hundred million today.

Only about half of the War's major battlefields are preserved by the National Park Service. Many of the other battles, no less important, weren't so lucky in the allotment of Federal dollars. Maybe they had bad politicians or, more likely, didn't want to celebrate their defeats. Many of these *other* battlefields have been lost to time or urbanization, but many remain, preserved by states or local governments.

The bluffs of Port Hudson were first fortified in August 1862, by the Confederate general John C. Breckinridge, the Vice-President of the United States until 1861. In November of the same year, Lincoln appointed Gen. Nathaniel Banks as commander of the Federal Army of

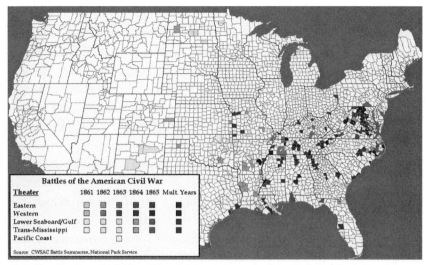

Battles of the American Civil War

Theater	1861	1862	1863	1864	1865	Mult. Years
Eastern						
Western						
Lower Seaboard/Gulf						
Trans-Mississippi						
Pacific Coast						

Source: CWSAC Battle Summaries, National Park Service

Civil War Battles, Civil War Sites Advisory Commission, National Park Service

the Gulf. Army general-in-chief Henry Halleck told Banks, "President Lincoln regards the opening of the Mississippi River as the first and most important of all our military and naval operations."

Banks, Speaker of the US House of Representatives and a former governor of Massachusetts, was a political instead of military general—and a bumbling one at that. It's no wonder it took four years to win the War. The country boys in Louisiana eventually sent Banks back where he belonged, behind a desk. More on that later.

Banks arrived in New Orleans in December with a contingent of more than thirty thousand men and moved to Baton Rouge, thirty miles south of Port Hudson. After several months of planning, Banks set out for the main Confederate stronghold on the Mississippi in Louisiana, Port Hudson, which had been harassing Yankee gunboats. He hoped to quickly subdue the river bastion, move onto Vicksburg, 130 miles to the north, and support the military general Ulysses Grant in his simultaneous siege of the other remaining obstacle to opening the Mississippi River.

Initially, Banks sent Adm. David Farragut and seven gunboats upriver in an attempt to get past the Rebel stronghold, now defended by about seven thousand rebels and under the command of Gen. Franklin Gardner, a West Pointer, skilled professional soldier, and another Yankee who decided to fight for the South. The New Yorker married the daughter of a leading Louisiana family.

Banks planned to attack the port with a fifteen-thousand-man diversionary force that would distract the Rebs. The overland assault sputtered, and the Confederate cannons sank one of the gunboats and damaged four more, forcing the Yanks to abandon the affair. This foray was a testament to the fortress perched on the precipitous banks of the river. Mr. Farragut was not a man easily dissuaded. Two years later, in Mobile Bay, he uttered the famous words: "Damn the torpedoes, full speed ahead!"

What transpired over the next few months were two massive Federal frontal attacks on Port Hudson, guarded by four and a half miles of earthworks, redoubts, and fortified artillery that failed miserably, forcing Banks to lay siege to Port Hudson.

Banks's first attempt to take Port Hudson occurred in May 1863. Supported by artillery and gunboats, his five divisions were left to attack "at the earliest moment." This led to a Federal disaster as Gardner shifted his men to meet each attack individually. When the smoke cleared, almost two thousand blue uniforms were left strewn over the battlefield to a Confederate loss of just over two hundred.

It was here, during this initial attack, that colored soldiers fought under the command of black commanders for the first time in the War. The most notable of these units was the First Louisiana Native Guards, colored troops, formed by the state of Louisiana from "free men of color," but now in the service of the Union.

A thousand of the colored soldiers charged into a well-defended gauntlet on the Federal right. The Native Guards fared no differently from the rest of the Federal forces. That is to say, they were repulsed with heavy losses, but the valiant attack garnered headlines in the North and became a rallying cry for the recruitment and utilization of colored soldiers in the Federal ranks.

Banks made a second attack two weeks later that turned out to be as big a boondoggle as the first, leading him to abandon attempts to take the stronghold by open assault. He surrounded and blockaded the fort, hoping to starve the Rebs out. With many of the Federal troops reaching the point of mutiny, the remaining 6,500 Confederates, having eaten all their mules and dogs and sustained on a diet of boiled rats, finally surrendered on July 9, 1863, and then only after General Gardner received word that Vicksburg had fallen on July 4. Hence, there was little strategic value in fighting on. The siege lasted forty-eight days. The Federal victory had been costly: ten thousand soldiers dead, wounded, or captured against only about a thousand for the Confederates.

For me, a veteran myself, analyzing the battle from afar and a century and a half later, the affair and its cost can be summed up as the consequences of pitting a novice general against a professional general.

The Port Hudson Historic Site is twelve miles north of I-110 and Baton Rouge and ten miles south of the historic town of St. Francisville, the latter the home to the highest concentration of antebellum plantation homes in Louisiana, if you're into that sort of thing.

I arrived at the historic site's museum to meet Mike Fraering, a native of New Orleans, curator of the museum, and a thirty-year veteran of the battlefield.

Mike gave me a brief history of the park that incorporates the northern half of the battlefield, obtained by the state of Louisiana in the 1960s and turned into a State Historic Site in the early 1980s.

The museum and park have a wonderful collection of artillery pieces and shells excavated onsite. Due to the nature of the siege, much of the battlefield served as the setting for a colossal artillery duel between the Federal Army's more than a hundred guns and the Confederate's fifty or so well-entrenched artillery pieces, some of the latter's forty-two-pound Navy cannons mounted on steel pivots along the river that could strafe most of the battlefield. One of these sits right outside the museum.

During the siege, some of the mighty guns and parapets gained such notoriety that the soldiers gave them names like the "The Baby," "Old Demoralizer," and "Lady Davis"! Before the launching of General Bank's second doomed offensive, the *New York Times* reported, "The most terrific cannonade commenced along the whole line that ever stunned mortal ears."

The museum also hosts one of the best collections of Civil War photographs anywhere. According to Mike, it was one of the most photographed battles of the War. General Banks, having higher political aspirations after the War, brought in a photographer to document his victory. The collection contains the only known photograph of a Confederate Army surrendering in the field.

I asked Mike, "How come Vicksburg is so well known and not Port Hudson? Why is Vicksburg a National Battlefield and not Port Hudson?"

Mike took in a deep breath. "Well, we were the last stronghold on the Mississippi, not Vicksburg. But they had General Grant. He saved the nation. We had Banks . . . and it would have probably helped if Hudson had a 'burg' or 'berg' behind it. Seems like all the famous battles were something-or-other 'burgs!'"

Mike lamented that Port Hudson had not been included in Ken Burn's wonderful and award-winning documentary, the *Civil War*. To add salt to the wound, some of the pictures shown in the documentary for the Battle of Vicksburg were actually pictures from the Siege of Port Hudson.

Mike provided me with some other facts about the park. Port Hudson is very preserved. After the War, the rugged terrain prevented the battlefield from being cleared or leveled for farming.

He also told me the little-known story that Port Hudson was once the holy grail for Civil War treasure hunters. In the twenty years between the property's acquisition by the state of Louisiana and the formation of the park, the land was public, but with no one at the site to discourage artifact collectors.

The museum has a small theater that shows a short film about the battle and siege and several neat interactive models, the best of which portrays the 1st and 3rd Louisiana Native Guards' assault on May 27.

I watched the film, inspected several of the artillery pieces around the museum, and then grabbed my backpack to set off for the park's main attraction, its six miles of trails. I soon discovered that the Port Hudson Battlefield is not a park with big vistas. There are almost no vistas. Thick stands of trees covered steep hills bisected by slithering creeks and ravines. By the end of the battle, many of the trees had been felled, either by artillery barrages or for defenses to hamper any Federal advance.

Mike Fraering, head interpretive ranger at the Port Hudson Historic Site, with one of the site's forty-two-pound cannons

Mike explained that because of the area's heavy rainfall, almost sixty inches a year, clearing the battlefield would subject the treasured earthworks to erosion, and keeping it cleared would be a never-ending battle against Mother Nature.

It didn't take long walking the park's trails to comprehend the futility of the Yanks' overland assaults. The trail went up and down, weaved here and there, through thick vegetation and over steep gullies. The battlefield looked more like an ideal setting for a Vietnam War movie than a Civil War battle. Much of it resembles a jungle. In fact, the largest group I saw at the park the day I visited consisted of a college ecology class viewing the park's flora and fauna.

It also didn't take me long to realize the trails are a rough hike, off limits to bikes, and not for free spirits in sandals or debutantes in high heels. Fortunately, I packed a bottle of water and, more importantly, insect repellent. Advice to future hikers: spray your feet. The hills are full of redbugs and ticks—and look out for snakes.

My first stop on the trail was the best-preserved earthworks in the park, Fort Desperate. The Confederate redoubt manned by Arkansas and Alabama veterans was a focal point of the battle that the Federal

9

Fort Desperate Earthworks, Port Hudson Historic Site

forces twice assaulted. It was smaller than I thought, maybe a hundred yards square. Looking over the earthworks and deep ravines, I could only imagine the carnage and mayhem that once transpired here. None of the saps, or deep trenches, dug by the Federals during the siege to approach the fort remain today.

A Confederate soldier commented after the battle that the ground around the fort was "literally covered with bluecoats." The birds chirping overhead gave no hint to the past: the ground shaking, the deafening blasts of cannon and crack of muskets, the young men of the North hurled back in a desperate fight disintegrating into a deadly back-alley brawl.

Before the battle commenced, General Gardner said, "The enemy are coming, but mark you, many a one will go to hell before he does Port Hudson." Federal general Thomas Sherman, no relation to William T., said his orders were "worse than folly." He was one of the first to fall, losing his leg to a rebel shell.

I ambled on. The steep, rugged landscape struck me the most. At one point, I spooked two deer that startled me probably more than I scared them, and all kinds of critters slithered, fluttered, and popped just off the trail. I can only imagine the fright the soldiers must have suffered almost continually, surrounded by tens of thousands of men toting loaded muskets, itchy trigger fingers at the ready.

During the June 14 assault, Col. Simon Jerrard of the 22nd Maine said, "If General Banks wants to go in there, let him go in and be damned. I won't slaughter my men that way." Later in the day when General Banks ordered a second incursion, the regimental commanders balked, deeming this a "fool" idea. Another Yankee officer said, "Our instructions were simple madness."

If you're a real traditionalist, and want to get a good sense of the battle, come on down and walk the trails on an afternoon in July. The heat may have been the biggest variable in the battle. Even today, the Louisiana heat is dangerous. Outdoor work crews often shut down in early afternoon during the temperate months. The climate was particularly tough on the Bluecoats, most from New England. Sunstroke, malaria, diarrhea, and other ailments took the lives of five thousand Federal soldiers here. I know of nowhere in the War where noncombat casualties equate to this.

It's hard to explain the Louisiana heat, and especially the humidity, to Yanks. If I had a nickel for every time I've heard somebody say how torridly hot and humid it is in Washington, DC, well, I'd have a lot of nickels. I'm a self-confessed pansy to the elements, but I've spent most of my fifty years basting in Louisiana. My day job requires that I go to DC frequently. If I go for two or three days, my lips get chapped from the relative dryness.

The soldiers' diaries constantly derided the heat. A Northern major wrote, "The heat, especially in the trenches, became almost unsupportable."

As I terminated my three-hour, seven-mile hike through the battlefield, my sweat-soaked shirt reminded me of this, even on an early spring day.

If you don't feel like you're up to the physical rigors of the trail, the Fort Desperate earthworks can be easily viewed by a short walk from a special access point in the park. As I departed the trail, my only disappointment was that there was no place to view the river and its steep bluffs from the park. Old Man River has today wandered off a couple miles to the west of the battlefield.

I wanted to see another site before I left, the Port Hudson National Cemetery, a few miles away on the southern portion of the battlefield. As I got in my vehicle, I ran into what looked like two college girls getting into an SUV with Virginia plates.

"Find anything neat?" I asked.

"Yeah," one of them said, "and a big snake!"

I smiled as I climbed into my car, figuring they had bumped into a harmless king or grass snake. The big, bad moccasins hang out by the water, and I didn't notice any mud on the girl's shoes.

The cemetery was founded after the battle, and almost four thousand Union soldiers are interred here, most as unknown graves, along with over eight thousand veterans of other wars. The Confederate soldiers were largely buried in their own pits or trenches. The lines of white stones, towering trees, and handsome stretch of well-manicured green grass bore testament to the cost of this often forgotten battle that opened up the Mississippi River. After the fall of Port Hudson, President Lincoln stated, "The Father of Waters again goes unvexed to the sea."

In Tony Horwitz's bestselling book, *Confederates in the Attic*, Tony refers to Louisiana as a "backwater" of the Civil War. Tony's a great journalist and one of my favorite writers, but as I looked over the long lines of white headstones, I didn't get the feeling these heroes thought of this place as a backwater. These dead announced the mercilessness of a great battle for the destiny of the soon-to-be world superpower.

I didn't spend a lot of time researching Port Hudson's order of battle, but I did do some terse checking. Both the 24th and 26th Connecticut had fought here, some of their fallen likely lying before me. A tall obelisk in Norwich, Connecticut, honors the 26th's fight here, and in Middletown, Connecticut, a 16-foot-tall granite exedra honors the 24th, Port Hudson carved into its face. How many more hidden-away monuments to this battle lay scattered across the now-united country? The Port Hudson Historic Site was really a cool place, one that had essentially been in my backyard all my life, but somehow avoided me for fifty years.

The little hidden hilltop adjacent to the great river, the site of the longest siege in American military history, piqued my interest. I thought I might set off on a modern-day adventure, 150-something years in the making, to look for, find, and explore these once significant, critical places. So let's step further back in time, to the start of the greatest drama to ever unfold on the fruited plain. If you want to see Port Hudson, here are the details:

Port Hudson State Historic Site
236 Hwy. 61
Jackson, LA 70748
(225) 654-3775
http://www.crt.state.la.us/louisiana-state-parks/historic-sites/port-hudson-state-historic-site/index

CHAPTER 2

When Lincoln Wept

Ball's Bluff, Virginia

On April 12, 1861, the newly formed Confederate States of America bombed Fort Sumter. The War had arrived. That summer, the new armies finally collided in the first major battle of the War at Manassas. Then, blue and gray pulled back, everybody wondering what was next, if anything.

Washington and Richmond still felt each other out. Where was this going? Gen. George B. McClellan had been made the commander of the Federal forces in the East, and likewise, Joe Johnstone for the South. Both armies stood poised, green, and probably everybody just hoped the winter would arrive and cooler heads would prevail before the following spring.

In this setting, the only major battle occurred in the East that fall, really by accident. The battle wasn't really big, especially compared to the huge armies that lunged at each other later, but it had significant consequences for the rest of the War, and beyond, and garnered as many headlines as any battle of the War.

Until only recently, the only thing marking this battle was a small cemetery with only forty-four Union graves, the third smallest Federal cemetery in the country, hidden off in the woods on the banks of the Potomac River just outside of Leesburg, Virginia.

In Leesburg in the fall of '61, like many places, Confederate and Federal forces were encamped on their sides of the river, then an international boundary between two countries. The novice soldiers, mostly only accountants, farmers, or something only months earlier, had a convenient agreement—don't shoot at me, and I won't shoot at you. There's even some record of truces, trading, and correspondence between the citizen soldiers.

The Confederate and Federal commanders, Nathan "Shanks" Evans and Charles Pomeroy Stone, respectively, had been at West Point together.

On October 20, McClellan ordered Stone to conduct a "slight demonstration" across the river. Evans had been moving his army around, and the Northern officers wanted to find out what was up. Finding nothing, Stone ordered Col. Charles Devens across the unseasonably high and swift river, during the night, to further reconnoiter the area. This later turned into a raid when the rookie soldiers mistook some fruit trees for a Rebel camp!

Through the night, Devens moved his men up a steep but passable breach in the more than one hundred foot, almost vertical bluff that protected the Confederate side of the River. With daylight, Devens discovered there was no Rebel camp. Stone then sent him more troops and Col. Edward Baker, one of the most well-known politicians in the country, a US senator who commanded four California regiments. The California regiments were actually Pennsylvania boys. Every state needed to be in the fight, and nineteenth-century politicians, like every century, weren't afraid to misnomer a few small details for political expediency. US Senator Edward Baker was Abraham Lincoln's best friend. The two had been lawyers in Springfield, and Lincoln actually named one of his sons Edward Baker Lincoln.

What happened in the next eighteen hours was a massive Federal debacle that resulted in one thousand casualties, more than six times the Confederates, and a dead senator in a fight where the Federal troops outnumbered the Confederates four to one in the area. The Yanks also had a slight advantage in artillery during the battle.

As I drove through Loudoun County, one of the fastest growing counties in America, and to the north side of Leesburg to the Ball's Bluff Battlefield Regional Park, one of the lead stories on a local radio station was a current debate about renaming Jeb Stuart High School somewhere nearby. Just that morning as I sipped coffee in my hotel lobby, CNN ran a lead story about the removal of Jefferson Davis's statue in New Orleans a day prior. More than 150 years later, the Civil War still dominated the news. The fate of the Confederate heroes would be decided in the future. I was heading to the past.

I drove through an impressive upper-class neighborhood on the north side of an ever-expanding Leesburg, a pretty, suburban town, thirty-two miles northwest of the White House. The park's entrance is actually accessed by the cul-de-sac of one of the neighborhood streets. There, I met Pat Mountain and James Morgan, two members of the Friends of Ball's Bluff Battlefield, a nonprofit organization whose goal is the battlefield's preservation.

James had written a book about the battle, *A Little Short of Boats*. It's a great book. I had actually read the book a few months earlier but didn't correlate James with the book until we talked a while . . . I'm getting a little slow with age, in both mind and body! I simply contacted the Park and asked to talk to somebody who knew something about the battle. James was actually born in Louisiana, his family from the tiny river-delta town of Morganza.

Anyway, Pat and James, both retired Federal employees, gave me a free walking tour of the park that the Northern Virginia Regional Park Authority (NOVA), a public entity, had begun restoring in 2004 after NOVA made a deal with the developer of the adjacent neighborhood. The restoration is an ongoing project.

I got the show-and-tell of what happened after Senator Baker and the Massachusetts and Pennsylvanian boys arrived on Southern soil. Pat and James immediately showed me the battlefield's topography. The Ball's Bluff area has deep ravines on each side of the battlefield, meaning when the Northern troops arrived, they only had two options—retreat back across the river or go forward. There were no other escape routes.

Early in the day, Devens men exchanged fire with a Mississippi regiment. Word got back to Baker, now in charge but still on the Northern side of the river. Baker ordered all available troops across the river, but due to a shortage of Federal boats, this took some time to ferry the troops across the rushing waters and up the bluff. By this time, old Shanks got organized, and three regiments, two from Mississippi and one from Virginia, converged on the now seven hundred or so federal troops. By mid-afternoon, the Rebs started to gain the upper hand, mostly because they could feed men and material to the battle much faster than the Federals. Like many early battles, adding to the confusion, some of the Yanks wore grey and some of the Rebs donned blue.

Worse for the Federal cause, Col. Baker, dressed in a flamboyant uniform, was shot late in the afternoon. Captain Caspar Crowninshield of

Friends of Ball's Bluff Battlefield members James Morgan and Pat Mountain

the 20th Massachusetts recounted the senator's death. After Baker was initially shot, he "got up again and then fell, struck by eight balls." Baker remains today the only US senator ever killed in battle. Hand-to-hand fighting occurred before the Yankee troops could retrieve Baker's body.

As the day wore on, Evans continued to feed more men into the battle. Devens, desperate for a solution to his straits, formed his men, and tried unsuccessfully to break out of the trap the Federal Army set for itself.

The rout was soon on. Like fleeing cattle, it started slow, but then swept to a tide. A Confederate soldier described it, "a kind of shiver ran through the huddled mass upon the brow of the cliff; it gave way; rushed a few steps; then, in one wide, panic-stricken herd, rolled."

The northern boys fell back the way they came. The only problem . . . the few Federal boats available for the retreat, overcrowded and under fire, quickly sank. More than a hundred Northern soldiers drowned or were shot by the Rebs as they tried to swim the river. Most of the remaining men bunched up on the riverbank under the bluff where they were killed or eventually captured.

By midnight, it was all over. Northern soldier G. W. Davison braved the river, swimming for his life. "I never felt so near death, in the water, weak, and out of breath, and balls whizzing." Ironically, Federal Col. Milton Cogswell, captured here, had the eye of one of Gen. Robert E. Lee's daughters while Cogswell was at West Point and Lee, the commandant.

I walked the park's verdant, pristine trail along the riverbank with Pat and James, listening to the battle's details. Ahh, the panic and fear, the tragic drama that unfolded and must have gripped these men—trapped in a pin beside the rushing river, awaiting their unknown fate. In all, 450 Northern troops were killed or wounded, and more than 500 surrendered. For days, bodies washed up in Washington, DC, one even as far downstream as George Washington's Mount Vernon. The press had a field day.

It is said that when Abraham Lincoln got word of Baker's death, he wept and his knees buckled. Funerals were held for Baker in Washington, Philadelphia, and New York, before his body was sent back to California for final interment at the Presidio.

The ramifications of the battle were far-reaching. Following several major Union defeats earlier in the year, Ball's Bluff and the death of a US senator led to the formation of the Congressional Joint Committee on the Conduct of the War. The committee injected nasty politics into the War, forever second-guessing the president and generals and creating a conflict between the army and the elected bosses never seen in America before or since, all to the good of no one.

The committee was especially hostile to the democratic generals, of which most of the rank and file belonged. They especially loathed the professional West Pointers who didn't push political positions. Committee member Zachariah Chandler summed up the committee's general feelings: "I do not believe there can be found an institution on the face of the earth . . . that has turned out so many false, ungrateful men as have emanated from this institution. Half are downright traitors and the other half sympathize with the South."

McClellan investigated the battle, his report placing most of the blame on Baker. But Congress would hear nothing of it, the degrading of their colleague and now-dead war hero. General Stone would be the scapegoat. In one of Mr. Lincoln's less finer moments, he allowed Stone to be arrested and locked away in a military prison at Fort Lafayette for six months without formal charges or a trial.

The army eventually released Stone without charges, but his career in the army was essentially over. He did reclaim his name and reputation. On the recommendation of General Sherman, he took the position of commanding general of the Egyptian Army, and later in life served as one of the chief engineers on the Statue of Liberty; he was the grand marshal of the ribbon-cutting parade. Ironically, his cavalry inspector in Egypt was Walter Jenifer, the Confederate cavalry commander at Ball's Bluff. Shanks Evans would go on to serve out the war, though he survived two court-martial attempts for disobedience and drunkenness.

Pat and James took me back up on the bluff to the Park's lookout where we looked out over the green waters of the Potomac to the Maryland countryside across the river, a carpet of rural, rolling farms dotted with a few barns. We then walked over to the National Cemetery that sits within the park. For more than a hundred years, the small federal cemetery, probably fifty feet square, stood as the only significant monument at the battlefield. A road was not even built to the cemetery until forty-two years after the War.

Pat and James showed me another interesting site, a monument to the color bearer of the 8th Virginia. The exact history of the monument is still being researched, but it was apparently donated by Massachusetts veterans after a visit to the battlefield in 1900. The old Yanks got to retelling the fight's events and remembered the tall, brave, redheaded Confederate sergeant shot down in front of his regiment, and sent the monument to Leesburg. Like the cemetery, it was all that marked the momentous, but lost battle until modern times.

Despite the battle's relative small size, only 3,400 troops engaged, the fight had an amazing number of participants who later gained prominence. Among these was Winfield Featherston, the commander of the 17th Mississippi, who served in Congress with both Baker and President Lincoln. Col. Charles Devens, who led the initial Federal crossing and was wounded in the battle, went on to be the attorney general of the United States under President Rutherford Hayes. Captain William Bartlett led the 20th Massachusetts. He lost a leg at Yorktown, then almost had his hand shot off at Port Hudson where he was the Federal officer forced to command from horseback, and ended the War a general. And last but not

Ball's Bluff National Cemetery

the least, future justice of the Supreme Court Oliver Wendell Holmes was wounded in the battle. Ball's Bluff taught the Bluecoats the consequences of bad leadership, and they learned fast. Eleven Yankee officers present went on to become generals before the end of the War.

I could have stayed for days, walking the picturesque park and picking the brains of Pat and James, but I had to move on, fresh in an appreciation for their help and work. They're dedicated to the battlefield, to say the least. I actually got an email from Pat a week or so after my visit inviting me back to the Park for the Fourth of July . . . James was leading a crew of the Friends in the firing of a six-pound cannon! Before I left, I stopped by the historic Jackson House, in the adjacent neighborhood, where the fighting commenced. It was purchased in 2013 by the Civil War Trust.

If you're in the area, stop by the Park. Admission is free. Here are the details:

Ball's Bluff Battlefield Regional Park
Ball's Bluff Rd.
Leesburg, VA 21076
(703) 737-7800
https://www.novaparks.com/parks/balls-bluff-battlefield-regional-park

CHAPTER 3

Stymied by a Goat

Pensacola, Florida

As you drive south on Highway 98 through Pensacola, Florida, and across Pensacola Bay, you land on Santa Rosa and Okaloosa Island (they're the same island, just called different things depending on which end you're on). For generations, Confederate families and college kids have flocked here for the white sand and fresh gulf air around the beach resorts that stretch east from Pensacola. It's called the Emerald Coast and the perfect quartz sand has been classified as some of the whitest in the world. It actually squeaks when you walk on it.

The Denmons were no exception. For as long as I can remember, I've traipsed here, first on family vacations and then for numerous spring breaks. I still come occasionally, but rarely now to parade around the beach with my shirt off, unless induced by too many spirits! I was amazed to find out an old fort inhabited the island, much less one that played a major role in the Civil War.

Fort Pickens, on the western tip of Santa Rosa Island and hidden in the Gulf Islands National Seashore, is not on the way to anywhere. Who wanted to go down there where there's nothing but sand, seagrass, and seagulls when the other way led to the party? But now on the hunt for the lost War, I turned my nose away from the lovely smell of sunbathing oil and the awful sound of boom-boxes thumping on the beach.

Florida has two state parks that memorialize Civil War battles at Olustee and Natural Bridge, both in the panhandle. But Fort Pickens, and the defenses around Pensacola, are the most significant. The forts on Pensacola Bay protected the US Navy yard before the War, the Federal's major naval presence in the Deep South. Actually, Fort Pickens could have easily been the country's Fort Sumter. One of the few forts in the

South the North didn't abandon, many thought this might be the fuse that lit the ticking time-bomb.

The Confederates made their first futile attempts to take Pensacola's defenses months before they first fired on Fort Sumter. When Mr. Lincoln got in office, one of his first military actions was to send two naval forces to relieve the isolated garrisons at Forts Sumter and Pickens. General Beauregard ordered the firing on Fort Sumter that started the War on April 11 when the Navy arrived to supply the fort. Yankee reinforcements landed at Fort Pickens one day later but only because a naval officer demanded the clarification of his orders before landing troops. Pickens could have easily been where it all started.

So, one early June day, I took off down Fort Pickens Road. Abruptly, the condos and high-rises of the beach town of Gulf Breeze stop, and the lonely road weaves another seven and a half miles through the serene shoal and turtle grass and sugar-white dunes of the Gulf Island National Seashore. The Seashore, America's largest and established in 1971, is twenty miles of pristine barrier islands, one of the most splendid plots of land owned by the federal government, and probably one of the most expensive.

On these pristine islands, dramatic events unfolded at the start of the War. Upon Florida's succession, the governor ordered the occupation of the Navy yard and the three federal forts that guarded Pensacola Bay: Pickens, Barrancas, and McRee. Cdre. James Armstrong surrendered the Navy yard without a fight, an action the Navy court martialed him for.

The army commander of the forts wasn't so easily persuaded. In January of 1861, thirty-one-year-old First Lt. Adam Slemmer abandoned all of Pensacola's defenses and moved his seventy-six men to Fort Pickens, the most defendable of the area's forts.

The Confederates and Col. William Chase, who built the forts, soon arrived to demand its surrender. "I have full powers from the governor of Florida to take possession of the Fort."

Slemmer would have nothing of it. "I am here by authority of the President of the United States, and I do not recognize the authority of any governor to demand the surrender of United States property." Hence, a tense standoff ensued, nobody wanting to start the War. The army eventually relieved Slemmer in the spring of 1861, but not with the nation's finest. The new troops included the 6th New York Volunteer Infantry, Wilson's Zouaves, commanded by William Wilson, a Tammany Hall enforcer and prize fighter. Yankee Col. William C. Holbrook called these rowdies, "thieves, plug-uglies, and other dangerous characters." The 6th New York's mascot was a goat, dressed in uniform.

Finally, after months of Fort Pickens's harassment of Southern shipping, the Confederate Commander in Pensacola, Gen. Braxton Bragg, sent over a thousand-man force to attack Pickens. Bragg turned out to be one of the Confederate's worst generals, and why he only sent a thousand of his seven thousand men over is still a mystery. There's some evidence that he only wanted to punish Wilson and his raucous New Yorkers. Gen. Richard Anderson led the Rebs' foray, boating across the bay under the cover of darkness, and then running into the encampment of the 6th New York where a fight ensued.

The New Yorkers quickly fled to the fort's defenses, including the goat. With daylight, Anderson had second thoughts about storming the fort's steep walls and dry mote. With almost ninety casualties, Anderson, shot in the elbow, abandoned the attack. The New York papers lauded the 6th as Pickens, "brave defenders!"

Realizing a general assault would be too costly, the Rebs undertook a second approach. A massive artillery duel ensued in November between Fort Pickens and the two Confederate forts, Barrancas, on the mainland, and McRee, on an adjacent barrier island. Two Federal gunboats also got involved. Over six thousand rounds flew over the bay, and Fort McRee was almost leveled. A little more than a month later, a second duel erupted. This time, the Northern gunners hit McRee's powder magazine, blowing it to pebbles.

In March of 1862, the eight thousand Rebels in Pensacola were sent off to fight in Tennessee, and Federal forces reoccupied the coastal city. The 1,800 Northern boys, many becoming ill with scurvy or other ailments, survived the fifteen months of isolation, outnumbered more than four to one.

At Fort Pickens, I got the tour from Ranger Bruce Nickel. The Fort's size immediately struck me. Constructed in 1834 by slaves, it has over twenty million bricks. It still has some authentic thirty-two-pound

Fifteen-pound cannon at Fort Pickens

smoothbores. Also unique are the fort's cisterns. There's no water on Santa Rosa Island, so the soldiers collected rainwater. I looked at the mine shafts, not for people, but to be packed with powder. These were designed to blow if the fort was ever in jeopardy of being overrun. Bruce told me that the fort even held Geronimo once after his capture.

All the concrete at Pickens is post–Civil War. Soldiers manned the fort into the 1940s. After World War II, the fort became a state park, until its incorporation into the Seashore in 1971. Fort Pickens is missing one of its five sides. That's not Civil War damage either. In 1898, an accidental fire got to the garrison's magazine. One side of the fort ended up in the Bay.

From atop the fort, olive- and lime-colored salt-grass and bleach-white dunes span the narrow island, sided by blue waters. A mile or so to the east on the entry road is where the battle between Rebels and the 6th New York transpired. In the distance, a mile across the Bay's choppy, turquoise water, the red bricks of the Navy Yard and Forts Barrancas glisten like toy houses. It's all a magnificent setting, cool ocean breeze, white sand, and no high-rise condos! For some reason, probably because it's been largely forgotten, there's not much literature about Civil War Pensacola. David Ogden, the cultural resources manager for the Seashore, told me of several recent articles about wartime Pensacola.

Fort Barrancas

I drove over to Fort Barrancas, which is a little more trouble to get to. It's in the Pensacola Naval Air Station, and you'll get a good review from the military police before entering, but it's worth it. Barrancas sits on a perch. From here, the view is much better. Below, across the bay, the antique crimson bricks and green roofs of Fort Pickens poke up a tad against the distant horizon, below the infinite sheet of water and above the white thread of beach. The Navy flyboys and sailors are still at it a century and a half later. When the fighters buzz the fort, cover your ears. Barrancas has a second fort, the Advanced Redoubt, on a tall hill further inland, but it requires a guided tour to visit.

Unfortunately, they didn't have any tours scheduled while I was in town, but that was okay. I had my own adventure in mind. I wanted to go see Fort McRee on Perdido Key, or what remained of it. The problem is, to get there, you have to drive around to Alabama, about two hours, and then walk five miles in. Or you can take a boat. McRee was the real lost War. It's just been sitting out there since its abandonment by the War Department in 1947.

I had a tip—a guy with a boat who might take me to McRee. I quickly rang him. He promptly told me, "No, I won't take you. I don't know you, and I'm tired of these Northern assholes."

Pensacola Bay from Fort Barrancas

I quickly explained to him I was from Louisiana. I'm one of the abused. And I was just writing a book about old Civil War sites.

"Nope," he said. "If there's anything I hate more than Yanks, it's reporters."

I thought the War ended 152 years ago. Maybe I wouldn't get to see McRee? I located a marina, just down the road, the Pensacola Beach Marina. I gave them a call and talked to Betsy, a tad friendlier. Maybe it was my charm, or more likely, she'd gotten over the Union occupation? She said she'd try to find somebody to take me out to McRee. She called me back an hour later with the good news.

I met Forrest Klein and his girlfriend, Amanda, at the marina and we embarked on the thirty-minute boat ride to McRee. The fort's in the Seashore, but it's so remote it's not maintained. Forrest told me that as part of the British Petroleum oil spill settlement, Pensacola is getting two ferries to access Fort Pickens directly from Pensacola.

After bumping over Pensacola Bay's blue water, we finally pulled up to the eastern shore of Perdido Key, populated today with only brown pelicans, blue herons, and a few Confederate beauties sunbathing on boats anchored offshore. Forest and I took off to explore the Fort, stomping through sand, piles of old concrete, and thick, grown-up brush which included some type of beach cactus that sent us back the way we came several times.

Most of what's left of the fort is concrete, remnants of the twentieth-century fort, but we kept looking for the old fort.

"What are we looking for?" Forrest asked.

"Some bricks. The old fort was made of bricks. Just like Pickens."

We stumbled on and on through the brush. Finally, about to give up, I crawled up on a thick concrete wall on the eastern end of the fort and then crawled down on the sand. In the bushes, at the base of the wall, were piles of old bricks, probably pushed here to make way for the new concrete. After a few minutes searching, we found a bunch of bricks. I was tempted to take a souvenir but decided a few pictures would be enough. Wow, now I found some of the War few people know about. Certainly, nobody on the half-dozen pleasure boats anchored at the bay's entrance had any inclination that the stunning backdrop was sacred ground where the country's fate was, at least to some degree, settled.

Lieutenant Slemmer, who with eighty-one men refused to surrender Fort Pickens, went on to face Bragg again, in another of the Confederate general's defeats, Stones River, where he was severely wounded. Slemmer went on to become a general. He died three years after the War from typhoid fever, contracted at Fort Pickens.

I highly recommend Pensacola and the Forts. The sand, the ageless old stacks of bricks surrounded by salt grass, the timeless waves crashing on the beach, and the wind and seagulls whistling through the old forts all make for a superb, pristine setting, all in complete contrast to the forts' violent past. The forts are easy to get to, except McRee, and there's plenty to do just down the beach. Forest led me to one last discovery after my day of ambling the dunes, Shaggy's, a bar and restaurant, where I had a great burger looking over the bay.

Fort Pickens Area, Gulf Islands National Seashore
1400 Fort Pickens Rd.
Pensacola Beach, FL 32561
(850) 934-2600
https://www.nps.gov/guis/planyourvisit/fort-pickens-area.htm

CHAPTER 4

"Say Nothing About it. We're in for it"

Kernstown, Virginia

Gen. Thomas Jonathan Jackson garnered his initial fame and nickname, "Stonewall," in the first major battle of the War, First Manassas. Late in 1861, Gen. Joseph Johnstone ordered Jackson to the Shenandoah Valley to raise an army and check Gen. Nathaniel Banks, whom we met back at Port Hudson, then commanding an army there, and keep him occupied and away from the eminent federal push on Richmond. The campaign started with Jackson's only defeat, if it can truly be called a defeat.

The battle commenced when Jackson's crazy-brave cavalry commander, Turner Ashby, stumbled onto a Federal Army commanded by Gen. Nathan Kimball in the small village of Kernstown at the northern end of the Shenandoah Valley. Ashby's 450 soldiers were quickly repulsed by Kimball's much larger forces.

Kimball quickly fortified his position, posting sixteen big guns and about three thousand men around and atop the commanding Pritchard Hill. Ashby got word to Jackson of the federal force, but failed to include a critical detail: the size and disposition of Federal forces in the area, about eight thousand in all.

Jackson, unaware of the size of Kimball's army and not one to let such details dissuade his plans, moved his little army of 3,500 men toward Kernstown. After an initial reconnaissance of the battlefield, Jackson was still not deterred. Though it was the Sabbath, a day he didn't like to fight on, and his men had just completed a blistering thirty-seven-mile hike in an astonishing thirty hours, he quickly arranged his artillery on an adjacent hill, Sandy Ridge, and readied for an attack before he was discovered. This was Jackson's first independent command, and he meant to win it.

Kimball, perplexed by Jackson's prompt actions, thought the Confederates arrived with a much larger force, and he moved more of his reserves forward.

As Jackson opened up his artillery, and the battle got going, one of Stonewall's aids informed him of the battle's composition. Jackson, realizing that he was now in a battle for survival, said, "Say nothing about it. We are in for it!" The South's most accomplished general quickly turned from the offensive to the defensive.

As I arrived at the Kernstown Battlefield, now in the hands of the Kernstown Battlefield Association, a private entity formed in 1996 to preserve the 375-acre battlefield that they recently purchased, I met the association's current president, Stephen Vaughn, on a Friday afternoon after the park had closed.

"I've got nothing else to do," Stephen said. "I'm on standby. I can't do anything fun, and I'm just watching my phone."

I quickly learned that the sixty-two-year-old ex-Navy F-14 fighter pilot flew an Airbus for United Airlines, and he was on "call" this weekend. As I wondered if he had ever bumped me around at thirty five thousand feet, he stood by to fill in if another pilot came up lame for one reason or another.

Loitering outside the association's visitors' center, my eyes were immediately drawn to Pritchard Hill. A couple of hundred yards behind the center, the apex of the little green hill, its slopes covered with freshly-cut, lush grass, jutted up fifty feet above everything.

"Let's take a look around," Stephen said, and I hopped into his jeep.

Instead of trudging up Pritchard Hill's gentle slopes, we rode up there to view the area and the adjacent Sandy Ridge from the promontory, the Blue Ridge Mountains off to the east.

Stephen then showed me some of the Visitor Center's attractions, including a four-foot by six-foot tablet titled The Confederacy Etched in Slate. The plaque has tremendous detail. Every Confederate general is etched on the slate, all four-hundred and something of them, with accompanying portraits of forty-eight prominent generals. The origins of the plaque are still unknown, but they've traced it as far back as the late nineteenth century.

View from atop Pritchard Hill, Kernstown Battlefield

He also gave me a tour of the Greek Revival, Pritchard House, built in 1854, and the home of Helen and Samuel Pritchard during the battle. The Pritchards farmed 206 acres and ran a thriving wagon-wheel business. Helen, then pregnant, Samuel, and their three children hunkered down in their cellar during the battle, only to emerge to discover their house converted into a hospital, where they were forced to nurse the wounded as the armies moved on.

Actually, the Kernstown Battlefield and the Pritchard House hosted two major battles during the War. The Second Battle of Kernstown was fought in July of 1864, when Gen. Jubal Early, who assumed Stonewall's command, and seventeen thousand Rebels dislodged Yankee Gen. George Crook and twelve thousand Yanks entrenched around Pritchard Hill and sent them fleeing for West Virginia.

Gen. John Gordon, with brigades of Louisiana, Virginia, and Georgia boys, led an attack near the Pritchard House against Northern forces that included a future president, Col. Rutherford Hayes, and James Mulligan, a Chicago attorney who raised an Irish brigade. Hayes fell back and survived the battle, but Mulligan, rallying his men behind the stone wall beside the Pritchard House fell wounded. His men gathered around him, including his nephew, Lt. James Nugent. The Rebel sharpshooters zeroed in, killing Nugent. When Mulligan's men tried to move him, the colonel said, "Lay me down and save the flags. Now you can do me no good. Save your colors!" Two days later, in the care of the Pritchards and sheltered in their house, a Rebel priest from the Louisiana Tiger Brigade gave the colonel his last rights before he passed this world.

As Mulligan fell, the battle raged on. At one point during the rebel advance, the Johnnies having obtained the wall, Early ordered a halt to the assault. The testy Virginia regiments, ready to end the shelling, would have no part of this. In open disobedience, they jumped over the wall and pressed the attack. The Rebel charge was so intense that Jewett Palmer of the 36th Ohio under the future president later said, "We were cut down by the score . . . enlisted men went down as I never saw them fall." Another Ohioan commented that the Rebs "pressed forward yelling like demons and poured volley after volley into our flank, which we could not return."

Among the other famous soldiers who fought for the green grass and hill over my shoulder on that warm July afternoon 153 years ago were future president William McKinley, Colonel Hayes's aide on the Hill, and Col. George S. Patton (the grandfather of Gen. George S. Patton Jr., of World War II fame), whose brigade assaulted Hayes's left. Despite the humiliating defeat, General Crook went on to redeem himself in several major battles, but was eventually captured, imprisoned in Richmond, and then paroled to fight again. After the War, he became a famous Indian fighter, best known for his pursuit of Geronimo. He was portrayed by Gene Hackman in the excellent 1993 movie *Geronimo*.

Later in the War, Northern Gen. Albert Torbert took over the house again, making it his headquarters, and pillaging the farm. So prominent was the house during the War that famed artist James E. Taylor did a sketch inside the house. After the War, and with the support of many Yankee officers, the Pritchards unsuccessfully made claims to the federal government for war damages. Within a decade, Samuel, now deeply in debt, was forced to sell the once prosperous farm.

The association has almost fully restored the house. They have some pictures on display of the house only a few years ago, dilapidated and

Pritchard House, Kernstown Battlefield

grown up in brush. Stephen showed me some furniture the association recently obtained that has been appraised at almost $30,000.

I laughed and said, "Y'all need to get that slate plaque appraised. If that old furniture is work 30K, that plaque may be worth hundreds of thousands."

Finished with the tour of the Pritchard House, I hopped into Stephen's jeep to go look at the rest of the association's work. As we rode along, he pointed out the window at several tracts of land they had either recently acquired, or planned to acquire, and we stopped at a small clearing where Jackson observed the First Battle of Kernstown. The site is under construction. Stephen pointed out the view of Pritchard Hill. Across the street, a half mile away, the green hill stood, almost unobstructed, commanding over a few tidy farms.

"We're planning to clear a few more trees to improve the view."

This was all fine and dandy, but it wasn't what I came to see. I finally exhaled. "When are you going to take me to see the wall?"

"That's all anybody wants to see," Stephen said, "the wall. Okay, let's go."

Back to the First Battle of Kernstown. The wall is a half mile, L-shaped, shoulder-high, stone wall that became the focus of the battle.

Kimball, bringing the reserves up, rushed a regiment under Col. Erastus Tyler—2,300 men from Ohio, Indiana, West Virginia, and Pennsylvania—to the rear of Sandy Ridge, threatening to take the Rebel artillery on the Ridge and encircle much of Jackson's army. Now, fully aware of his army's desperate straits, Jackson rushed the 27th Virginia, the Stonewall Brigade under Col. John Echols, to intercept Tyler. The 27th took up a position behind a portion of the wall. Outnumbered, ten to one, the 27th poured fire into the oncoming Yanks.

Both commanders suddenly determined the value of the wall, and a frantic, life-or-death race ensued for the remainder of the stonewall on the backside of Sandy Ridge. The Virginians won the race, but only by seconds. When the race ended, the Yanks were a hundred yards short of the wall.

The stone wall now became the only thing between Jackson and his demise, maybe even his capture. In the next few hours, both armies pumped soldiers into the fight for the wall, now cloaked in smoke and stabs of red flares. Confederate general Richard Garnett, a West Pointer, arrived to lead the defense. At best, the Rebels were outnumbered two-to-one for most of the afternoon. Jackson's new plan was simply to hold on until dusk, and then retreat. But late in the day, the beleaguered Confederates began to run out of ammunition as Kimball brought another three thousand men forward to the assault on the wall.

Garnett finally ordered a retreat, much to the dismay of Jackson who rode forward in an attempt to rally his troops. After the battle, Jackson court martialed Garnett, but it became a moot point. Less than sixteen months later, both men would be dead—Jackson at Chancellorsville in a friendly fire accident and Garnett on Cemetery Ridge at Gettysburg— just twenty yards from the federal lines.

The men who defended the wall stated that the top of the stones were literally saturated with blood from the minié balls' collision with Rebel flesh. James Simpson of the 14th Indiana later wrote, "A perfect blizzard met us. The very air seemed to grow heavy with bullets, which striking our men, sounded like the dusting of carpets with rods." Robert Lemmon, behind the wall with the 21st Virginia said, "It was not the sound of one or more bullets flying, but the rushing mighty wind of leaden hail as it howled past." Jackson's aides remembered the fighting as fiercer than Manassas. Stonewall commented later, "I do not recall ever having heard such a roar of musketry."

The 4th Virginia lost four color bearers and had its flag pierced with fourteen bullet holes. The 5th Ohio lost five color bearers.

Only recently has a park and trail at the site of the wall and Sandy Ridge, called Rose Hill, and adjacent to the Kernstown Battlefield, been opened, and the wall made public—so new that Google Maps didn't even have it plotted when I visited in 2017.

As Stephen drove to the wall, he pointed out a nice, upper-middle-class neighborhood. "This is where I live."

"Do your neighbors know they live in a battlefield?"

"Probably don't know and don't care."

We both chuckled. As Stephen pulled up to the brand new trailhead and parking lot, he told me that there's a debate in the valley about where to invest the tourism dollars. "Some of the younger generation wants eco-tourism-type trails."

Stephen and I thought a lot alike, more from the old school. He pointed out the window. "The wall's down there, but I can't get that far away from the truck and cell service is bad. You'll have to come back to see it."

I did come back, the next morning, and found the wall. The thick gray stones, stacked three to four feet high, and a foot and a half wide, weaved through knee-grass and scrub trees. I stumbled into a meadow below Sandy Ridge to check it out. Fortunately for me, the park has cleared one section of the wall, near their interpretive signs, where I got a good picture. The wall is somber today, surrounded by serene fields, still fluttering free and untouched by man. Touching it, I wondered if there might be some traces of the Southern blood in the pores somewhere.

I also walked up the back side of Sandy Ridge. Stephen told me the association has plans to clear some trees from the ridge. Even now, it's easy to tell how beneficial this will be to grasping the battle. In the future, we'll be able to see both hills, and maybe the stone wall from Sandy Ridge.

Though fate cost Jackson the battle (most of his army believed they would have held out with ammunition), it was a major strategic and media victory. The Southern papers hailed the general and his soldiers, fighting almost to a draw, though outnumbered more than three-to-one, as heroes. Lincoln planned to send Banks' army to support McClellan in his push on Richmond, but changed his mind. In fact, during the battle, Banks was on a train to his new post at Manassas. By late spring, Jackson's small band of seventeen thousand men occupied fifty thousand Bluecoats. And yes, Jackson would be back in two months to take the Shenandoah Valley and send the Federal forces fleeing.

Kernstown Battlefield
610 Battle Park Dr.
Winchester, VA 22602
(757) 593-8227
http://www.kernstownbattle.org

CHAPTER 5

The Night the War Was Lost

New Orleans, Louisiana

As the modern traveler drives or flies to New Orleans, he gets some sense of the city's isolation from terra firma. All approaches to the Crescent City require the crossing of large stretches of water, much of it unnavigable and laced with marshes. It's a hard place to get to, or get out of, even today, as has tragically been played out over and over during hurricane season—the only thing I've ever seen that interrupts the non-stop party in its streets.

At the start of the Civil War, New Orleans was the second biggest port in America and by far the largest city in the Confederacy, its population greater than the next five biggest cities combined: Charleston, Richmond, Mobile, Memphis, and Savannah. Its fall, largely without a fight, in the first year of the War has often been relegated by the historians and the Republic as a second-tier event, not getting the attention as other early battles like First Manassas, Wilson's Creek, or Fort Donelson.

In 1860, New Orleans had the Confederacy's best factories, foundries, and ship-building facilities. Its port's annual receipts totaled $180 million. It controlled sea access to most of the United States, producing an estimated $400 million in yearly river commerce, and was the banking capital of the South, its vaults full of cash and $12 million in gold, all in 1860s values. In a war that would eventually be decided by the North's industrial superiority, the fall of New Orleans was the most strategically important battle of the rebellion.

Seventy miles south of New Orleans in Plaquemines Parish sits the location where the fate of the city on the river was decided. Forts Saint Philip and Jackson sit on the banks of the Mississippi River, the latter adjacent to State Highway 23. Once out of greater New Orleans, there are only two major roads in the entire parish, one on each side of the river. Low-lying marshes built from thousands of years of river alluvial constitute the remainder of the parish.

These two forts protected New Orleans' only viable avenue for invasion, the Mississippi River. Philip stymied the British in the War of 1812. The Navy tasked Flag Officer David Farragut with surmounting them in 1862, and his second in command, David Dixon Porter, with the support of fifteen thousand troops under Gen. Benjamin Butler, another of Mr. Lincoln's political generals.

Farragut, a hard-fighting, no-nonsense veteran of two wars hailed from Tennessee and grew up in New Orleans, often said, "The best defense is well directed fire from your own guns." At the onset of hostilities, he sided with the North, telling the secessionist, "You fellows will catch the devil before you get through with this business."

Gen. Mansfield Lovell, a native of the District of Columbia and the deputy commissioner of streets for New York City before the War, commanded New Orleans' defenses. Lovell thought the river and forts were impregnable, largely based on the failed British efforts in the War of 1812. What Lovell and the Rebels didn't factor was steam. The British had been forced to circumnavigate the river by sail, almost impossible on the raging, shifting river and under cannon fire.

In the spring of 1862, the forts were defended by about 1,700 men, under Gen. Johnson Duncan and more than 120 big guns, including some forty-two pounders. To augment the two forts' defenses, a chain stretched across the mile-wide river.

In March of 1862, Farragut readied his forty-six ships, armed with almost 350 cannons, to steam up the river. He had a problem that forced the issue. In New Orleans, the Confederates were constructing two massive ironclads, the *Louisiana* and the *Mississippi*. The construction of both nearing completion, the latter would be the largest warship in the world, one that even gave the fearless Farragut shivers.

On April 18, Farragut ordered his ships to move up river and commence bombarding the forts. For six days, the forts and the Navy exchanged cannon fire. The Navy, its guns with a little more range than the Rebs, maneuvered so that they could fire on the forts, most of the Southern balls landing short of the Federal Fleet. The barraged opened with 1,400 rounds the first day.

After seven days of bombardment, the raining shells caused little damage to either side. The cannonading destroyed a few of the Rebel cannons, most of the forts' wood buildings, and breached the levee, putting a few feet of water in Jackson, but only discomforting the Confederates. Both forts maintained most of their fighting capacity.

Farragut, growing impatient with the battle, ordered his ships to run the gauntlet on the night of the twenty-fourth, preceded by a massive artillery barrage. He camouflaged his vessels with branches and sent men ahead to cut a portion of the river chain.

Though both forts held out, they failed to halt the Navy. Farragut got thirteen boats past the forts. The bulk of the battle transpired when the Confederate Navy got into the fight. The Southern navy launched its fire rafts, boats soaked with oil, then lit a fire, which were sent to collide with the Federal Navy.

The nighttime battle degenerated into a mass of confusion. The Navy lost its lead gunboat, the *Varuna*, and the Confederate *Governor Moore* was sunk. In all, the Navy fired more than fifteen thousand projectiles at the Forts. Several Federal boats were severely damaged or forced back, but the fight annihilated the Confederate Navy.

Yankee General Butler described the perilous passage. "The crash of splinters, the explosion of the boilers and magazines, the shouts and cries, the shrieks of scalded and drowning men; add to this, the belching flashes of the guns, blazing rafts of burning steamboats, the river full of fire, and you have a picture of the battle."

Now Farragut sailed north, nearly unmolested, to the biggest prize in the South.

Where were the Confederate Armies at the War's most critical moment? If you're one of those diehard, long-live-the-Confederacy types, instead of coming to New Orleans to protest the removal of Jeff Davis's statue, you should really be trying to chop the thing down and throw it into the river. He didn't seem too worried about all this. Through the winter, he stripped Lovell of his troops and warships. They were off fighting for some wheat field, remote fort, or crossroads. This entire affair demonstrated the ineptness of the generals and leaders to understand the evolution of modern war. By the end of the conflict, the cities became both the targets, prizes, and more importantly, the industrial engines that decided victory or defeat.

On April 25, the Federal fleet arrived in New Orleans. The city lay in chaos. Thirty thousand bales of cotton burned, valued at $20 million. Farragut demanded the city's surrender. The Confederates balked, but three days later, Farragut threatened to shell and burn the city.

Apparently, Mr. Farragut was rather convincing, and the city finally surrendered on April 28. The North's cost to take the South's biggest and probably easiest-to-defend city: 37 killed, 147 wounded or missing! The Confederate losses: seventy-three dead, seventy-three wounded or missing. Historian Charles Dufour titled his book about the fall of New Orleans, *The Night the War Was Lost*.

With nothing left to protect, Forts Jackson and Philip soon surrendered to Butler's men left behind by Farragut below the forts.

Today, Forts Jackson and Saint Philip still stand, guarding the river, two of the most interesting and forgotten relics of the War. Unfortunately, neither are open to the public.

The army occupied Jackson until it was turned over to the Parish in the 1960s. The Parish built a ring levee to protect the fort and opened it as a park. Hurricane Katrina put twenty-eight feet of water over the fort, and then in 2012, Hurricane Isaac put twenty-two feet of the river over it. Jackson has been closed to the public since Katrina, but I finally found somebody to show it to me.

After a dozen or so calls, I got in touch with James Madere, the former president of the Plaquemine Parish Historic Society, and the parish employee with the keys to the fort. He agreed to meet me at Fort Jackson's recently rebuilt museum one morning. The museum was built in 2015, but as of this writing, it is not open to the public.

James showed me the museum's artifacts, all of which were salvaged from the museum after Katrina. We then rode down to Fort Jackson and were met at the gate by one of its current occupants, a raccoon. The masonry fort, completed in 1832, has been hammered over the years by floods and hurricanes. The fort's tall, red brick walls are heavily scarred. The long, symmetrical lines are blotted with missing bricks, huge cracks, and severe differential settlement, easily identified where the straight lines bend and the mortar has fallen away. Still, the fort looked formidable, ready for a Yankee artillery barrage.

James told me there's no levee big enough to keep out the big floods but the ring levee keeps out annual flooding. This is a tumultuous land. Katrina inundated the entire parish. Of almost thirty thousand homes, only a dozen or so were habitable after the storm.

He told me they are in the process (filling out the government paperwork) to incorporate both Jackson and Philip into the National Park System (NPS). James showed me some of the fort's interesting components. The iron tongues for most of the cannon casements are still there. These are extremely rare. I went to more than a dozen forts and never saw any of these. He also showed me another distinctive aspect of the fort, the Hot Shot oven. Here, cannon balls were cooked until they turned red, then they were dropped into a cannon already packed with powder. These were intended to start fires on the ships they bombarded.

James Madere, Plaquemine Parish Historic Society, at Fort Jackson

They've only got one cannon at Jackson, and it's currently being analyzed to determine its origin. James walked me over to another interesting item, a spiked cannon in the fort's old mote that Katrina unearthed.

"The mote area," James said, "has never been excavated, and it's where all the junk went. In fact, we've found a bunch of cannon balls buried in the fort, but these have also been left in place."

As James explained, the hope is if the NPS takes over the fort, they will conduct a proper survey. James is the guardian to ensure its all left in place until that happens.

"There's no telling what's buried in here," he told me.

We spent a good hour walking the fort, on and off the brick ramparts and grass lawns, into the nooks and casements, dodging the raccoons, and most prevalent guest, awful deer flies buzzing and biting. James showed me the old museum in the fort, housed in an old powder magazine, only a brick tunnel with an arched roof, like a musty, old basement. Katrina covered it with almost thirty feet of water.

He lamented and moaned, recounting the removal of the artifacts. "There was two feet of muck in here. We shoveled it out, sifting through every grain to find everything."

In the new museum, they have a rack with some mini cannons they used to sell at the old museum that they recovered, still covered in rust and grime, and now part of the fort's history.

I asked James to take me to Fort St. Philip on the other side of the river. It's currently on private property, and there's no road to it, but it is visited on rare occasions. You have to boat across the river and then plow through the swamps.

"No way," James said. "There's too many snakes over there. It's a snake pit, and it's too dangerous."

"I'm from Louisiana," I argued, feeling my Confederate roots. My forefathers dodged all those cannonballs, so what's a few snakes? "I've been dealing with snakes all my life."

"Nope. It's too dangerous. We only go over there during December, January, and February. They love to sun up on those stone walls. And it's surrounded by swamp."

James Madere, Plaquemine Parish Historic Society, and a spiked cannon at Fort Jackson

The author at Fort Jackson

I pondered this. Louisiana only has 4.5 million people, but it has 2.3 million alligators. There's no telling how many tens of millions of poisonous vipers we have. Maybe James was right. I'd come back in the winter. Unfortunately for my readers, that schedule didn't accommodate my writing bosses.

"Hopefully," James said, "the feds will eventually build us a nice ferry across the river, and they can clean out the snakes! If you need some pictures, I've got some I will give you."

After my visit, I got an appreciation for James's lifetime of dedication to the forts. There's no place I visited, and probably no place in America with this importance that is in as much danger of being lost forever. I'm not the biggest fan of the federal government coming in and taking over everything, but to their credit, the NPS is probably the only entity that can save the forts and our history for future generations. Let's all hope they decide to take the forts in.

We'll run into General Butler and Mr. Farragut again. General Duncan surrendered. Later paroled, he contracted malaria somewhere and died seven months later.

If you do decide to go to the forts, you have to go through New Orleans. It's a one-way trip from the Crescent City. And if you're in the

Big Easy, it has several other sites for Civil War enthusiasts. The most important of these is Confederate Memorial Hall Museum, the second largest Confederate museum in the world.

I'd say, in the spring of 2017, there's no place in the world of Civil War preservation that feels more under siege or defensive than the museum. I've been to New Orleans hundreds of times. I lived outside the city for years, and never went. I wanted to stop by while in town, so I called, explained that I was writing a book, asking if there might be someone I could speak with before my visit.

A young lady promptly told me they would be out that day for Confederate Memorial Day.

"I didn't even know the Confederates had a Memorial Day," I said.

"*Sir*," she said, "the Confederates invented Memorial Day."

Thinking I might catch up with somebody after hours, I asked, "Do you live in New Orleans?"

"No, I live in Metairie. There's no way I'd call New Orleans home. And what kind of book is this? Who's the publisher, and what's it about?"

I investigated. There *is* a Confederate Memorial Day, and it was observed before our current Memorial Day. I decided I'd have to come back another day. Which I did.

On Camp Street, the church-like red-brick-and-terra-cotta building and museum, on the National Historic Register, has been a fixture for more than a century. The museum is a nonprofit. Philanthropist Frank Howard donated the building in 1891, but ownership disputes have been ongoing for almost a hundred years. Several attempts have been made to evict the Hall, but the courts have, to date, sided with the museum.

When you walk into the building, you feel like you've entered an old library, the wood floors squeaking. The stained glass windows, twenty-four feet ceilings, and wood walls produce a hushed ambiance. The museum also has a film about its history and many of the artifacts. After viewing it, it's best to just wander the museum. Not any replicas here. This is all real. They've got it all: weapons, artifacts, and a large collection of manuscripts. The uniforms grabbed my attention. The coats depict how small the soldiers were, even the generals. I had read somewhere that the average Civil War soldier weighed 143 pounds. A hundred and fifty years ago, especially during the War, calories were sparse—no double cheeseburgers or breakfast buffets. The details on the brass buttons amazed me, even for the privates.

There's also plenty of flags, more than 140. There's the flag that draped over Jefferson Davis's casket when he lay in state here during his reinternment from New Orleans to Richmond. More than fifty thousand people came to the museum that one day to pay their respects. I love the battle flags, with their bullet holes. I wanted to see the battle flag of the 14th Louisiana, stolen from the museum and recovered thirty years later by the FBI. At least eleven men were either killed or wounded while carrying the flag. Unfortunately, I didn't see it on display. A lot of the flags are stored downstairs, awaiting restoration funds.

As of 2017, the biggest Civil War attraction in New Orleans is right behind the museum at Lee's Circle. There sits a pedestal, more than seven stories tall, in the center of the traffic circle. But Bobby, the work of famed New York sculptor Alexander Doyle in 1884, has been removed and stored in a secret warehouse somewhere. Will they rename the circle? Where will Bobby and the other generals end up? The city's had hundreds of requests from people and places that want the statues, including the state of Louisiana. The Civil War, at least in the spring and summer of 2017, is a hot topic on Bourbon Street. Everybody's got an opinion.

There's a few more Civil War sites I recommend in New Orleans. *Forbes Magazine* has ranked Metairie Cemetery as one of the World's Ten Most Interesting Cemeteries. It's a popular travel stop for anybody coming to New Orleans, annually ranked by visitors as one of the best things they saw while in town. Keep in mind, New Orleans is below sea level and everybody's buried above ground.

Interred here, on an abandoned horse tract, in sheets of aged stone, and below the broad oaks are Civil War Gens. P. T. G. Beauregard, Richard Taylor, and John Bell Hood. Jefferson Davis and Gen. Sidney Johnston were both initially buried here, both later reinterred elsewhere. The tombs are still there.

There's also P. B. S. Pinchback, one of the Louisiana Reconstruction governors, and the first African American governor in America, and dozens of governors, senators, politicians, famous madams, business leaders, and Millionaires Row, where those who made it big in the city on the river, display their wealth for eternity, or at least until the "big" hurricane hits. Anybody that was somebody is here.

One of the cemetery's most famous sites is the army of Tennessee Louisiana Division Monument, a mausoleum, capped with Gen. Albert Sidney Johnston atop his horse, Fire Eater. We'll run into these boys again. There's plenty of tour companies that will show you the cemetery, or go it alone. It's a solemn, but enjoyable stroll or drive. Warning, this *is* New Orleans. Don't walk it on a midsummer afternoon!

While in New Orleans, if you go down to all the madness in the French Quarter, beside Jackson Square sits the Louisiana State Museum in the historic Cabildo. The 225-year-old building was the site of the famous Plessy-versus-Ferguson trial. The museum has a Civil War section. One of its prominent exhibits is General Lovell's coat and sash. Maybe he was in such a hurry to get out of town, he forgot to pack?

Fort Jackson
38039 LA-23
Buras, LA 70041
Confederate Memorial Hall
929 Camp St.
New Orleans, LA 70130
(504) 523-4522
http://confederatemuseum.com

CHAPTER 6

Lee Takes Command

Malvern Hill, Virginia

Numerous well-respected contemporary Civil War historians consider the Seven Days Battle fought outside Richmond, Virginia, in the summer of 1862 to be one of the major turning points of the War—right alongside Gettysburg, Vicksburg, Antietam, or Atlanta.

The battle, at the time, did constitute the bloodiest week in American history. There's also the plain fact that during the battle, the cautious, defensive commander of the army of Northern Virginia, Gen. Joseph Johnstone, was wounded and replaced with Robert E. Lee. But the real reasons are much deeper.

We have to put ourselves back in the summer of 1862. Since the Confederate victories at Manassas and Wilson Creek, almost a year earlier, the War had been a disaster for the South. With the exception of Stonewall Jackson's campaign in the Shenandoah Valley, and a few other small victories, the South had been defeated almost everywhere. New Orleans had fallen, and the South had lost most of the major battles in the west to include the biggest to date, Shiloh. Numerous Southern coastal fortifications fell, and the largest American army ever put in the field stood only a few miles outside of Richmond under the Command of Gen. George B. McClellan, dubbed the Young Napoleon by the press.

Lincoln's plan was simple. He sent Gen. George B. McClellan and the army south from Washington to end the rebellion. The army sailed down Chesapeake Bay, landed on the Virginia shore, marched inland eighty miles, and now stood poised to take the Confederate capital and end Secession. This offensive would mean the Civil War would go down in the history books as only a rebellion that was quickly put down once the nation got serious.

Honest Abe's plan had some big obstacles. The young Napoleon wasn't much of a general, and the new Southern commander who took over with McClellan only a dozen miles from Richmond was. General Lee gathered all available forces, reorganized his army, renamed it the army of Northern Virginia, shored up Richmond's defenses, and counterattacked. Lee was a fighter, win or lose, he attacked. A month later, McClellan was in full retreat to the coast. If McClellan had taken Richmond, the War might have been over before Lincoln ever made his Emancipation Proclamation.

After the Seven Days Battle, Lincoln, and almost everybody else, realized that the War would be much bigger and costlier than anybody had yet imagined. This was to be more than the whipping of a few renegade states back into line. Only a few weeks after the battle, Mr. Lincoln outlined the Emancipation Proclamation and disseminated it to his cabinet. The war that started to restore the Union would now be fought for more.

The culmination of the Seven Days Battle that constituted a half dozen clashes east of Richmond transpired on July 1, on the gentle slopes of Malvern Hill, where McClellan skedaddled, his army now in a defensive position, its back at the James River. Here, for the first time, all the forces of both armies were combined, and almost sixty thousand troops engaged.

In fact, in all but one of the Seven Days Battles, the Federal Army prevailed, but due to Bobby Lee's aggressive tactics, McClellan thought he was greatly outnumbered. Here, Lee showed, for the first time, his masterful ability to know what his opponent thought. Lee ordered his army on an almost suicidal charge up the long, open slope of Malvern Hill against what some historians believe the best artillery position of the entire war. The rebels were decimated, but true to form, McClellan again retreated from victory!

Before I drove out to Malvern Hill, I met with Robert Krick, a historian for the National Park Service's Richmond National Battlefield Park. There are only a few stops on my journey that have any federal participation, and Malvern Hill is the only one included in a national battlefield. But most of the battlefield has only been recently made available to the public since 2000, to include land obtained by the Civil War Trust and put under NPS management in 2012. It's kind of new, and I wanted to see it.

According to Robert, the NPS obtained the original 130 acres that constitute the crown of Malvern Hill in the 1930s, but today, the Park Service manages almost 1000 acres at the battlefield. The park has over three miles of trails, some very new, and the Park Service leases much of the land to farmers so that the property stays in a condition similar to the battle.

The urban area of Richmond today has over 1.2 million people. And as I drove out of town, along a busy four-lane road, BMWs and tractor trailers competing for space, through affluent, antique Southern neighborhoods and past shiny new malls where people of every race and background mingled openly and together, I couldn't help but ponder this city's transformation. Presidents Lincoln and Davis, in their wildest dreams, likely couldn't imagine what the dusty town of forty thousand, the focus of the world in their time, would look like a century and a half later!

Not far out of Richmond, the suburban sprawl gives way to a land-scape of rural farms and winding two-lane roads slicing through gentle rolling hills covered with a checkerboard of timber and corn. Just north of the meandering James River, Malvern Hill pokes up just a little higher than the surrounding ridges.

The Malvern Hill battlefield is a simple interpolation. There a two parking lots, maybe twenty spots total, one at the small crest of Malvern Hill where Federal Forces under Gen. Fitz-John Porter set up their 238 pieces of artillery and two divisions of 18,000 men and another division in ready reserve. McClellan spent the early portions of the battle dining on a gunboat on the James River, only arriving on the battlefield midafternoon, inspecting the lines before spending the battle displaced from the action on the far Federal right.

The other parking lot is at the ruins of the Methodist parsonage where the Confederate troops under Gen. Daniel Harvey Hill gathered to storm the hill. There are no NPS personnel at the battlefield and no visitor's center. There is a small visitor center at the Glendale National Cemetery two miles down the road, filled with Northern tombstones from the battle, that is open during the summer only. There were no photos taken of the battlefield during the war, and no drawings, at least not by anybody with a smidgen of talent. Though Malvern Hill is considered the best preserved battlefield in Virginia, no original structures from the battle remain.

A three-mile trail weaves through the battlefield with interpretive signage. Please note, that as of 2017, the newer one and a half miles of trails do not have signs. The NPS has a brochure for it, but you have to either get it at the Richmond Battlefield or online when the cemetery is closed. They also have a neat, online app for your phone that can be quickly downloaded.

The crux of the battle can be fathomed from the crest of Malvern Hill. To the north, there is a field, a half-mile wide and a mile long. Surrounding the field, impenetrable gullies and slopes fall off to swamps or creeks. In the distance, three-quarters of a mile away, you can see three Rebel cannons. It was a simple plan, fifteen thousand Confederates charged up the open, long slope.

I took Mr. Krick's advice. I walked the battlefield from the Rebel Lines up to the Yankee batteries on the crest. It's a peaceful stroll, birds chirping,

Federal twelve-pound Napoleon atop Malvern Hill

oats and wheat fluttering. In my sneakers, it took me about thirty-five minutes, the tiny Federal cannons atop the hill slowly coming into form. Of course, I wasn't carrying a ten-pound musket plus an ammo satchel and canteen. No grape and canister exploded around me, shaking the ground. And I didn't have to walk through the waist-high crops. Lucky for me, the NPS had cut a nice, wide grass path for me to wander up at my own pace. It's a solemn walk, part killing field, part sacred ground, part cemetery. I couldn't help but notice the scant depressions where the brigades of Gens. Ambrose Wright and Little Billy Mahone, the latter all of five feet five and one hundred pounds, took shelter as the Rebel charge waned.

As you walk up the battlefield, you easily get some sense of the lunacy of the charge that commenced about 5:30 p.m., on a warm summer evening. How and why did the South's greatest general concoct such a bloody disaster? Historians started debating before the battle's smoke cleared. Some argue that Lee was overly fatigued from the week's long work. Lee knew he had the enemy on the run. He was on a hot trail, and didn't want to let McClellan slip away. The day before, Lee grew frustrated when plans to strike a decisive blow against the Bluecoats at Glendale fell apart. On July 1, the Federal Army was backed up to the James River, and now was the time to destroy it before it escaped.

The catastrophe resulted from an ill-conceived plan coupled with an uncoordinated attack largely due to Lee's vague orders and unrealistic expectations. In fact, the bulk of the battle commenced by accident when Confederate general Prince John Magruder misinterpreted one of Lee's vague orders that he thought meant "storm the Hill with all available forces."

Lee did try to find a way to flank the Hill, and his chief subordinate, Gen. James Longstreet, executed a plan to form two grand artillery batteries to level the Northern defenses. When all these failed, the attack over the open, "long slope" was all that remained. Confusion, poor communications, shoddy generalship, and the hot pursuit of an army that Lee thought might escape led to the Confederate army's charge over a mile of open ground and up the Hill. Lee made the costly mistake of many amateur generals in the war, moving his men and artillery onto the battlefield piecemeal in the face of a large, stationary force.

By all accounts, the Yankee artillery barrage that ripped Lee's men to shreds was one of the most terrific and deadly of the entire War. Lt. Adelbert Ames's single six-gun Federal battery expended 1,392 rounds in the afternoon. The soldiers' diaries portray an apocalyptic scene, the shelling deafening, the ground shaking as if the earth literally disintegrated around them.

Col. John Gordon, leading an Alabama brigade in the heat of the battle, had seven bullets pierce his uniform. The 3rd Alabama lost six consecutive color bearers. Despite five separate charges, the Rebs never got to the top of the hill. There's a marker about three hundred yards short of the Yankee cannons to mark the Confederate High Water Mark.

Here, somewhere, Louisiana Private Edwin Jemison, from a leading Southern family, was decapitated by a Northern shell. Recent research has identified a photograph of the eighteen-year-old Jemison, who almost unbelievably to me, enlisted in the 2nd Louisiana in my home town of Monroe, Louisiana, in 1861. The photo has become one of the most celebrated and famous symbols of the waste of the War. Most believe, like thousands of other Confederates, he is buried in an unknown grave somewhere on the battlefield. The 2nd Louisiana lost two commanders on this day and their casualties were second only to the 3rd Alabama.

The northern portion of the trail wanders by the ravine where Confederate general Lewis Armistead's men hunkered down. Of note, Armistead would die a year later at Gettysburg, his story prominent in the Pulitzer Prize–winning novel *The Killer Angels*.

The Confederates suffered more than 5,600 casualties compared to about 3,000 for the North. Today, the killing fields on Malvern Hill are tranquil, but the day after the battle, Col. William Averill of the 3rd Pennsylvania Calvary, part of the Federal rear guard, stated, "Over five thousand dead and wounded men were on the ground, but enough were alive and moving to give the field a singular crawling effect." Confederate general D. H. Hill, Stonewall Jackson's brother-in-law, who recommended against the charge, was more to the point: "It was not war, but murder." A year later, as Johnny Reb stood poised to charge up Cemetery Ridge at Gettysburg, many of the men moaned that this was another "Malvern Hill."

Why McClellan didn't move on Richmond after the battle has also been debated for more than a century. It's difficult to figure. The evidence suggests that he still believed he was greatly outnumbered. Unlike Lee, Little Mac, as his men affectionately called him, didn't like to chance it. In reality, he had thirty thousand more men than Lee and the support of the Navy fleet on the James River.

After the battle, McClellan's generals fumed with anger, begging their commander to attack. Northern general Phil Kearny wrote, "I, Philip Kearny, an old soldier, enter my solemn protest against this order for retreat. We ought instead of retreating should follow up the enemy and take Richmond. And in full view of all responsible for such declaration, I say to you all, such an order can only be prompted by cowardice or treason."

But Robert E. Lee and his brave Southern soldiers ran the hated Yanks out of Virginia and changed the entire momentum of the War. Lee hadn't so much defeated the Blue Coats, but simply bluffed the Young Napoleon off Southern soil. Here, better than anywhere else in Virginia, the twenty-first-century onlooker can see how this unfolded. The result: the South had a new hero in Lee, and a hope they would win the War. There would be three more years of blood and carnage, and a War that meant more to the nation than just the restoration of the status quo.

Malvern Hill Battlefield
9175 Willis Church Rd.
Richmond, VA 23231
(804) 226-1981
https://www.nps.gov/rich/index.htm

CHAPTER 7

"I Must Have Kentucky"

Richmond, Kentucky

In August of 1862, despite its setbacks earlier in the year, the Confederate armies were back on the attack. In the West, Gen. Kirby Smith marched into the border state of Kentucky with twenty thousand men in what he called a "bold move, offering brilliant results." The bluegrass state was the birthplace of both countries' Presidents. Though a slave state, it voted against secession. Smith hoped to augment his ranks with Kentuckians that most Southerners believed were desperate to be saved from Northern tyranny.

Kentucky's fate that fall was sealed at probably the War's most forgotten battle, one that may have been the Rebel's greatest victory, and the Civil War Sites Advisory Commission ranks as one of the War's forty-five decisive battles, Richmond, Kentucky.

There's no battle I investigated with less print or general information available. At the Louisiana Tech Library, I searched the index of fifty years of *Civil War Times* and found not one reference. The library doesn't subscribe to the *Times* anymore, so maybe they've done something lately, but in fifty years, with at least thirty articles a year, I'd say the battle's lost to even Civil War buffs. But there's a battlefield, run by Madison County, and a Richmond Battlefield Association. I reached out to both and decided I'd go find this place, so critical a century and a half ago but forgotten today.

In August of 1862, when Kirby Smith invaded Kentucky, the North responded, quickly raising seven Ohio and Indiana regiments that were sent to Kentucky under the command of Kentuckian general William "Bull" Nelson. The raw Bluecoats, organized in two brigades under Gens.

Mahlon Manson and Charles Cruft, took up a position at Richmond, thirty miles south of Lexington and fifty-five miles south of the capital, Frankfort.

On a lovely summer morning, I pulled into the Battle of Richmond Visitor Center to meet with the center's administrator, Phillip Seyfrit. Phillip told me the story of the battle's preservation, all a recent affair. In 1999, after a large portion of the battlefield, vacant since the War, was sold for development, the citizens got involved purchasing an initial sixty-two-acre plot and then forming the association. The center has only been open since 2008, but as of 2017, the county and the association have preserved almost six hundred acres of the battlefield.

The museum's got some great items, including the recent acquisition of General Nelson's commission as a major general, signed by President Lincoln. They've got a couple of good movies, artifacts from the battle, and a neat laser light map. I'd never seen one of these, but it's better than most of the dynamic light maps I'd seen. The Rogers House, built in 1811, houses the museum. Significant fighting took place right outside, and the house became a hospital during and after the battle. For many years, it served as the commander's residence at the Army Blue Grass Depot, just behind the house.

The Battle of Richmond transpired over six or seven miles as the Confederates attacked up the Richmond-Kingston Pike, today the Battlefield Memorial Highway. One of the Confederacy's finest commanders, the Arkansan and Irish immigrant, Gen. Patrick Cleburne and his seven thousand Shiloh veterans, mostly Arkansas and Tennessee lads, supported by a division of Gen. Thomas Churchill, marched north toward Richmond. On a hot August 29, 1862, Cleburne's cavalry, under Col. John S. Scott, lured the Federals to a strong Confederate defensive position.

About six miles south of Richmond, Generals Manson and Charles Cruft formed a line around the Mt. Zion Church, right on the Battlefield Highway, with their Indiana and Ohio boys, about seven thousand, most only mustered in a few weeks earlier. The next morning, just south of here, near the Pleasant View house, also right on the highway, the fight opened with an artillery exchange.

I drove down to Pleasant View which constitutes the initial sixty acres purchased to preserve the battle. Here, on August 30, Cleburne commenced a day of textbook Civil War attacking and flanking that sent Manson's troops fleeing. Most of the battle occurred east of the highway in what is now the Blue Ridge Army Depot. It's on ground in the depot where Cleburne was wounded, shot through the cheek, the bullet and some teeth exiting through his mouth. He later said that he "caught the bullet in his mouth and spit it out."

Here at Pleasant View, Cleburne sent Churchill's division into a draw to flank the Federals. Today, it's called Churchill's Draw, and can be viewed in the park—a deep, wide trough cutting through the Kentucky soil and cloaked in thick trees and brush. Soon, there will be more of it to see. Both the Pleasant View house and the Mount Zion Church served as hospitals and sustained damage during the battle. The congregation at the church still gathers there today. Pleasant View and Mount Zion can be toured, but only by making arrangements with the association in advance.

I walked the park's trail, sucking in the clean Kentucky air. Getting to the Mount Zion Church from Pleasant View requires walking through the Battlefield Golf Course. I saw a first on a Civil War battlefield, a sign that read: "Watch for Golfers and Golf Balls." The Palmer House, one of the four or five structures from the battle still around, is today the pro-shop for the golf course. It also served as a hospital and suffered damage during the battle.

Completely outflanked, and after losing two regimental commanders, the federals took up a disorganized retreat that, General Cruft said, "fast became shameful."

Manson reformed a defensive line around the Rogers House but again got outflanked in heavy fighting, and the Federal forces stampeded back to Richmond, forming a final line in the Richmond Cemetery. The Battlefield Memorial Highway generally follows the axis of the battle, through the gentle green hills covered with a patchwork of trees and new development. Almost all the battle fought on the east side of the road is in the Bluegrass Army Depot. You can go in and look with the standard security check and pending the national threat level.

Sign at the Battlefield Golf Course, Richmond Kentucky

The depot has more than fifteen thousand acres. I don't know why they need all that. Most of it looked like fenced pasture or trees to me, but the battlefield's presence in the depot has saved much of it from development and, as Phillip told me, may be a blessing. Like the Rogers House, someday the army may decide they don't need all that land, and more of the battlefield could be given back to the county or city to expand the Richmond Battlefield Historic Park.

At the cemetery, the three-hundred-pound graduate of the Naval Academy, Gen. Bull Nelson, finally arrived at the battle to take command. Rallying his men, he climbed up on a tombstone and yelled: "If they can't hit something as big as I am, they can't hit anything." Seconds later, a bullet struck Nelson in the thigh.

As the fighting in the cemetery hung in the balance, one of the War's more interesting characters, Camille Armand Jules Marie, the Prince de Polignac, a French soldier and nobleman whom the soldiers called Prince Polecat, and an aid of Kirby Smith, rushed to the front and grabbed the colors of the 5th Tennessee. Waving the flag, he stormed forward into the wall of lead.

In the fighting, Col. William Link, the charismatic commander of the 12th Indiana fell wounded. He died the next day in the Holloway

House in Richmond (still around). His remains were sent back to Fort Wayne, his funeral one of the largest ever held in the city.

The Federal line soon broke and fell back into Richmond, running pell-mell through the streets and headed further north, but Scott's cavalry encircled the town. The entire Federal Army, now trapped, surrendered. The Cemetery is still there, a great piece of turf, filled with weathered tombstones and monuments to the Confederate's dead and Richmond's accomplished residents.

I drove into Richmond, population about four hundred during the Civil War, but now more than thirty thousand and home to the University of Eastern Kentucky and fifteen thousand students. The pretty college town is ever-expanding, its population almost doubling in the last twenty-five years. I got stuck in a traffic snarl, moving into town slower than Scott's cavalry did.

The federal losses were staggering, more than a thousand dead or wounded, and 4,303 captured. The Rebels lost less than five hundred killed, wounded, or missing. The battle had been one of the most complete Confederate victories of the War. There are no pictures or sketches of the Battle of Richmond, but Cleburne corralled up the captured in and around the Madison County Courthouse. The courthouse is still there today. It's a massive antebellum structure, probably thirty-five feet high, fronted with four big columns and capped with a twenty-foot cupola.

In a village of four hundred, the structure, surrounded by the two armies must have been a sight to behold. Two days later, thirteen thousand Rebels and more than four thousand Federal prisoners marched into Lexington, and a few days later, occupied Frankfort, the only Northern state capital to fall during the War. On September 4, the Kentuckian and notorious Confederate cavalry raider, Col. John Hunt Morgan, and his men rode into Lexington. One of Morgan's lieutenants, Basil Duke, recalled, "The command entered Lexington about 10 A. M., amid the most enthusiastic shouts."

The South had reclaimed Kentucky, or at least its capital and eastern half. The Battle of Richmond, even in its day, fell to the back pages of the news. It occurred on the same day as the Second Battle of Manassas. The fall of Kentucky got Lincoln's angst up. He said, "I hope to have God on my side, but I must have Kentucky."

The War had moved north, onto federal soil, the Confederates apparently reclaiming Kentucky, and in a few weeks, Robert E. Lee would successfully invade Maryland. Could the South actually succeed militarily? Most historians agree that the month after Richmond constitutes the Confederacy's high water mark of the War.

Kentuckians would soon lose one of their heroes. General Nelson, who had displayed brilliant military skills at Shiloh, was shot less than a month after the battle by another officer, Gen. Jefferson C. Davis, no relation to the Confederate president. During an argument in Louisville, Nelson backhanded Davis and said, "Go away, you damned puppy." Davis called for a pistol and shot the "Bull" dead! Charges were never brought. General Manson, captured in the battle and later paroled, served in Georgia before being severely wounded.

We'll bump into some of the Rebel commanders later. Patrick Cleburne would survive his wounds and go on to be known as the Stonewall of the West. Many of his juniors would join him, painting themselves in Southern glory. Three of the four, Preston Smith, Evander McNair, and Benjamin Hill became generals by the end of the War.

I had a sandwich in a trendy restaurant in antique downtown Richmond and then headed back to the Rogers House for something different. The Battle of Richmond Association held their meeting the day I visited, and Phillip told me I was welcome to come. Seven members attended the meeting, an informal affair held in Phillip's office. I got to see what real Civil War Preservationists do.

Mr. Robert C. Moody, a feisty, elderly gentleman, who appeared to be the godfather of the group, quickly solicited me for a membership. "It will help us cover the more than $10,000 we just paid for that General Nelson Commission with Abe Lincoln's signature on it."

In the blink of an eye, he sucked a Ben Franklin from me, and I found myself filling out my membership form! Robert's a retired lawyer whom the governor appointed to the Kentucky Civil War Sesquicentennial Commission. It didn't take me long to figure out I wouldn't want to find myself in a courtroom opposite Bob.

Before the meeting, I discussed the War with several of the members, many of whom had traveled far and wide in a journey similar to mine. I even learned that Bob owned one of General Nelson's pistols.

The meeting was your standard stuff: talk of the budget, general business, the purchase of new items for the park or museum, and a lot of discussion about the Battlefield's upcoming reenactment. Phillip allowed me to introduce myself—quickly recognized as the guy from the state where they're pulling down all the Confederate monuments. Of course, Kentuckians are really Yanks, though they all disagree with this assertion—strange country we live in!

After introducing myself, I asked, "Since there weren't any Louisianans in the battle, who's somebody interesting that my readers might want to hear about?"

Several people spoke up. "There were Louisiana troops here."

"Who?" I asked.

"Scott was from Louisiana, and so was one of his regiments," two members informed me. The association certainly knew the battle.

I might note that when I undertook this Civil War journey, I had no intention of accentuating the Louisiana boys' participation in the War, or point out their heroics or failures. But I found myself, especially after discovering their significance at Kernstown and Malvern Hill, looking for them everywhere I went. I couldn't help it. It's part of my story. We all have one. They weren't everywhere, but there were, like the men from every state, in more places than I could ever have imagined.

I hadn't seen anything about Louisiana in any of the Richmond battle records I read, but while the association went on about their business, discussing vendors for the reenactment, I put the internet browser on my phone to work.

The 1st Louisiana did participate in the battle, one killed. The regiment's commander, James Nixon, turned out to be another one of those interesting characters who just won't go away, a New Jersey native and the brother of a Garden State congressman during the War, a Republican no less. James moved to New Orleans before the War. He's still in the news today. He's the third grandfather of Missouri Governor Jay Nixon, who's caught up in the Confederate battle-flag issue. Governor

Nixon backed removing it from public buildings, but the press is constantly reminding us of his third grandfather. I read one headline: "Nixon unwilling to restore Confederate battle flag despite Civil War family ties to both sides."

This War and its participants are still there, every day. That's good. As my mind wandered off to other things, the association's members worked hard to do their part here at Richmond. Come see their work. Events here are moving so fast that by the time you get here, there may be more of it to see.

Battle of Richmond Association
101 Battlefield Memorial Hwy.
Richmond, KY 40475
(859) 624-0013
http://battleofrichmond.org

CHAPTER 8

To Die in the Mud

Chantilly, Virginia

If there's any place in the early twenty-first century that represents prosperous suburban America better than Fairfax County, Virginia, I haven't been there. The county, its population over a million, has, according to the Census Bureau, the second highest per-capita income in the nation. One hundred and fifty years ago, the county only had a little over ten thousand residents, but sitting twenty miles southwest of Washington, DC, found itself at the crossroads of the War. Armies traipsed all over the county, but amazingly the county avoided most of the War's major clashes—with the exception of one nasty fight.

In August of 1862, Bobby Lee defeated the Northern army, this time under Gen. John Pope, for a second time at Manassas. In the days that followed the battle, Pope, his army in shambles, struggled to get his men back to the defenses of Washington, as Lee tried to get between Pope and the capital in an attempt to destroy the Northern army. On a rain-soaked day in early September, the little town of Chantilly played host to the War's largest battle in Fairfax County, known as the Battle of Ox Hill or Chantilly.

If you're ever wondering why so many Civil War battles have two names—well, both armies gave them names. It depends on where you grew up.

Lee sent Stonewall Jackson and twenty thousand men trying to force the final battle against the beleaguered, disorganized Federals. Pope got wind of it and sent two divisions under Gens. Isaac Stevens and Philip Kearny to intercept Jackson. They collided near Chantilly on a low little ridge known as Ox Hill. The battle ebbed, the Federals gaining an early advantage. But eventually, the Rebs brought superior numbers to the field. In the midst of the fighting, a violent, intense thunderstorm enveloped the battle, producing a nightmarish scene of thunder, cannon roar, lightning, dead and bleeding men, and sheets of rain.

The battle is best noted for the deaths of both Federal generals, each trying to lead their men on charges as daylight waned in a final push to carry the day, but each not knowing the Confederates had reinforced their lines. The tempest and sheets of rain eventually rendered muskets useless, and both armies realized there was little to gain. Blue and gray fell back, but not before more than 1,500 men lay dead or wounded in the two-hour fight. Lee, begrudgingly let Pope retreat to Washington, which he promptly did, where Lincoln removed him from command two weeks later.

The battlefield's preservation, or lack thereof, is also noted as a key event in modern Civil War preservation. After a long struggle, in 2008, Fairfax County opened the Ox Hill Battlefield Park.

In the park, General Stevens's 79th New York, the Highlanders, pushed back a regiment of Louisiana troops into some thick woods. As the Yanks pressed forward, the Confederates unleashed a storm of musketry that crippled the Federal line, injuring Stevens's son, Captain Hazard Stevens.

Confederate general A. P. Hill ordered a brigade of South Carolinians into the fight to assist the Louisianans.

As Stevens's line faltered, the 79th lost five color bearers, and Stevens ran forward and grabbed the colors of his old regiment, yelling, "Highlanders! My Highlanders! Follow your general!"

The Yanks charged forward, to the rising crescendo of gunfire. Overhead, the sky darkened, black clouds and stiff wind engulfing the scene. As lightning dashed across the sky and thunder boomed, a Rebel slug pierced Stevens's head. Instantly dead, the general fell, the colors draping his body. In a flash, the Federal Army lost one of their most promising commanders. A West Point graduate and Mexican War veteran, he had already displayed his gallantry on several occasions in the Southern rebellion, most notably personally leading his men on a costly charge at the Battle of James Island in South Carolina.

It's here that the North also lost another general, this one also a Mexican War hero and proven fighter. Gen. Winfield Scott called Gen. Philip Kearny "a perfect soldier" and "the bravest man I ever knew." Kearny had been bold enough to openly admonish McClellan after Malvern Hill, and rumors circled that he was on the list of generals to replace McClellan in command of the army of the Potomac.

As darkness and storm encased the battlefield, now nothing but a confused mass of men struggling for survival, Kearny rode to Stevens's position, reported to be in jeopardy. Finding the 21st Massachusetts, Kearny ordered them forward.

The Massachusetts boys complained that their weapons wouldn't fire and that Rebels lay in force in the cornfield opposite their lines. They produced two captives from the 49th Georgia to make their point.

Kearny, riled and believing Federal troops held the cornfield, scoffed, "Damn you and your prisoners."

The Federal troops again warned Kearny, who replied. "The Rebel bullet that can kill me has not yet been molded." He then galloped into the cornfield, his uniform hidden beneath a rubber raincoat. The general, already minus an arm from the Mexican War, quickly found out the Massachusetts men knew their business. He ran smack into the 49th Georgia.

In the pelting rain, the Southern boys yelled, "That's a Yankee officer! Shoot him!"

Kearny wheeled his horse around, leaning on its neck, and made a mad dash for the Federal lines. Rebel muskets erupted. A minié ball entered Kearny's hip, shattered his pelvis and lodged in his chest. He fell from his horse, dead instantly.

The ground and guns saturated, the sky dark, but flickering with white flashes, the heavens emptied. The battle dissolved into nothing, the men and officers only trying to find cover and friendly lines.

Gen. A. P. Hill later looked upon Kearny's body. "You've killed Phil Kearny. He deserved a better fate than to die in the mud."

The next day, General Lee, a friend of Kearny's, sent the fallen general's body through the lines under a flag of truce with a personal note. Instead of destroying the army of the Potomac, Lee would instead look North and march his army into Maryland. In Washington, Lincoln would again try and find a general capable of checking the Rebs.

After the horrid storm, the fighting at Chantilly settled down, at least for another one hundred and twenty-five years. In the 1980s, the ever-expanding Fairfax County threatened the battlefield, largely still intact. The fight to save Chantilly, and two or three other Civil War battlefields initiated the modern preservation effort, largely with the formation of the organizations formed to protect these battlefields, the Association for the Preservation of Civil War Sites, and the Civil War Trust, which later merged into the Civil War Trust. Chantilly was the battle that the preservationists lost, all but the setting aside of five acres for a future park, today the Ox Hill Battlefield Park, around the two original monuments to the Generals Kearny and Stevens.

The park has about a quarter mile of trails and some good interpretive signs in the area where Stevens and Kearny fell. An audio tour can be downloaded from the park's webpage that further describes the battle and sites of interest. I visited on a weekday afternoon, but seven or eight people strolled the park or read the interpretive signs. The park is green space, set in a dense urban area. Most striking, adjacent to the battlefield and across the street, the eight-story concrete and glass headquarters of a software company looms over the once bloody field—quite a contrast, and something I only saw at this battlefield on my expedition.

One of the signs has a photo of the battlefield in 1907 . . . this was wilderness then. The park has a couple of signs that tell the interesting story of how the monuments came about, and how we know the exact location of General Stevens's death. After the War, a Confederate veteran owned the property and placed a large quartz stone where Stevens had fallen. There's also the 'Kearny's Stump' monument (marking a tree stump), today replaced by a granite stump, but this marker was used in the original 1915 survey for the conveyance of land for the Kearny and Stevens monuments. The sign has a copy of the survey plat showing the exact measurements of the monument lot and the original easement.

Who knows where the War would have gone if Stevens and Kearny hadn't run into Jackson's corps that fateful September day. The War certainly lost two of its boldest and most interesting characters. Both are memorialized from sea to shining sea. Stevens, once the governor of the Washington Territory, has several counties, towns, forts, schools, and buildings, etc., named after him. Kearny, from New Jersey, is even more celebrated. There's plenty of statues, counties, and towns, and even the *SS Philip Kearny* in his honor. His statue represents New Jersey in Statutory Hall in the US Capital. They're still honoring Kearny in the Garden State, inducting him into the New Jersey Hall of Fame in 2016.

This small battlefield represents a lot of "what ifs?" Without the storm, would Lee have been able to isolate and destroy Pope's army? That would have made things interesting early on. We'll never know what would become of the two generals and their impact on the War.

I rang up Ed Wenzel, one of the original members of the Chantilly Battlefield Association and a one-time board member for the Association for Preservation of Civil War Sites. He suggested we catch up at a local Irish pub in picturesque Fairfax for a beer. Ed was a Civil War preservationist who thought like I did.

It didn't take me long to figure out Ed was a fighter as he recounted the struggle to save the battlefield. "When I was born," Ed said, "there were 40,000 people in the county. Now, there's more than a million, most from somewhere else that don't care about our history."

He told me the story of the late 1980s, when Fairfax County planned to develop the battlefield into a commercial and residential area. Few knew what the county and the developers were doing, and by the time they found out, there was little ground left to save. It really forced the Civil War community to get organized.

Ed continued, "Back in the late 1980s, the county wanted to move those monuments to another location and allow townhomes to be built on the actual battlefield where the generals fell."

Eventually, the association saved the monuments. The Civil War Trust has stated publically that "the Chantilly Battlefield Association is widely thought to be the first Civil War battlefield preservation organization of the modern era . . . Ed Wenzel and two colleagues, Brian Pohanka and Bud Hall were the original voices advocating on behalf of the Chantilly/Ox Hill Battlefield, the destruction of which ultimately led to the creation of the first national battlefield preservation group."

Since Chantilly, the trust has preserved more than four thousand acres of battlefields across the country.

I also learned from Ed, as we ate a burger, that the next day, after a two-year debate, the Fairfax County School Board would be voting on whether to change the name of J. E. B. Stuart High School. Ed let me know that he had already voiced his opinion on the matter in a letter to the School Board and local paper.

I recommend Chantilly if you're in the area. It's a great little stop. And if you're a diehard Civil War preservationist, this little battlefield, and the fight for its centerpiece, the two stone monuments to Stevens and Kearny dedicated in 1915, resulted in the Ox Hill Battlefield Park and much of the Civil War that's saved to date . . . including almost everywhere I went.

Two days after I visited Ed, I bought a hard copy of the local newspaper. J. E. B. Stuart High School will be no more at some point. The School Board voted to rename it.

Ox Hill Battlefield Park
4134 West Ox Rd.
Fairfax, VA 22033
(703) 324-8702
http://www.fairfaxcounty.gov/parks/oxhill

CHAPTER 9

"Damn My Soul to Hell"

Harpers Ferry, West Virginia

Every American school kid knows that John Brown was hung at Harpers Ferry, West Virginia. They're also taught that this was one of the significant events leading up to, and even inciting, the War.

What they're not taught, and few Americans realize, is that at least on a numerical scale, Harpers Ferry was the biggest Confederate victory of the War. Until Douglas MacArthur's army surrendered at Bataan in the Philippines during World War II, more Americans had surrendered in the ferry town at the confluence of the Potomac and Shenandoah Rivers than at any time in American history—more than twelve thousand.

I drove into Harpers Ferry from the west and ran into the cozy, vintage, postcard town that popped up out of the hills. On all sides, tall green hills and their precipitous bluffs, almost a thousand feet above the river, abruptly closed in on the town. Just moseying along, you get a confined, almost claustrophobic feeling. It doesn't take much military competence to see that the town is a military caldron, a cemetery. You're in a hole, looking up at whomever or whatever might want the place.

Before the War, the little town housed the United States Armory and Arsenal, what later became called the US Musket Factory, yearly churning out guns, ammo, and other war materials. Fearing the weapons factory might fall into Confederate hands, the Federal Army torched the armory at the start of the war. Even without the armory, the ferry town had a supply garrison, and vast strategic importance due to its location. Two great rivers converge here, as did the Baltimore and Ohio Railroad, the capital's main connection to the rest of the country.

By the fall of 1862, a little more than a year since the commencement of fighting in earnest, the tiny river town had already changed hands twice. In September of 1862, only two months since Bobby Lee took over with the Federal Army at Richmond's doorstep, the army of Northern Virginia had pushed the Federal Army back out of the Confederacy, into Maryland.

Now, less than two weeks after his brilliant victory at Second Manassas, Lee concocted a daring new plan. Rumors swirled that the European powers considered recognizing the Confederacy, and he might also sway the upcoming congressional elections. Now was the time for Lee to apply pressure, invade the North, threaten Baltimore, Philadelphia, or maybe even the nation's capital, or have a decisive victory on Northern soil. He set out for Pennsylvania, McClellan, reluctantly put back in command after the calamity of Second Manassas, in pursuit.

As Lee marched north, he sent Stonewall Jackson with about half of his men to take Harpers Ferry. This would remove the threat to his rear and capture the immense trove of military supplies.

Actually, West Virginia didn't really exist in 1862. If you weren't paying attention, like me, in your eighth-grade civics class, the non-secessionist counties in the Old Dominion voted to secede from Virginia in 1861, but they weren't admitted into the Union until 1863. Nobody really knew what West Virginia was in 1862.

For the attack, Lee augmented Jackson's forces, giving him troops under Gens. Lafayette McLaws and John Walker. The Rebels would separate into three forces, and approach Harpers Ferry from the three mountain tops that encased the town, Maryland Heights to the east, Loudoun Heights to the South, and Bolivar Heights to the west. This required the Confederate forces to split up, as each apex demanded a significantly different approach. Jackson marched sixty miles over several days to reach the approaches to Bolivar Heights. His first forces under McLaws arrived near Maryland Heights on September 12.

Defending the garrison was Col. Dixon Miles and fourteen thousand green troops. Miles was a West Pointer but had recently been suspended from service for drunkenness at First Manassas. Much of the Federal command thought the arsenal indefensible and recommended it be evacuated, but general-in-chief Henry Halleck ordered it held "until the last moment." The North really had some bad commanders to start the War! It's a wonder they didn't lose it early on.

As I got into town, I found a parking spot and decided to hike up to Maryland Heights, where the bulk of the fighting occurred. I strolled across the exquisite old rail bridge built in 1894. The piers to the old bridge, in existence during the War, still pierce the water beside it. It's more than a thousand foot climb up the heights, steep and winding. I've been up some big hills, to twenty thousand feet, but this two-hour climb hurt . . . maybe I'm just getting old and soft. I hiked past the old Federal Naval battery (no guns today), just earthworks. Here, the garrison's big guns swept the town and the two other heights, but the slope is so steep, they couldn't be turned to defend Maryland Heights itself.

At the crest of Maryland Heights, there's an old stone wall, a fort, and wonderful views. A thousand feet below, the Potomac River parts the verdant emerald mountains, cutting a steep canyon and splashing over rapids as it slices its way to the sea, much of northern Virginia visible to the east. I sucked in the clean air, and stood up on some of the big rocks to gawk.

It was here that two of General McLaw's brigades, Kershaw's South Carolinians and Barksdale's Mississippians, the latter responsible for

The author at the remnants of the Stone Wall atop Maryland Heights

retiring General Stone at Ball's Bluff eleven months earlier, found a path up the backside of the hill. Unthinkable to Miles and the Federals, the Rebels even managed to lug four cannons up the hill. A brigade of mostly Ohioans, under Col. Thomas Ford almost fought off McLaws, but when the brigade's second in command, Col. Eliakim Sherrill, fell injured during the fight, the Yanks put it in reverse.

Ford, a lieutenant governor from Ohio and not a professional soldier, eventually ordered a full retreat, an action for which he was later arrested, tried, and dismissed from the army. Sherrill would recover from his wound, but like Barksdale who bravely led the Mississippians this day, they would both fall mortally wounded the following summer on the fields around Gettysburg.

The previous night, some of Miles's officers suggested abandoning Harpers Ferry and defending Maryland Heights.

Miles refused, saying, "I am ordered by General Wool to hold this place and God damn my soul to hell if I don't hold it against the enemy!" Throughout the fight on Maryland Heights, he refused to reinforce the retreating troops.

While on the heights, I decided to walk down to the overlook cliff. The view is magnificent over Harpers Ferry and both rivers and probably worth the thirty-six stories I descended and ascended to get there, though I had second thoughts on the climb out.

From the overlook, I peered down the almost vertical mountain to Harpers Ferry, my stomach turning oozy, the antique village like a model in a museum. Off to the south, across the narrow valley, General Walker arrived on the equally steep and rocky Loudoun Heights, his guns looking down on the town from the south side of the Shenandoah River. In the distance, behind the tranquil town, a slight rise known as Bolivar Heights emerged over the town from the west.

On the first night of the battle, Miles reluctantly allowed a column of cavalry, some 1,400 men under Col. Grimes Davis, to cross the pontoon bridge over the Potomac in an escape attempt. They carried the message from Miles of the condition of the garrison. The cavalry managed to get out. The day before, McClellan had sent a sufficient force to retake Maryland Heights, but as usual, they dallied.

Looking down on Harpers Ferry from the Maryland Heights Overlook

On a fall day 155 years ago, when Stonewall Jackson arrived on the western side of town, the Confederates succeeded in cutting off all communications from the garrison to the world. Stonewall Jackson was the right man to take Harpers Ferry. His first command of the War was here and he knew every crook and cranny. He would attack Bolivar Heights from the west, the only approach unguarded by a river, with eleven thousand men. His intimidating reputation carried as much weight as his position.

Back to town I went and up to Bolivar Heights. If you decide to do the full Maryland Heights trail, it's four tough hours. With a little juice left in my legs, I hiked up the Bolivar Heights trail. It's not as high and steep, but is still a nice trek. From Bolivar Heights, everything is in view, the town just below, the valleys and mountains over your shoulder, all a wonderful mix of color and landscape. Here, the park service has some replica cannons overlooking the town. It was here that Jackson set up his command and began the initial artillery barrage of the town on the fourteenth. Somehow, at least in Colonel Miles's mind, General Walker also managed to get artillery up on Loudoun Heights. The Yankee soldiers' diaries recount the barrage from the hole in the mountains being akin to an erupting volcano, but the initial barrage didn't produce the desired results on Jackson's schedule. That night he sent A. P. Hill's division down the west bank of the Shenandoah River. The next morning, the Federals were surrounded not only on the heights, but around the town also.

Miles held a war council where he suggested surrender. One of his commanders replied, "For God's sake, Colonel, don't surrender us. Don't you hear the signal guns? Our forces are near us. Let us cut our way out and join them." But Miles opted for the white flag. After the meeting, he was injured by an artillery shell and died the next day. We don't know if his soul ended up in Hell or not.

The garrison and its huge stash of war supplies, including seventy-three pieces of artillery and two hundred wagons, and the railroad, now belonged to the Confederacy. Jackson sent a message to General Lee, waiting on the garrison's capture before moving further northward, "Through God's blessing, Harpers Ferry and its garrison are to be surrendered."

I planned to also hike up the Loudoun Heights, but balked. I was now completely out of gas.

On the hunt for the lost Civil War, early the next morning, my legs sore and suffering, I hobbled into the park headquarters to meet with Dennis Frye, the NPS's chief historian for Harpers Ferry. Like many of the gracious people whom I had met, and would meet, who helped steer me along this wonderful journey, Dennis has spent a lifetime bringing the War back to life. He's authored a half-dozen books, been on numerous national TV shows, to include production assistance on award-winning features on the Battle of Antietam and the abolitionist John Brown, and an associate producer on the movie, *Gods and Generals*. He's also a co-founder and a former president of the Civil War Preservation Trust. Like many of the people I met along the way, he's not an amateur enthusiast, he's all in—it's a job, a life, not a hobby.

As we discussed my journey back in time to the lesser-known War, he told me about several of my destinations where he actually signed the purchase of parts of the battlefields during his years with the Trust.

I asked, "Tell me about the hidden Civil War stuff around here. I hiked up Maryland Heights yesterday, all the way to the Stone Fort."

"That's our toughest hike," Dennis said.

No kidding.

Dennis had a long list of forgotten sites, including the Murphy-Chambers Farm on the Shenandoah River, recently acquired by the park service and where A. P. Hill made his daring night-time pincer to surround the garrison. He said, "Portions of the old pontoon bridge, where the cavalry escaped are still down by the river." He pointed to a picture to show me where.

I asked about something I was on the hunt for—damage to the Chesapeake and Ohio Canal. This canal, used to transport coal and other goods through the Alleghenies to Washington before, during, and after the war, was a constant target of Lee and Jackson. They made numerous attempts to destroy it, with little luck. A portion of the canal and one of the old locks sit on the east bank of the Potomac in town, almost under the rail bridge.

"You can go up to Williamsport," Dennis said. "Jackson shelled the dam up there. The house beside the lock still has bullet holes, and there was some more damage up north of Paw Paw tunnel, but I don't know exactly where."

Tired of hiking up and down the winding streets of Harpers Ferry, I drove up to Williamsport, about thirty miles north. There, I got a really good look at the canal, constructed of stone and mortar, and then drove up to Dam 5. Caution, this is *very* rural Maryland . . . nothing there but the dam, the neat old lock, and the house with bullet holes. I drove on up to the Paw Paw Tunnel, the most impressive engineering marvel on the canal. It's still there, a neat old structure, a canal tunneled through a mountain, heading off into the wild, and worth viewing if you're in the area. Its construction ended up costing twenty times its initial estimate. Not finding any War damage and my legs too beat to go looking through the hills of the Green Ridge State Forest, I drove back to Harpers Ferry to finish investigating.

I checked out all of Dennis's recommendations, including the Lockwood House, a huge stone and brick edifice that served as the armory paymaster's residence until it became a hospital during the battle.

There's too much to do in Harpers Ferry. There's the Harpers Ferry National Historical Park's Visitor's Center, and numerous museums, all

Dam 5 on the Chesapeake and Ohio Canal

with great historical pictures and sketches, and the Appalachian Trail's Visitor's Center, plus cafes, books stores, and the old B&O Rail Station where you can still catch a ride on Amtrak or the Maryland Regional Commuter Rail through the charming mountains. And there's all that John Brown stuff too. Who knows what else is really here? I'm sure Dennis does, but it's a great stop, the scenery splendid, the War everywhere. If you want to go, just go to Harpers Ferry, you can't miss it.

Harpers Ferry National Historical Park
767 Shenandoah St.
Harpers Ferry, WV 25425
(304) 535-6029
https://www.nps.gov/hafe/index.htm

CHAPTER 10

"I Will Send You Trophies"

South Mountain, Maryland

As I drove east through the wonderful Maryland countryside, through rolling golden corn fields, on Highway 68, the road narrowed to cross a stone bridge over a little valley stream. The sign on the bridge read ANTIETAM CREEK. A dozen miles ahead, a tall mountain, draped in green and a thousand feet above, loomed over the landscape.

In September of 1862, while the Federal army suffered the grand calamity at Harpers Ferry only fifteen miles south of here, General McClellan stumbled on one of the luckiest breaks in the history of warfare, one that possibly provided the greatest opportunity for an early Northern victory in the War. As a result, one of the War's most strategic, consequential, and lesser known battles transpired here in the Battle of South Mountain.

As General Lee continued to march north to Pennsylvania, he halted at Hagerstown, West Virginia, to wait on Jackson after his investment of Harpers Ferry. But Lee got behind schedule, Jackson's operation taking longer than expected. Divided, Lee knew his army was exposed, far from friendly terrain and any supply base. His forces, just under forty thousand men and divided into several commands, could easily be swallowed up by Little Mac and his massive army of eighty-five thousand troops one after the other. Lee fretted, his divided army only shielded from the Federal Army by the 1,300-foot-high South Mountain, a finger of the Blue Ridge Mountains running north and south, and his knowledge of McClellan's tendency to dither.

On September 13, as Bobby Lee waited anxiously to hear from Jackson, two Indiana soldiers found three cigars wrapped in a piece of paper lying in a field. Enjoying the tobacco, they looked over the paper, covered in ink. A sergeant read the words and quickly passed the paper up the chain of command, where it eventually reached McClellan. The paper was the notorious Special Order 191, Lee's detailed plans and troop dispositions for the Harpers Ferry operation written out to Gen. Daniel Harvey Hill. Even better for Little Mac, Lee's adjutant, Robert Chilton, transcribed the order, and since Chilton had once been a paymaster for the army, McClellan's staff easily confirmed its authenticity.

Little Mac and his staff quickly realized the obvious. Lee was vulnerable.

McClellan joyfully exalted. "Here is a paper with which, if I cannot whip Bobby Lee, I will be willing to go home." Delighted, he later wrote, "My general idea is to cut the enemy in two and beat him in detail," and later telegraphed Washington, "Will catch them in their trap . . . will send you trophies."

For McClellan to succeed, as he knew, required prompt action, and though not acting as boldly and rapidly as most historians agree the situation dictated, Little Mac, at least for him, picked up the pace of his operations. On the morning of September 14, he sent three corps to take the gaps through South Mountain, hoping to fall onto Lee's divided forces.

Lee, getting wind that maybe McClellan had some intelligence to his desperate straits, sent his rearguard, under Gen. D. H. Hill, into Fox's and Turner's gaps, South Mountain's northern passes, with orders to hold the passes, "at all hazards." Hill, with only five thousand men, had to stretch his men along several miles to defend the gaps.

Seven miles to the south, less than a thousand Confederate cavalry guarded Crampton's Gap, which protected a route not only to Lee's Army, but also Jackson at Harpers Ferry.

Everywhere, the Rebels were heavily outnumbered but held the high ground and only needed to hold off McClellan for a day until Jackson rejoined the Confederate Army.

On the morning of September 14, two army corps, under Gens. Joe Hooker and Jessie Reno, assailed the northern gaps, and later that day, another corps under Gen. William Franklin attacked Crampton's Gap.

Gen. D. H. Hill, who initially arrived on the mountain with only two brigades, later recounted a view from the Mountain that day.

"The vast array of McClellan spread out before me. The marching columns extended back as far as eye could see in the distance; but many of the troops had already arrived and were in double lines of battle, and those advancing were taking up positions as fast as they arrived. It was a grand and glorious spectacle, and it was impossible to look at it without admiration. I had never seen so tremendous an army before, and I did not see one like it afterward."

By nightfall, the cost of the battle littered the mountain—more than five thousand men killed, wounded, or missing including the death of several generals.

The Battle of South Mountain is often overlooked today, largely because it is overshadowed by the epic battle it enabled three days later. Outside of Sharpsburg, Maryland, along the banks of Antietam Creek, the armies clashed in the single bloodiest day in American military history.

The battlefield at South Mountain is still there, and there I went one summer morning to meet Steven Stotelmyer, a native of the area, guide at both South Mountain and Antietam, and a founding member of the Central Maryland Heritage League. I met Steven at the Old South Mountain Inn, D. H. Hill's headquarters during the battle, astride the Old National Pike in Turner's Gap.

Steven first drove me down the Dahlgren Road, showing me a few hilltop meadows where the Rebels set up artillery as I looked down some of the steep, rugged inclines, falling down hundreds of feet into deep, tree-lined ravines.

"General Meade's division attacked up this road," Steven said. "You need to tell your readers to drive down Dahlgren Road. It's too steep and winding to drive up it. But this gives you some sense of the precipitous, rugged terrain the battle was on. Probably the roughest terrain of any battle in the east."

I quickly concurred as we bounced along on the gravel road, getting an occasional overlook into the Catoctin Valley to the east, a flat plain of farmland five hundred feet below and every shade of green in the morning sun.

"Up this road," Steven said, "Joe Hooker's corps pushed back Hill's left flank."

"How long have you been associated with the battlefield, guiding and working?" I asked.

"Longer than I've been alive, literally," Steven said with a chuckle. "I've been coming here and Antietam since before I was born. I have a picture of my parents at Antietam. My mom was a few months pregnant. That was me!"

I might note that South Mountain is not a walking tour, though the top of South Mountain is traversed by the Appalachian Trail. The battlefield is too spread out, broken, rocky, and entwined with private tracts. To really see the battlefield requires a driving tour. The state of Maryland has one that can be downloaded, but you really need a guide. It's all a very confusing maze of hills, roads, draws, and thick trees around the old cast-iron battlefield signs, put up in the late twentieth-century but still around.

To get started, I suggest driving up to the Washington Monument where Steven took me. The conical stone lookout tower was America's first monument to President Washington. The top of the monument has the best view of the Mountain, draped in verdant trees, a single ridge slicing through the rich farmland on each side. Below the fresh mountain air, the roads bisected the farms and connected the little valley towns, their shiny roofs and tall churches visible.

The monument was here during the battle but only used as an observation or signal post. The state of Maryland also has a small museum at the monument with a great, dynamic light model of the battle. Watching it will help visualize the battle's events before you head out slicing here and there, round and round, up and down over the small roads that bisect the battle and mountain.

We drove down the Old National Pike, today Highway 40, where Union general John Gibbons's Iron Brigade, Wisconsin, and Indiana boys fought it out with Col. Alfred Colquitt's Georgians. In one of those ironies of the War, Gibbons served as the best man in D. H. Hill's wedding.

"Colquitt's boys were really the only Confederates that held their ground that day," Steven said, pointing out the window. "The wall they held is still there, but it's on private property. You can see it in a new snow."

Who in the hell would be driving this narrow, winding road with a fresh snow?

Steven Stotelmyer, Central Maryland Heritage League, at the Washington Monument on South Mountain

Steven then took me over to Fox's Gap. Here, the fighting got underway at 7:30 in the morning, commencing an eleven-hour struggle for the gap. Late in the morning, Confederate general Samuel Garland, commanding a brigade of North Carolinians fell mortally wounded. Union colonel and future President Rutherford Hayes also fell severely wounded here, but by midday, Union general Jacob Cox's division of worn-out Ohioans held the gap. But instead of pressing the attack, they paused, took stock, and consolidated units, giving the Rebels time.

As the day wore on, General Lee, in one of the few battles he didn't command in the field due to injuries to his hands, sent reinforcements under James Longstreet to the mountain, as did Union Corps Commander Jessie Reno, in a desperate attempt to hold the passes.

Arriving at Fox's gap, Steven pulled over to show me the original "sunken road." It's still there, today called Reno Monument Road, cut about eight feet into the mountain at the gap. Late in the day, as the Federals overwhelmed the Rebs, a brigade of South Carolinians and Georgians under Thomas Drayton found themselves on the road, surrounded on three sides by angry Yanks.

Lt. Peter McGlashen recalled what happened next: "The men stood their ground nobly, returning the fire until nearly two-thirds of their number lay dead or wounded in that lane. Out of 210 carried into the fight, over 125 were killed or wounded in less than twenty minutes. The slaughter was horrible. When ordered to retreat, I could scarce extricate myself from the dead and wounded around me. A man could walk from the head of the line to the foot on their bodies."

Steven showed me some recent research on the fight at the road that further documents the toil. The 3rd South Carolina, sometimes called the "Lost Legion," had 136 of its 160 men killed or wounded here in less than thirty minutes.

The 9th New Hampshire arrived at Fox's Gap at the height of the turmoil. Its colonel, Enoch Fellows, sent his men into the melee. "I want every man of the 9th New Hampshire to follow me over that wall. Now, men of the 9th, it's time to cover yourselves in glory or disgrace. Any man that does not cross this wall I will report to his state!"

The Rebel situation growing critical at Fox's Gap, the Confederates outnumbered at least two to one, Hill rushed some of Longstreet's just-arrived reinforcements, a brigade of Texans under Gen. John Bell Hood, to Fox's Gap.

Hood had recently been removed from command for stealing some Yankee ambulances, but the day desperate, Lee reinstated Hood, whose men ran straight into General Reno, who had arrived at the Gap, and put a minié ball into the general. Reno's men carried him back down the mountain where he died, the most senior Federal officer to fall in the War to date.

At Fox's Gap, the state, the Appalachian Trail, and preservation groups have the most land accessible to the modern Civil War tourist, with big chunks on both sides of the "sunken road," available for perusing.

Steven showed me the Reno Monument, beside the "sunken road," dedicated in 1889, and a bunch of old pictures of the mountain in the late nineteenth century. Most of the trees that cloak the mountain today didn't exist, and the views of the mountain during the battle were much more open. He also walked over to show me something of personal interest right beside the Appalachian Trail on the site of the Wise

House, present at the Gap during the battle but torn down in the early twentieth century.

"This is the Wise Well." Steven pointed to a few stones.

I had heard about the well. For more than 125 years, legend had it that Mr. Wise dumped fifty-eight dead Confederates in his well, and was paid handsomely, one dollar per burial by the Federal Army. After the War, this didn't do much for Mr. Wise's reputation, and according to lore, the state forced him to remove the bodies and give them a proper burial.

Steven later emailed me an article he wrote about this for *Blue and Gray Magazine*. According to Steven, the Yankee soldiers dumped the bodies in the well, and Mr. Wise never got a penny for it. In 2002, an archeological survey was done of the Wise property, and the famous well was finally located. The survey only excavated enough to confirm the location of the abandoned well, found to be filled with old debris.

We then drove south, seven miles down the mountain to Crampton's Gap, weaving through the patchwork of roads and cornfields. Steven pointed out at least a half-dozen old houses present during the battle. He also pointed to several vacant lots where modern houses have been purchased and removed, and one house recently purchased and scheduled to be removed in an attempt by preservation groups to restore the entire area to its 1862 condition.

"The roads are pretty much where they were during the battle," Steven said. "Except for the trees, it's largely the same."

As Steven talked, I plucked a tick off my leg and then gave myself a good inspection!

At Crampton's Gap, the Federals had their best opportunity to breach the mountain. Early in the day, they outnumbered the Rebs more than ten to one, but Corps commander general William Franklin waited until late in the day to attack. Initially facing only dismounted cavalry, the Yanks easily swept around the Rebels, who then rushed two thousand Georgians under Gen. Howell Cobb to Crampton's Gap.

A former Governor of Georgia and Speaker of the US House of Representatives, Cobb was considered one of the founders of the Confederacy. He was so loathed in Unionist circles that during the Federal Army's march to the sea two years later, General Sherman made sure his men didn't miss Cobb. He ordered his plantation burned, instructing his men to "spare nothing."

The ex-speaker didn't fare much better at Crampton's Gap. Franklin's corps, more than ten thousand strong, easily pushed the Georgians off the mountain. Cobb raised the colors trying to rally his men, but Yank lead soon shot the flag from his hands.

Cobb lamented. "What can be done? What can save us?"

James Toomer of the 16th Virginia described the Federal attack. "They came over the field grandly, the officers all in place and cheering the men onward, the men well aligned on the colors, with the Stars and Stripes floating above them . . . like devils let loose in the infernal regions."

Darkness actually saved Cobb. The battle at Crampton's Gap was the most decisive Union victory of the day, the Confederate losses at about one thousand, half of which were captured, against similar Union losses, but the Blue Coats held the Gap. Franklin's corps, the least bloodied of the battle, sat poised to cause major chaos for Lee's Army. But Franklin decided they had done enough for one day.

Crampton's Gap is not as preserved as Turner's and Fox's Gaps. In 1884, Civil War correspondent George Alfred Townsend purchased the Gap and built a huge estate in the pass. He did erect the mammoth, fifty feet high, War Correspondents Memorial Arch, which is still there today. It's neat-looking and dominates the pass, a thick stone monolith, capped with a castle-like cupola, but it has nothing to do with the battle.

Steven drove me around Crampton's Gap, including down the Mountain Church Road at the east base of the mountain where the Confederate cavalry made their initial stand behind a stone wall that still stands beside the road.

We then drove back up to the top of the mountain and hiked up to the Washington Monument. As we strolled up the winding trail, Steven told me he has a book coming out that reconsiders McClellan during the Maryland campaign.

"That will arouse some attention," I joked.

"Yeah," Steven said. "I'm making my case. Mac's gotten a bad rap here. This was his best generalship."

Steven Stotelmyer, Central Maryland Heritage League, at the National War
Correspondents Memorial, Crampton's Gap

I read several other respected opinions that mirrored Steven's
thoughts on McClellan during the Maryland campaign. Meade certainly
was no Stonewall Jackson, but looking down the steep, broken hills and
off to the east to the spires of Middletown, ten miles distant, it's hard to
criticize the Federal Army. They marched here and then fought up this
rugged mountain. As my chest heaved in and out from the short hike up
to the monument, I tried to fathom the Yank's exhaustion. Ahead, down
the mountain lay the only sure thing . . . a massive and battle-tested Rebel
army somewhere at the mountain's base. You have to come look at this
battle to understand it. Many thanks to Steven for showing it to me.

The night after the battle, Lee got word from Jackson of the immi-
nent fall of Harpers Ferry. He met with his generals, and then pulled all
his men off the mountain. The day's events forced him to abandon his
campaign north. He'd turn his army southward, but he bought enough
time to gather his forces.

McClellan and his men celebrated. For the first time in the War,
the army of the Potomac held the battlefield when the guns quit firing.
Around midnight, McClellan cabled Washington with the news of his

great victory, and the next day wrote his wife, "Have just learned that the enemy are retreating in a panic and our victory is complete."

But it was not long before the Young Napoleon's elation waned. Maybe he didn't yet have trophies to send to Lincoln. His pickets and observation posts soon reported a large Confederate Army forming for battle north of Sharpsburg, along the banks of then little known Antietam Creek. Though victorious, Little Mac squandered any advantage gained with the discovery of Order 191. He now had to fight the Rebel army, no longer separated, and on ground of their choosing.

Washington Monument State Park
6620 Zittlestown Rd.
Middletown, MD 21769
(301) 791-4767
http://dnr.maryland.gov/publiclands/Pages/western/washington.aspx
http://dnr.maryland.gov/publiclands/Pages/western/southmountain
battlefield.aspx

CHAPTER 11

"Yes, I Fear All"

Shepherdstown, West Virginia

Two days after both armies mauled each other on the blood-soaked fields at Antietam, Lee ordered his men back across the Potomac, not in retreat, but to regroup, rest, gather stragglers, and again move north. His army crossed the river at a ford about a half mile south of what is today Shepherdstown, West Virginia. As the army crossed and moved on, Lee left two brigades and forty-four pieces of artillery behind, atop some tall bluffs on the west bank of the river as a rearguard.

A few days earlier, Lincoln telegraphed McClellan: "Destroy the Rebel army, if possible."

Late on September 19, Federal general Charles Griffin sent two regiments across the Potomac on a reconnaissance mission. A brief scuffle ensued, and the Yanks captured four pieces of Rebel artillery. The next morning, Griffin's commander, Gen. Fitz John Porter, ordered two full brigades across the river. Porter had been relieved of command for alleged insubordination at Second Manassas but had been recently reinstated by McClellan.

The Confederate artillery commander, the preacher-turned-soldier, Gen. William Pendleton, got confused and alarmed. Pendleton named his first four cannons: Matthew, Mark, Luke, and John. During Griffin's initial attack, he took off for General Lee's headquarters. The artillery commander reported to Lee that the Federal Army captured his entire forty-four gun battery. "The enemy has taken the heights and captured all the guns."

"All?" Lee asked.

"Yes, I fear all," the preacher replied.

Understandably, Bobby got concerned. Was this a full-fledged Union thrust? Lee summoned Ambrose Powell (A. P.) Hill, fast becoming a stalwart of his army. Hill, a West Pointer, wore a red frock in battle and excelled at Second Manassas, Harper's Ferry, and Antietam. Lee sent Hill and his light division back to the Potomac.

Hill's division arrived and ran into the reinforced bluecoats. The Yanks, isolated, on the wrong side of the river, and now outnumbered began retiring. Hill's Light Division pushed back the Northern boys, but the Federal artillery, perched high on the opposite bank of the river tore into the Confederates.

In just a few hours, more than a hundred men met their maker, with almost six hundred more wounded or missing. Historians have often referred to Shepherdstown as a small skirmish after Antietam. I challenge the reader to find a veteran who has been in a fight with more than seven hundred casualties that they think was a skirmish. Shepherdstown was the bloodiest battle fought in West Virginia, and may have been more strategic than deadly.

In 2004, the Shepherdstown Battlefield Preservation Association was formed, and recently, the association and Jefferson County have purchased some of the battlefield. In 2017, if a Civil War time traveler wants to see what a virgin battlefield, one that's nearly intact and untainted and has yet to be restored, looks like, Shepherdstown is the place to go. And that's exactly what I did.

I met Kevin Pawlak with the association. We drove through marvelous, antique Shepherdstown, its main street lined with old brick buildings, cafes, and colorful banners—a magically charming mix of new and old hidden in the Appalachians. The two thousand citizens and four thousand students at Shepherd University enjoyed their lazy Saturday morning. Down German Street we went, until it turned into River Road, running beside the Potomac. About a mile and a half south of downtown sits an old cement factory. The road bisects it. There's only two signs, one installed by the War Department in the 1890s, and one recently put up. It's here, on the bluffs beside the river, where the Northern boys fled for their lives, the Rebs pouring fire down on them as the Yanks ran down the steep ravines and into the wide river.

We first walked through the old cement factory, a collection of old, grown-up stone walls along the river the resembled Roman ruins.

"The factory was shelled during the battle, but the site has never had any archaeology done on it," Kevin said. "A few years ago, one of my college professors found an old Enfield. The stock was gone and it was rusty, but it was vintage."

At the river's edge, Kevin pointed to the piers of the old bridge, burnt by the Rebels, and to the River's two crossing spots, a ford, and the remnants of the dam in the river for the cement factory, both today only ripples in the river. I planned and came prepared to cross the river, walk the ford. Many people do it today, but typical for me, my timing was terrible. The region got a rare three-inch summer rain the day before. Old Mr. River scooted along, the bubbling, wide sheet of brown water racing by too fast for me to tempt it.

We walked through the old cement factory, many of its walls still standing, and looked at four old kilns, in remarkable shape.

Kevin told me one story about some Yanks hiding in the kilns, one of which had a shell come through its opening. Those boys would be what

Kevin Pawlak, Shepherdstown Battlefield Preservation Association, at a kiln in the cement factory at Shepherdstown

Civil War historians classify as "missing." I looked at the kilns, tall stacks of damaged grey and tan stone and brick around arched holes.

I pointed to a section of one of the kiln walls with a large section of stone displaced. "Yankee cannonball?"

"We don't know. Probably some of it."

"I bet there's somebody that can tell you."

Kevin then took me up a steep trail, to the bluff. Below, I looked down on the cement factory and river, fifty feet below, and into several tight draws that split the hillside. "This was a killing field. There wasn't near as many trees then. The Yanks ran through these tight ravines, the Confederates firing from up here. The Yanks were in a death trap, but the Rebs were exposed up here to the Federal artillery. Bad for everybody."

The Yankee gunners had honed their craft. The 14th South Carolina lost more than fifty men in twenty minutes. A South Carolina soldier wrote: "It was the best artillery shooting I ever saw. Every shell seemed to burst immediately in front of our line."

During the fight, Porter sent two more brigades across the river, more to cover the retreat than anything, and the battle further intensified.

I wanted to see another spot, the 118th Pennsylvania's position. The 118th had two bad strokes of luck this day. The regiment, only in the army a few weeks, had been issued faulty muskets, many that wouldn't fire. They were so green; they had yet to fire them, only discovering their weapons' flaws at the moment of truth. The second mishap occurred when the 118th's commander, Col. Charles Prevost, refused to abandon his position because he didn't get his orders through the proper channels. Hill's boys decimated the 118th, inflicting 40 percent casualties.

Captain Francis Adams of the 118th described the retreat: "I shall never forget the scene as I worked my way across the dreadful causeway. The bullets struck all around me—men were shot in various places of the body, some falling, others again staggering and struggling to make the other side."

"Do y'all have the spot where the 118th got slaughtered?" I asked.

"Yes, I'll take you there."

Shortly, we looked up the draw where the Pennsylvanians ran for their lives through the storm of lead.

"Once y'all get some signs," I said, "and get all the brush cleared off the cement factory and kilns, this will be a really cool place."

"Yeah, Shepherdstown is the nearest place to eat or stay to Antietam. It's already a neat college town. It will be a great stop."

We walked back to the river to look across the waters to Maryland. After the Federals retreated back across the river, Lt. Lemuel Crocker of the 118th disobeyed orders and crossed the river alone to retrieve the wounded. Caught by the Rebs and informed that the armies had not called a flag of truce, Crocker explained himself. So impressed with Crocker's bravery and cause, the Rebs not only let him proceed, they provided him an escort. And Crocker soon returned with a surgeon to attend to both Blue and Gray.

Union Captain Frank Donelson summed up Crocker's deeds. "The daring of this man Croker is beyond all precedent. Think of it, crossing the dam alone, exposed all the while to the sharpshooters' deadly aim. Why they did not fire upon him is beyond comprehension."

"So this is where Crocker crossed the river," I said.

Kevin smiled. "That is my favorite story of the entire Civil War."

The fighting ended that night at Shepherdstown. The "skirmish" caused by "all" the guns that weren't captured, convinced Lee to abandon his second northern invasion. It put the brakes on McClellan's pursuit. The Maryland campaign was all but over. Estimates put the casualties in the seventeen-day campaign at north of forty thousand.

Nothing had been settled. In just a few months, the two armies, bigger, better armed, and bolder, would be clashing again. Lincoln sacked the Young Napoleon seven weeks later, and shortly thereafter, the army arrested and court martialed Fritz John Porter for his actions at Second Manassas, then convicted and dismissed him from the army two months later.

In the end, things worked out better for the battered 118th Pennsylvania than the Southern boys who chewed them up that day on the banks of the river. They would go on to be one of the more storied units in the army, invited by Grant to receive the arms and flags of Lee's army at Appomattox.

Hill and his brigade commanders didn't fare so well. William Pender would die the next summer at Gettysburg. James Archer would be captured there and die before the end of the War. Maxcy Gregg fell at Fredericksburg. Lee removed the preacher, Pendleton, from the artillery and gave him an administrative job. And we'll run into A. P. Hill again.

Shepherdstown Battlefield
4389 River Rd.
Shepherdstown, WV 25443
https://www.facebook.com/ShepherdstownBattlefieldPreservationAssoc
iation/

CHAPTER 12

"Death Came in a Hundred Shapes"

Corinth, Mississippi

In the early twenty-first century, Corinth, Mississippi, is a quaint little town of fifteen thousand, set in the foothills only a few miles south of the Tennessee state line. The town didn't exist in 1850, but in the next decade two new railroads crossed paths here, the Mobile & Ohio and the Memphis & Charleston, the latter the only major Confederate east-west line. In 1862, tiny Corinth, with a population of about 1,500, of which 400 were slaves, saw more than 200,000 troops occupy the town and hosted a Union siege and a bloody battle, all but forgotten today.

After the battle of Shiloh, both countries gasped. The almost twenty-four thousand casualties were fivefold the War's biggest battle to date, Manassas. If you didn't know, the Hebrew word "Shiloh" means "place of peace." The Rebels pulled out to their most strategic point in the area, Corinth, where the two iron roads crossed. The town, with only three hotels, took in almost seventy thousand Confederates who quickly entrenched themselves, and eighteen thousand wounded or sick men, turning almost every building in town into a hospital. The little village turned into a massive war-camp, almost every building occupied and tents stretching in all directions.

Gen. Henry Halleck, whom Lincoln would name general-in-chief a few months later, said, "Richmond and Corinth are now the great strategic points of the war, and our success at these points should be insured at all hazards." A huge Union army subsequently invested Corinth. After a month-long siege, the Rebels abandoned the hamlet to the Union Army.

The Union soldiers and generals generally thought Corinth a steamy, insect-infested hellhole. One Minnesota lieutenant claimed the women were "she-vipers" who looked like "shad-bellied bean poles," and the town's chief products "wood ticks, chiggers, fleas, and niggers."

I found an old book written by Otto Eisenshimal, *Historian without an Armchair*. Back in the '20s and '30s, Otto, the son of a Civil War veteran, toured a bunch of Civil War places, meeting with old veterans. He came to Corinth to inspect its earthworks and left to posterity his thoughts on the town. "Headquarters of well-known generals are too numerous to attract attention. I was shown the house where Albert Sidney Johnston stayed prior to the battle of Shiloh, and the ones where Pierre. G. T. Beauregard, William Rosecrans, US Grant and others held forth at one time or another. Plenty of beautiful homes were available for them to choose from."

The reality of Civil War Corinth is probably somewhere between two opinions! Even then, Corinth had been forgotten. Otto's most entertaining observation was a marker that commemorated a Texas Colonel, William Rogers, which read: "Will be honored and remembered by every Texan for all time to come." Otto noted, "Well, I've asked every Texan I've met if he remembered Colonel Rogers. I have yet to find one who does, or to whom the name means anything."

In the fall of 1862, the Confederate armies tried to reclaim the crossroads. It's here that some of the War's most interesting characters came together in a battle that ranked, as far as casualties, one of the thirty bloodiest battles of the War. In proportion to the troops engaged, Corinth ranked as one of the deadliest battles of the rebellion.

In the months after the fall of Corinth, many of the one hundred thousand Union soldiers who took the town were subsequently sent off to fight elsewhere. By October of 1862, Union general William Rosecrans commanded twenty-two thousand troops in Corinth, most occupying the abandoned Rebel earthworks around the town.

On a hot October 3, a Confederate army under the command of Gen. Earl Van Dorn, augmented by Gen. Sterling Price's army of the West, attacked the Federal lines north of Corinth. Van Dorn, in his own words, "proposed to march to a certain and brilliant victory." Price was a Mexican

War hero and ex-governor of Missouri. Van Dorn and Rosecrans graduated together from West Point; Van Dorn and Price had been bested at Pea Ridge six months earlier, and set out to reclaim their reputations.

The battle played out rather simply. Van Dorn's more than twenty thousand men stormed the Federal defenses on the north side of town on a sultry October day. By concentrating his men, the Rebs outnumbered the Yanks three to one on this side of town. But Van Dorn marched his men ten miles, and without water and little rest, sent them into battle. Still, they breached the Federal lines and almost carried the day. But dizzy with thirst and exhaustion, the Rebs ran out of gas.

Van Dorn renewed the attack the next day, but this turned into a bloody disaster. Rosecrans had reinforced his front. By day's end, Van Dorn romped off in full retreat, the ground strewn with Southern boys, 500 killed, almost 2,000 wounded, and 1,800 prisoners against Federal losses of about half these numbers.

Sergeant James Payne, of the 6th Missouri, summed up the failed Confederate charge, "They were under the concentrated fire of fifty cannon and ten thousand rifles. Not for a moment did they halt. Bending their necks as do men when protecting themselves . . . they pressed rapidly ahead. Every instant death smote. It came in a hundred shapes, every shape a separate horror."

The sweltering southern sun creeping above the green hills to the east, I drove through attractive, tidy, Corinth. This wasn't king cotton, but rural, rolling hills, the citizens of the county voting two-to-one against secession. The area didn't even get electricity until the Federal government's Tennessee Valley Authority put in a grid in the 1930s. For almost a century and a half, the preservation of Civil War Corinth was mostly a local effort, but this morning I drove to the Corinth Civil War Interpretive Center, opened in 2004 by the NPS, to meet Woody Harrell, the retired superintendent of the Shiloh National Military Park, now a resident of Corinth. The center opened after years of lobbying, when Mississippi finally had some bosses in Congress.

I recommend the Interpretive Center, as good as I've seen. The twenty-minute movie about Civil War Corinth is in high definition. Woody showed me some of the center's attractions, including the Battle

Flag of the 6th Missouri. The flag bearer was shot nine times during the battle at Corinth, but the flag survived and ended up at Vicksburg. Eight months later, knowing Vicksburg would soon fall, the wife of the 6th's commander, Josephine Irwin, snuck into Vicksburg to see her sick and wounded husband, Col. Eugene Irwin. She sewed the flag under her dress and snuck it out. Her husband died a few weeks later, felled by two Union minié balls.

They've got some other battle flags, pock-marked with bullet holes, and some of the best photos of any battlefield I went to, most notably by George Armstead. Woody told me this was due to the large number of troops in Corinth. The photographers came to make a nice profit, mostly on soldiers' portraits. Usually, I like to run off to the battlefield, the museums all largely the same, but this one I wandered for more than an hour. There's a twelve-pound James rifle, captured by the Confederates at Shiloh and recaptured by Union forces at Corinth.

Woody showed me two components of the center that he had a hand in. The first, the fountain behind the center, The Stream of American History, which Woody scratched out on a pad while stranded in Miami during 9/11. The second is the bronze mural at the center's entrance, the Bas Relief. The models for the six soldiers were NPS rangers. Woody showed me his fingerprints in the mural. I found a couple of newspaper articles about the opening of the center, one with the US senator thanking Woody for his dedication to the new Corinth Center. Outside sits the focal point of the battle, Battery Robinett, still astride the Memphis and Charleston Railroad, now Norfolk Southern.

Van Dorn and Price got the best of day one.

On the second day of the battle, Gen. Dabney Maury's division, and more specifically, a brigade under Gen. John Moore, had a titanic fight at Robinett. This is where Colonel Rogers fell. The United Daughters of the Confederacy have replaced the wooden plaque with another monument to Colonel Rodgers, the biggest monument I saw at the battlefield, a tall stone obelisk.

Intense fighting transpired here. I found two descriptions of the attack, each by common soldiers, one blue, one gray. Captain Oscar Jackson, of the 63rd Ohio, guarded the right of Battery Robinett.

"The rebels began pouring out of the timber and forming storming columns. All the firing ceased and everything was silent as the grave. They formed one column . . . then another and crowding out of the woods another, and so on. I thought they would never stop coming out of the timber. While they were forming, the men were considerable distance from us but in plain sight and as soon as they were ready they started at us with a firm, slow, steady step. In all my campaigns I have never seen anything so hard to stand as that slow, steady tramp. Not a sound was heard, but they looked as if they intended to walk over us."

Lt. Charles Labruzan of the 42nd Alabama described what happened next as he topped a hill. "Rising the crest of the hill the whole of Corinth with its enemy fortifications burst upon our view. The US flag was floating over the forts and in town. We were now met by a perfect storm of grape, canister and cannon balls and minié balls. Oh God, I have never seen the like, the men fell like grass. I saw men running at full speed stop suddenly and fall on their faces with their brains scattered all around with legs or arms cut off shrieking within a few feet of me. I gave myself to God and got ahead of my company. The ground was literally strewn with corpses. . . . We were butchered like dogs."

Colonel Rogers was a fighter. A veteran of the Mexican War, he served under Jeff Davis and, in fact, had a terrible falling out with him. One of the most famous photos of Corinth, on display in the center, is of Colonel Rogers, dead, lying beside a dozen of his fallen men in front of Robinett. Five Texas color bearers fell before Rogers took up the colors, this his undoing. We know where William Rogers is buried because after the battle, General Rosecrans visited the Battery and said, "He was one of the bravest men that ever led a charge. Bury him with military honors and mark his grave, so his friends can claim him. The time will come when there will be a monument here to commemorate his bravery."

Today, a middle-class neighborhood and the Interpretive Center, part of a larger city park, occupy the bloody contested ground, birds chirping in the trees, kids playing in the park.

Woody took me to several other sites around town, including the NPS's other site, the old contraband camp. At this time in the War, Lincoln had yet to issue his Emancipation Proclamation. Captured or runaway

Woody Harrell, retired Shiloh National Military Park superintendent, at Colonel Rogers' monument

slaves were simply war booty, called contrabands at the time. They were put into camps and paid to work for the Union cause. In Corinth, almost four thousand ex-slaves occupied the camp after the battle.

We drove by the four wonderful old houses that survive from the battle, all different, but all venerable in their Greek Revival architecture. They all harbored the great generals of the War: Grant, Johnston, Beauregard, etc. Only the Veranda house is open to the public. Woody told me the story of Rose Cottage, burnt in the 1920s, but rebuilt. The house served as Gen. Sidney Johnston's headquarters before the battle of Shiloh. The lady of the house, Augusta Inge, made Johnston some sandwiches before he left for the battle. His body brought back to the house to lay in state after the battle, Mrs. Inge found a half-eaten sandwich in the general's pocket.

Finally, Woody took me to the epicenter, what it was all about, the railroad crossing. It's still there, by the new railroad depot and museum, and a big, authentic thirty-pound Parrott Rifle. Woody and I took some great pictures, and he pointed out the town's war sights from here. Corinth today in this area is all post–Civil War, but there are plenty of photos of the old crossing in the museum, and the great painting at the museum done by Keith Rocco, is right here, at the Confederate high-water mark of the second day of the battle. The center's free pamphlet has the painting on its cover. Bring it with you to the crossing—you'll see why this is sacred ground.

After the battle, almost every building in town became a hospital. The center has numerous diaries depicting the horror and stench of the town, probably the smallest in the War to see so many troops and wounded. Sergeant Sam Byers described the town after the battle: "I saw the floors, tables, and chairs covered with amputated limbs, some white and some broken and bleeding. There were simply bushels of them, and the floor was running blood. It was a strange, horrible sight,—but it was war. Yes, it was hell."

The battle was costly, almost seven thousand casualties, more than four thousand Confederates. The Union had four generals wounded and one killed: Gen. Pleasant Hackleman, a personal friend of Lincoln. A second friend of the President, Gen. Richard Oglesby, thought to be mortally wounded, was saved by Grant, who sent a surgeon to Corinth to tend to the general. Oglesby survived and went on to be a three-term governor and US senator from Illinois. On the morning of the battle's second

The author at the rail crossroads in Corinth

day, Union colonel Joe Mower was wounded and captured but later recovered by the army. He would go on to be a corps commander by War's end.

Another survivor of the battle was the mascot of the 8th Wisconsin, a bald eagle named Old Abe. He sat on a perch in battle. General Price ordered the feathering of Old Abe at any cost. During the battle, a Rebel slug severed Abe's tether line, and he took to the sky to fly the lines. Needless to say, he soon became a hot target, and Rebel fire soon clipped a wing. The Wisconsin boys recovered Abe and tried to put him back on his perch, but Old Abe would have none of it. He found cover.

Old Abe went on to have a distinguished battle record at some of the War's biggest fights before finally passing in 1881, where his stuffed remains were put in the Rotunda of the Wisconsin capital. Teddy Roosevelt once viewed Abe, and he's on the patch of the army's 101st Airborne. There's plenty of statues and monuments around to Old Abe. A fire destroyed the Wisconsin capital in 1904, consuming Abe's remains. The proud eagle had a good run but came the closest to meeting his maker at Corinth.

The Yanks eventually abandoned Corinth, the typhoid- and dysentery-riddled locale too unhealthy to garrison. On their way out, they burnt the town's biggest edifice, the Corona Female College, and Corinth fell from the nation's headlines, never to return. The Corinth National Cemetery is there, with the Union dead, more than four thousand marked unknown. It's still taking interments.

One of the reason's Corinth has fallen from the collective American and academic memory is its commanders. Rosecrans went on to defeat at Chickamauga, Braxton Bragg's only major victory, before being relegated to lesser commands for the remainder of the War. The cocky Van Dorn got demoted to a cavalry commander after Corinth. A notorious womanizer, less than a year later, a jealous husband murdered him in his own headquarters. Generals Hamilton and Mansfield Lovell, who abandoned New Orleans before its surrender, were both soon cashiered. We will bump into Sterling Price again.

Thanks to Woody for his life's work and showing me around. Price for the tour? A trade, my old copy of Otto's book. He knew of him from his days at Shiloh but hadn't read the *Historian without an Armchair*.

Eisenshimal had his ashes spread over the Shiloh Battlefield. A few days after my visit, Woody e-mailed me a picture he pulled from his records showing the old wooden marker that Otto had found at Colonel Rogers's grave.

Come see Corinth, especially if you go to Shiloh. It's only thirty miles away.

Corinth Civil War Interpretive Center
501 W Linden St.
Corinth, MS 38834
(662) 287-9273
https://www.nps.gov/shil/learn/historyculture/corinth.htm

CHAPTER 13

"To Lose Kentucky is to Lose the Whole Game"

Perryville, Kentucky

In the fall of 1862, the apprehension in the Northern press and the public over the situation in Kentucky reached a fever pitch, Lincoln himself saying, "To lose Kentucky is nearly the same as to lose the whole game." Making matters worse, on the heels of Kirby Smith's success, Confederate general Braxton Bragg marched another army of twenty thousand men into Kentucky, Gen. Don Carlos Buell's army shadowing him to protect Louisville and Cincinnati.

Lincoln didn't just moan, he gathered forces. In Louisville, fifty-five thousand troops were put under the command of Buell, who soon set out to find Bragg, sending his army in three separate columns into Kentucky. Early in October, Bragg decided to turn and fight, hoping to attack one of Buell's isolated corps.

On October 7, the Kentucky landscape parched from the biggest drought in memory, the fighting got underway when the lead division of Gen. Charles Gilbert's III corps, in need of water and commanded by Gen. Phil Sheridan, ran into some Rebels around a water hole near Peters Hill, a few miles west of the small town of Perryville.

The next day, Bragg, thinking only a single Federal Corps occupied the area, commenced a general attack. Instead of running into Gilbert's corps, he unknowingly attacked another still deploying corps under Gen. Alexander McCook. Despite being outnumbered, the Rebs made a furious, uphill attack, sending the Yanks fleeing.

The Confederate success was likely due to the fine commanders under Bragg, one of the best assembled in any army during the War, and certainly this early in the rebellion. Five of Bragg's commanders, including William Hardee and Joseph Wheeler, would go on to be lieutenant generals. Hardee, once the commandant of West Point, wrote the army's manual of tactics. He also had some of the Confederacy's best fighters: Gens. Patrick Cleburne, A. P. Stewart, Simon Buckner, John Liddell, Daniel Adams, John Wharton, Preston Smith, and George Maney, who would go on to glory before the War's end.

By the end of the day almost 8,000 Americans, 3,400 Rebs and 4,200 Federals, would fall, killed, missing, or wounded. Though a Confederate tactical victory, as darkness fell Bragg soon realized the size of the forces aligned against him, and later than night began to fall back to join Kirby Smith's army. Both Rebel generals' dreams of Kentuckians flocking to join their armies did not come to fruition. Bragg's officers and Smith wanted to stay and fight, but Bragg decided to leave the State, marching south to Tennessee, and the Confederacy abandoned Kentucky to the Union.

Both Buell and Bragg came under widespread ridicule for their conduct during the battle, Buell for not pursuing, and Bragg for retreating. Both were summoned to their capitals to explain. The army replaced Buell, and he never got another command. Bragg survived, but his officers never regained confidence in the general.

The gargantuan battle of Perryville, the second largest in the west at its time, its consequences some of the most enormous of the entire War went unattended and all but forgotten until 1936 when the state of Kentucky opened a small park at the battle site. In 1954, its seventeen acres became the Perryville Battlefield State Historic Site.

In 1991, the Perryville Battlefield Preservation Association was created and since has aided in the purchase of twenty additional tracts. Today, more than 1,100 acres are preserved to honor our forefathers.

The hour's drive to Perryville from Lexington is wonderful, the roadside dotted with famous bourbon distilleries and thoroughbreds grazing on the fluttering bluegrass. Might I be looking at a grandson of Secretariat or maybe the triple-crown winner American Pharoah?

I met Chuck Lott, a historian for the Friends of Perryville Battlefield State Historic Site. Chuck gave me a walking tour of the battlefield. Perryville is one of the most undisturbed and pristine battlefields anywhere, from any war. The short, steep grass-covered hills, the wooden fence lines and roads, still in existence, and the remains of the Civil War structures allow the visitor to retrace the battle with almost perfection, the undisturbed spots of the battle's major events available for our perusing.

The state has planted the rolling hills with colorful black- and brown-eyed Susans—it's a beautiful scene under the big, clear Kentucky sky. From little hilltops, we can look down into the valleys (killing fields) and from hilltop to hilltop to the artillery pieces. At Perryville, there aren't many monuments, and no pieces of authentic artillery, but there's a battle-field, almost identical to 1862, where the Rebel forces pressed the Federal flanks with hammer-like blows that sent a Union Army, atop hills forti-fied with artillery, fleeing.

The five-hour battle left the rolling hills strewn with thousands of dead and wounded. Chuck took me on a hike on the Union left, where Benjamin Cheatham's division attacked. Here brigades under Gens. Daniel Donelson, A. P. Stewart, John Wharton, and George Maney undertook assaults into the wall of musketry and canister.

We walked up and down the short, steep rolling hills, Chuck showing me where the Tennessee boys stormed the hills. Donelson got the fighting started, attacking what he thought to be the Federal left, but actually into the heart of the Federal line. A reporter described his attack: "The whole line moved forward in beautiful order. All my conceptions of the hurrah and din and dust of battle were confounded by the cool, business-like operations going on before me."

Soon, General Maney commenced an attack on Donelson's right that did threaten the Federal left perched on a hilltop. All along the Federal left, the Northern boys held the hilltops, but they were green, and the Rebs were crack veterans. Sam Watkins of the 1st Tennessee, who fought in dozens of battles, and left one of the best manuscripts of the war to posterity, said, "We could see the huge war dogs frowning at us, ready at any moment to belch forth their fire and smoke, and hurl their thunderbolts of iron and death in our very midst."

As the Tennesseans approached the first hilltop, the Union general James Jackson said, "Well, I'll be damned if this is not getting rather particular." Seconds later, he fell dead from a minié ball. The Rebels took the hill, capturing seven of the eight Federal artillery pieces.

The Union soldiers fell back to the next ridge. Maney led his boys on. Trapped in a deadly pit, they had no choice but storm the hill. According to Sam, "It was death to retreat now to either side. . . . The guns were discharged so rapidly that it seemed the earth itself was in a volcanic uproar. The iron storm passed through our ranks, mangling and tearing men to pieces. The very air seemed full of stifling smoke and fire which seemed the very pit of hell."

On the second ridge, Union general William Terrill fell mortally wounded from shrapnel and the Yanks fell back to another ridge. General Terrill, a Virginian, had a brother James who fought for the Confederacy. James fell at Cold Harbor. It's said their father erected a monument to his sons with these words: "God alone knows which was right."

Many of the rookie Northern boys, their nerves frayed, fired away with their ramrods still in their muskets. Before the day ended, General Jackson and all his brigade commanders fell mortally wounded, the only time in the War a division lost its entire command structure.

Finally, Col. John Starkweather rallied his Wisconsin boys here to keep the entire Federal left from collapsing. No photos were taken at Perryville, but there are a few sketches. One of the most famous, by A. E. Mathews of the 31st Ohio, depicts Starkweather's desperate stand.

Starkweather's stand was doomed. On the Federal right, the Confederates under William Hardee got going. Hardee sent a division of Simon Bolivar Buckner into the fight. Buckner's grandson, Bill Buckner, is actually still alive, and participates in the reenactments. On this side of the battle, the Union troops were seasoned, but unfortunately they faced some of the Confederacy's best.

On Hardee's left, Bushrod Johnson, Patrick Cleburne, and a brigade of Louisiana Boys under Daniel Adams, who lost an eye at Shiloh, stormed across Doctor's Creek, destroying the 42nd Indiana, and then across the Bottom house grounds, owned by Henry Bottom. The house is still there, with bullet holes. It's not in the battlefield now, but there are plans to bring it in.

Bushrod's men ran out of ammo, but not before the general had five horses shot out from under him. But Cleburne, recovered from his wounds at Richmond, and Adams came online to press the attack. A savage fight took place at the Bottom House. There's another great sketch of the battle, done by William Davis, of the 15th Kentucky trying to hold off Adams and Cleburne behind the Bottom house.

Bottom's barn, being used as a Federal hospital, caught fire from an artillery round and burned to the ground, the wounded, screaming men inside incinerated. Chuck took me over, and we stood on the spot of the barn where the Northern boys burned to death—eerie. In Davis's dramatic painting, the barn burns behind the Kentuckians, with their hands full and too busy to save their wounded comrades in the barn. A lot of the battlefield caught fire, the soldiers' diaries depicting an apocalyptic scene.

Thaddeus Brown, with an Illinois battery, described Cleburne's charge: "They formed in division and charged across the cornfield their commander mounted on a splendid gray charger. Both rider and horse were killed, and the shells from Battery I made gaps in their column, but they closed up their ranks, and come on."

Brown was mistaken. Only Cleburne's horse, Dixie, perished.

E. J. Lewis of the 16th Louisiana gave his side of the story. "There was no cringing, no dodging. The men stood right straight up on the open field, loaded and fired, charged and fell back as deliberately as if on drill. The Yanks were whipped at every point."

We walked up to Loomis heights, the focal point of Hardee's attack, defended by a brigade under Col. William Lytle. Here, we viewed the rolling hills, like waves on the ocean, but covered with fluttering prairie grassland, where forty thousand men fought a five-hour life-or-death struggle.

Chuck pulled out his binoculars and we looked over the ridge-lines. On them, the Park has either placed replica guns or cannon silhouettes. Between the hilltops, we looked down into the smooth gently curved valleys, once strewn with dead and wounded soldiers, but today filled with wildflowers, a wonderful array of colors. According to Chuck, more than two hundred men are still there, buried in shallow graves below the yellow and white wildflowers. The only thing marring the view is a powerline crossing the battlefield east of Loomis Heights.

From here, Chuck pointed out several other things of interest. Off to the southeast, the New Orleans Washington Artillery peppered Loomis Heights. Their regimental flag was the first Southern Cross Confederate Battle Flag to be produced during the War, stitched together by Mary Lyons Jones, and given to General Beauregard. The Confederate battle flag has become the most recognizable and controversial symbol of the Confederacy, its image known worldwide. The Washington Artillery's original flag would be retired after Perryville and taken back to Alabama by Lt. Thomas Blair. Blair would die at Chickamauga, but his family kept the flag. Chuck told me about a great documentary that tells the story of this original flag, *The Southern Cross*.

If you're interested, the Washington Artillery, formed for the Mexican American War, was one of the units incorporated into the army after the Civil War. It's one of the oldest operating military units in the nation and earned a Presidential Unit Citation fighting the Nazis. Last time I checked, it was in the Middle East, still fighting it out for its country. Its unit patch, depicting its more than 160-year-old motto, says, "Try Us."

Chuck pointed further off to the west, to a distant hilltop, where Gen. Phil Sheridan and his division watched the battle. Phil, a newly promoted division commander, had recently been reprimanded for being too aggressive, and he had been directed not to do anything unless ordered.

It must have been tough on Phil. He got to see the Union I Corps defeated, while two full corps, more than thirty thousand men, relaxed in the area, while his commanding general was at Buell's headquarters, unaware that a major battle was underway.

Late in the day, Loomis Heights fell to the determined, undaunted Rebs, and both flanks of the Union Army fell back. Lytle was wounded and captured, most of his brigade commanders suffering a similar fate. Lytle, a celebrated poet, was exchanged. At Chickamauga, he fell mortally wounded. Confederate soldiers guarded his body where he fell, today called Lytle Hill at Chickamauga National Military Park.

Chuck took me to one more notorious spot on the battlefield. As the blazing sun fell below the horizon that fateful October day, Gen. Leonidas Polk, in field command of Bragg's army, arrived in General Liddell's area of the line. The shadows growing long, Liddell's men had trouble distinguishing between friend and foe, and Polk rode forward. He soon found himself in the midst of the 22nd Indiana. Asked who he was by a Yankee officer, Polk rode the Federal line yelling, "I'll soon show you who I am. Cease firing at once."

Polk spurred his horse and raced for cover. He found Liddell. "General, every mother's son of them are Yankees!"

A cry belched from Liddell's men, "Yankees!" A perfect flash of red erupted from the Rebel line. Two-thirds of the 22nd Indiana fell dead or wounded.

As darkness enveloped the Kentucky hills, the Union army had been dislodged, falling back on all fronts, but by now, Bragg learned that he had engaged only a third of the Bluecoats in the area. To linger until morning meant certain annihilation.

The story of Henry Bottom is emblematic of the War's toll, not only on the soldiers but also on the people. When the epic battle unfolded, Henry was one of the county's leading citizens, owning a 762 acre farm. When the armies arrived on his doorstep, Henry's wife, two sons, an uncle, and ten slaves lived on the farm. In addition to the loss of his barn and the damage to his house, the Bottoms lost nine cows, thirty sheep, thousands of pounds of pork and bacon, three thousand bushels of corn, fifty bushels of oats, two horses, and twenty-two tons of hay, either destroyed or consumed by the soldiers and horses.

In the days that followed the battle, the Federal forces tended to their dead and wounded. The Rebel army's retreat left the hills covered with dead or wounded Southern boys, and the army impressed the Bottoms and other locals into service policing up the dead and maimed, being feasted on by wild hogs. The little town of Perryville, population three hundred, turned into a horror scene and carried a stench for weeks.

Bottom buried the dead in a mass grave, cataloging those that could be identified. Henry and his family stayed on his farm after the War, spiritually and economically destitute. Henry filed a claim with the US

Chuck Lott, Friends of Perryville Battlefield State Historic Site, at the Bottom House

government for damages after the War, but was denied on the grounds that he was an ardent secessionist. He died in 1901 a broken man. His son refiled the Bottom claim in 1902, and finally in 1914, Congress awarded the Bottoms $1,715 for a farm valued at over $16,000 fifty years earlier.

Bottom is remembered today for his cemetery. After the War, he tried to build a stone wall around it, but financially strained, he never finished it. The cemetery languished, grown up in weeds until the United Daughters of the Confederacy built a twenty-eight foot tall monument on the battle's fortieth anniversary, the battle's only monument until the state of Kentucky got involved in the 1930s.

The battle decimated the command structure of McCook's I Corps. Only three brigade or division commanders survived the battle unscathed, one of which was General Lytle, who would fall at Chickamauga.

Col. John Wharton, who got around the Union left flank, would go on to be a major general, but was shot in a feud back in Texas by a fellow Texan and Confederate officer near the War's end—maybe the War was a safer place than the Lone Star State! As stated earlier, many of the Confederate generals, not to include Bragg, would go on to lead massive armies in the great struggle, but on the night of October 8, 1862, they would depart and leave the hills, meadows, and farms of Perryville to the dead and then to generations of Kentucky farmers who tilled the dirt, the rural way of life reclaiming the peaceful land until the country came back almost a hundred years after the violent, bloody afternoon.

The two-month fight for Kentucky produced more casualties than Shiloh. If you're a Civil War traditionalist, Perryville is a must see. Ed Bearss, the NPS Chief Historian Emeritus, has stated, "The Perryville Battlefield today is as handsome and unspoiled as it was one hundred and forty years ago . . . enabling you to walk in the footsteps of history." Ed is a classic national treasure. If you don't recognize the name, you've probably seen him on TV. He's the old-school, Marine Corps World War II veteran always giving animated descriptions of Civil War battles.

The visitor's center has a video for sale. You can get a walking tour of Maney's charge from Ed. It's great, and yes, he moans about the powerline, but the winter day he films the video, he says, "It's cold, but I feel warm."

I'm going to take the reader to a lot of places, but nowhere does the setting more closely resemble the 1860s than here. Michael Weeks, who writes and updates a guidebook to five hundred Civil War sites, calls Perryville his favorite. Walking the battlefield, it's almost like the lines of blue and gray could appear at any second, the sounds of artillery disrupting the calm of the rural day.

Perryville Battlefield State Historic Site
1825 Battlefield Rd. (KY 1920)
Perryville, KY 40468
(859) 332-8631
http://parks.ky.gov/parks/historicsites/perryville-battlefield/

CHAPTER 14

"I Want the Glory"

Helena, Arkansas

If there's a state that doesn't get its due during the War, it's got to be Arkansas. Only six of the fifteen states that saw most of the fighting had more battles than Arkansas. Of course, there's Pea Ridge where the NPS has a national military park, and Prairie Grove, the state of Arkansas's biggest Civil War park. In the southern half of the state are a handful of parks where some of the Red River campaign's battles were fought. These latter parks are small with little left except a few acres and a couple of signs.

It should be noted that there's not much of the War left in southern Arkansas, but the Red River Campaign's battles in 1864, as we shall see, were extremely bloody, with little quarter given by either side. At Poison Springs, the Confederates massacred the surrendering colored soldiers, and at Jenkins Farm, the colored troops, in response, took no prisoners. If you've seen the opening scene of the movie *Lincoln*, it depicts the brutal fighting in these battles, and then Lincoln talking with two African American soldiers, his concern growing that the War might degenerate into something much worse.

I was looking for something more than just a battlefield. Helena, Arkansas, has it all and is still emblematic of Confederate Arkansas. Today, as in 1863, if you drive from Memphis to the hills of Vicksburg along the Mississippi River, about 250 miles, the delta spreads out on both sides of the Old Man, flat as a board, for hundreds of miles, the alluvial soil some of the richest in the world and covered with row-crops. The only topography of any significance between Vicksburg and Cape Girardeau, Missouri, is the geologic anomaly, Crowley's Ridge. The narrow, 150-mile-long windblown ridge rises as much as five hundred feet above the floodplain. Before modern levees, it stood like an island in high-water years over the unchecked Mississippi.

The ridge collides with the great river at only one place, the only place in 250 miles where the topography allows an army to look down at the river from bluffs, Helena, Arkansas. The portion of the ridge around Helena is today the St. Francis National Forest, a jungle of trees above the table-flat delta stretching in all directions to the horizon. As you can imagine, the little town of Helena, where the hills meet the river, was a valuable spot during the War, and it often filled the headlines of Northern newspapers. Its decline in the collective history of the War is likely due to the fact that the battle of Helena was fought on the same day that Vicksburg fell and General Pickett made his charge at Gettysburg. This became the other thing that happened in that busy first week of July 1863.

Today, life in the delta, aside from modern technology, is not much different from 150 years ago. These river counties are some of the poorest in America, agriculturally driven and predominately populated with African Americans. Except for a few rich farmers, there's not much there. Helena is no different. Today, it has fifteen thousand residents, two-thirds of which are African American, and the city's per capita income only about 40 percent of the national average. For the last century, this is not where the young American family dreamed about moving when they made it.

During antebellum times, these towns in the heart of the delta were some of the richest in the Southern states, where the plantation class spent its money, socialized, threw their balls, and did their business, the river the avenue to move their produce. The towns themselves were much more progressive than the plantation class, the citizens better educated and mercantile. Most of the Jews in the South lived in the trading cities, like Helena. Before the War, Helena, the seat of Philips County, was second only to the state capital in importance, the county the richest in the state. Slaves constituted a majority of the population in the four river counties around Helena.

Having grown up in the delta, I'm familiar with these once-affluent towns. We've got one in northeast Louisiana, on the river, Lake

Providence. Today, it's unequivocally the poorest, most depressed place in the state (often ranked in national surveys as one of the ten worst places in America), but it once had an opera house, and until the 1960s, though well into its decline, it still hosted the Miss Louisiana Pageant, evidence to its past eminence in Southern society.

Unlike most of the delta, Helena is well preserved, the community making strides to crawl out of poverty. Its population has stabilized in the last twenty years, some of which is due to the casino industry just across the river, but also what the city has done to reclaim its history. Helena sits adjacent to the only bridge across the big river for more than a hundred and fifty miles, a twenty-first-century testament to the physical barrier of the mile-wide sheet of water scooting to the gulf.

Union forces under Gen. Samuel Curtis occupied Helena early in the War. Curtis confiscated slaves from the surrounding area, freed them, and either put them to work for the army or enlisted them. The better-educated merchant and trading classes of Helena, not as enthused about secession as the rest of the state, supported Curtis. The problem was that the Confederacy surrounded Helena, and it could only be supplied via the river. But it, and its garrison of Union troops, became a citadel and, more importantly, a refuge of Unionists, Confederate deserters, and, more disheartening to the hostile neighbors outside of town, slaves, who now had somewhere to flee to. Helena became a thorn in Jeff Davis's behind that the Southern armies spent tremendous men and material, without luck, to remove.

Arriving in Helena, I was pleasantly surprised. Things are slow, but its lovely main street, Cherry, has been restored. It looks like something you'd find in a neat American college town, and riding down it, you certainly get the sense that Helena was once a happening place. One-hundred-year-old warehouses and trading posts have been converted into offices, stores, and restaurants, under the heights to the west commanding over the town and river. Shiny, new blue signs point here and there to Helena's historic sites, tucked around cozy brick side-streets, new light poles, and repurposed old buildings. This is what the Civil War was about, a rich shipping and market town surrounded by hundreds of miles of plantations, all of which earned its wealth on the backs of slaves.

I pulled into the town's restored old railroad depot that today houses a Civil War museum run by the Delta Cultural Center (DCC), dedicated to interpreting the heritage of the delta and promoting economic growth. The center manages the town's Civil War sites, and many of the town's historic buildings, one of which is the Beth El Synagogue. The museum tells the story of Civil War Helena. I also learned, announcing its importance to the Confederacy, Philips County produced seven Rebel generals. I think all of Louisiana only had about twenty generals, and we had almost twice the population of Arkansas.

In town, I met Jack Myers, a retired historian for the DCC. Jack showed me around. First, we drove up to a park at Battery C, on Graveyard Hill west of town where artillery commanded the town and the river. From atop the hill, Helena and its grid of streets spread out to the mighty Mississippi, all in view.

By the summer of 1863, the Confederacy set out to retake Helena, now under the command of Gen. Benjamin Prentiss. Confederate general Theophilus Holmes, who Bobby Lee sacked after the Seven Days, was then sent west, first as the commander of the Trans-Mississippi Department, but then reduced to the command of only Arkansas. He decided he needed to do something to reclaim his name. He rounded up Sterling Price and his Missourians and set out from Little Rock to reclaim Lincoln's little island in the South. Holmes told Price, "The invaders have been driven from every point in Arkansas save one—Helena. We go to retake it . . . I want the glory!"

Homes's plan had hope. He had under his direct command for the attack almost twice the four thousand Union troops in the enclave, almost all Arkansans and Missourians. Homes had some interesting characters as commanders: Gen. John Marmaduke, the son of a Missouri governor; Gen. Lucius Walker, the nephew of President Polk who had already been captured and paroled; Gen. Mosby Parsons, the ex-US attorney for Missouri; and Joseph Shelby, who led a company of border ruffians in Bleeding Kansas in the '50s.

Homes's plan soon went awry. He bumbled his way to Helena, slowly, giving Prentiss the heads-up. And when the Rebs did attack on the Fourth of July, Homes issued a vague order, attack, "at daylight." Several of his commanders interpreted this differently, leading to a piecemeal attack. From there, the battle turned into a complete boondoggle. The only bright spot were attacks by Price's Missourians that took Graveyard Hill, and Gen. James Fagan and his Arkansans who managed to get to the top of Hindman Hill southwest of town. But these led nowhere. A brief attempt on Fort Curtis, in the center of town, was undertaken, but quickly torn to pieces.

Historians are still trying to figure out what Homes planned to do about the Union Gunboat *Tyler*, moored in Helena. With all the trees around Helena felled, the *Tyler's* eight-inch guns had an open field of fire across almost all the battlefield. The Confederates on the exposed hilltop were ducks on a pond.

An even bigger failure was Homes's flanking movement around the north side of town by Marmaduke and Walker that went nowhere. Marmaduke actually shot Walker in a duel two months later in Little Rock—Marmaduke's punishment: after the War, the citizens of the Show-Me State elected him governor!

Unfortunately, Battery C, atop Graveyard Hill, is the only one of the four batteries open to the public. The rifle pits are still there, but you have to look into the kudzu to see them. The other three are undeveloped but on private property. In 2004, six bodies that became known as the Fagan Six were discovered on Hindman Hill. They were reinterred in the Helena Confederate Cemetery. Despite outnumbering the Yanks two-to-one, Homes's losses of over 1,500 were more than eight times the Union losses. Instead of glory, the grand debacle resulted in Homes being put out to pasture.

The Battle's been largely lost to history. For the last year and a half of the War, all that garrisoned the pride of antebellum Arkansas were colored federal troops. Despite his decisive victory, and a worthy showing at Shiloh, Printess, not in favor with the rising Grant, left the army later that year and saw no more service.

Jack showed me the current focus of the DCC, highlighting Helena's role in the Underground Railroad. The city has a new park, Freedom Park with interpretive displays, and has another park under construction to emphasize General Curtis's proclamation in town to free the slaves.

Tappan House, Helena, Arkansas

Apparently, this didn't go over well with Mr. Lincoln, yet to issue his Emancipation Proclamation. The president was supposed to be in charge of the nation's policy on slavery!

There's more to Civil War Helena than just the battle, and Jack showed me around. The DCC has recently constructed a replica of Fort Curtis, though not in the exact location, with neat replica twenty-four pounders. Helena has hundreds of grand old houses from its heyday, many in disrepair, but Jack pointed out two, the Hornor Home, occupied by the Federals, and the Tappan House, the home of Confederate general James Tappan, still occupied by the Tappans, but used as Curtis's headquarters. Perched on a hill, the colonial mansion has a big white front, four columns, and porches on two floors. General Sherman spent a night here while in town. Like Lake Providence, Helena's old opera house is long gone.

I stopped by the Helena Museum of Phillips County where Greg Cook, the museum's historian, gave me the tour. It's got some good models of the battle. Most interesting to me were the museum's book collection, including a full set of the magazine *Confederate Veteran*, the voice of the United Daughters of the Confederacy and the Sons of Confederate Veterans, until it ceased publication in 1932. There's also a first edition of

The author at Fort Curtis in Helena, Arkansas

Grant's memoirs and a lot of other old first editions and histories of the War. The museum's feature book is a signed copy of *Life on the Mississippi* by Mark Twain, who gave it to the town after stopping there on a book tour. Jack also told me that Earnest Hemingway stopped for lunch in the town at one time.

The museum's got a bunch of other great things from the county's history, to include a large collection from Helena native and Confederate general Thomas Hindman, a Mississippi transplant and congressman before the War. Wounded at Shiloh, he later took command of the Trans-Mississippi Department. Hindman's firm hand in that role caused him to fall out of favor with most Arkansans. He went on to fight in many of the epic battles in the Atlanta campaign before fleeing to Mexico. One of the few Confederate generals not to get a post-war pardon, he returned to Arkansas anyway in 1867 where he was promptly arrested. He then tried to gear up his old political machine. Six months later, he was murdered in his house in Helena. Who did it? It's still the great unsolved crime of Helena 150 years later.

Helena's got a few more attractions. This is the heart of the Blues Highway. The little town on the river host the Peabody Award-winning blues radio show, the *King Biscuit Time*, the longest-running American radio broadcast. There's also the Confederate Cemetery stacked on Maple Hill where three Rebel generals are buried, including Arkansas's most famous, Patrick Cleburne.

Delta Cultural Center
141 Cherry St.
Helena, AR 72342
(870) 338-4350
http://www.deltaculturalcenter.com/

CHAPTER 15

"Bury These Poor Men and Let Us Say No More About it"

Bristoe Station, Virginia

By the fall of 1863, the tiny Orange and Alexandria Railroad Station at Bristoe had already changed hands several times—the railroad being the only train link between Washington and Richmond.

Then, the station sat in rural farmland. Today, though there is no station in Bristoe, the Norfolk Southern Rail still scoots by through Prince Williams County, thirty miles southwest of Washington, the landscape contemporary urban sprawl. Since 1990, the county's population has more than doubled from 216,000 to over 450,000.

Only recently has the county gotten involved to stop the onrush of concrete, neighborhoods, and strip malls, to preserve the little spot of Virginia where many of the War's most famous generals fought two battles, one, Robert E. Lee's last offensive of the War. Today, the battlefield sits right off the Prince Williams Parkway, wedged between a new housing development, a golf course, and Broad Run Creek.

The first battle occurred in August of 1862, often called the Battle of Kettle Run, when General Lee sent Stonewall Jackson and Jeb Stuart around the Federal Army, commanded by Gen. John Pope, to cut the Yank's supply line. The 2nd Virginia Cavalry and Louisiana Tiger Brigade captured the lightly defended station, intent on putting it out of action. Busy celebrating, the Rebels let the next train slip by but soon began ripping up track. The next train derailed and the one after that, shot up with musketry, collided with the wrecked train to put the line out of action.

Jackson's men ripped up more track and burned the trains. General Pope, seeing the fires in his rear and knowing he had to restore his communications, got baited into attacking Jackson's entire corps, not knowing a second Confederate corps under Gen. James Longstreet also camped in the area. The next day, he marched onto the battlefield at Second Manassas saying, "We shall bag the whole crowd." History tells us this turned into a gargantuan Union disaster that cost Pope his command.

As Jackson trotted off to fight Pope, he left a division under Richard Ewell to defend the station. The next day, Fighting Joe Hooker's division arrived to retake the station but got in a nasty fight with the 5th, 6th, and 8th Louisianans. With the damaged trains still smoldering, and the station ransacked, Hooker's boys eventually ran off the Rebels, but not without the cost of more than three hundred dead or wounded. The 2nd and 73rd New York, the latter the famous Fire Zouaves, took their highest casualties of the War this day. Late in the day, Jackson ordered Ewell to retreat to Manassas where the real undoing of the Yanks was about to take place. The first battle only had about a third of the troops as the second battle, but it was a spirited and deadly fight.

A year later, in the summer of 1863, the War reached an apex at the epic battles of Gettysburg and Vicksburg. Everybody wondered where this was going? Could and would it ever end? The Confederacy retreated on all fronts, but their armies, though bloodied, remained intact and dangerous, as did the bulk of the South.

As Lee slowly retreated from Gettysburg back into Virginia, General Meade, to Mr. Lincoln's chagrin, pursued leisurely. In the three months since the epic Pennsylvania battle, there had been a few minor skirmishes, but nothing of significance. The hundred-mile retreat had been protracted, Lee's army weaving and maneuvering to avoid the Federals and licking its wounds, both armies staying an arms-length apart. Everybody knew another battle was inevitable, but where?

On October 14, Gen. A. P. Hill attacked what he thought was the rear of the Union column, the V Corps. But behind it, marched the II Corps under Gen. Gouverneur K. Warren. General Hill was well into his attack before he figured out he was in way over his head. Before the day ended, almost 1,400 Rebs fell, nearly threefold the Northern losses.

On a spring afternoon, I sat on a bench atop the hill west of the railroad, studying a map and some notes, looking down at the battlefield trying to correlate the second battle with the landscape.

Below this hill on that October day, the Federal Army marched along the railroad, pulling back to the heights of Centerville. And down this hill, Gen. Henry Heth's two brigades of North Carolinians under William Kirkland and John Cooke attacked the Yanks. Cooke was the son of famous Union Cavalry general Philip Cooke, Jeb Stuart's brother-in-law who remained loyal to the North. This wasn't just a war of brother versus brother, but father versus son. Both Cooke and Kirkland would be seriously wounded in the fight, a mauling by any interpretation that left the hill west of Bristoe blood-soaked with dead and wounded North Carolinians.

Though initially outnumbered, the Yanks formed a strong defensive line behind the railroad embankment. Several of the New York regiments surrendered at Harpers Ferry and had since been paroled, and meant to reclaim their reputations.

It all transpired in lightning-quick speed, less than an hour. Captain James Graham of the 27th North Carolina later described the approach to the railroad: "The enemy arose and gave us a volley which cut down more than half the remainder of our regiment. I doubt if such carnage was ever known in the same short period." His regiment suffered 70 percent losses this day. After the battle, General Hill tried to explain away the calamitous attack, but Bobby Lee, known for his politeness, but not in the best of moods, rudely cut off Hill, admonishing him, "Well, well, general, bury these poor men and let us say no more about it."

As I continued to study the map, beside me, a young lady held an unruly six-month-old disrupting my thoughts. Another wannabe Scarlett O'hara walked by looking at the yapping, annoying baby and said, "You've got such a beautiful baby."

I can't even fathom that a beautiful six-month-old baby ever existed! But today, the one-time killing grounds where so many boys fell was filled with people carrying on their daily lives, enjoying a serene afternoon on the blanket of green grass.

Finally, Bill Backus, the park's historian, arrived to give me a break from the baby and explain it all. I quickly learned that Bill is yet another

Yank down here spending his life preserving the War. We took off on one of the park's almost three miles of trails, ambling down the hill toward the railroad mimicking the death march for so many Tar Heels on the pleasant afternoon a century and a half ago.

"Was it this open during the battle?" I asked.

"Pretty similar," Bill said. "The guy that owned the land was the sheriff, but he was a Unionist, and moved away for the War. The ground was an abandoned farm then."

The sheriff, Thomas Davis, latter summed it all up: "From the breaking out of the war until 1863 I was farming and merchandising at Bristow Station where the Rebels burned me out twice on account of my political sentiments. I was a Union man straight out from the beginning to the present day. I farmed until 1862 when the Rebels stopped me."

"What about the station?" I asked.

"It's long gone," Bill answered.

"Any original structures here?"

"No, the sheriff's house was near the Robinson Cemetery," Bill pointed to a few rows of tombstones, fenced in, adjacent to the park, "but it's post-war."

Bill told me the story of the park. In the late 1980s, the site was actually considered for a landfill. Due to opposition, this was abandoned. Over the next few years, the state tried to have the site put on the National Register, but this too drew opposition from local landowners. This sounds like Congress! Over the next decade, the debate went on. Even the state legislature got involved in the fight between preservation and the ever-expanding county. Finally, in 2006, after numerous studies, several compromises and agreements, the initial park tract of 133 acres was transferred to the Historic Preservation District of Prince Williams County and the park was created. The Bristoe Battlefield opened to the public the next year.

We walked up to the railroad. To the left, near present-day Bristow Road, the North Carolinians, peppered with Yankee lead, actually broke through. Here, Union colonel James Mallon, rallying his New Yorkers, fell dead, the victim of a Rebel minié ball. The railroad, its three-foot-high embankment cutting through the slight hills, provided cover and a perfect firing position for the Federals as the Rebels charged down the hill.

Bill and I walked on, to the southwest. Here, Union shelling landed a fatal blow to Confederate general Carnot Posey, who died a month later at the University of Virginia, where he is buried. Bill pointed out the historical marker near the ravine where the Louisiana regiments gave Hooker fits in the first battle of Bristoe.

"Yeah," Bill said, "it was actually your Louisiana boys that got after the sheriff and burned him out!"

I chuckled. "Are his relatives still around? I hope they're not still holding a grudge."

We walked on, to the only War-related cemetery on the site, where soldiers of the 10th Alabama are buried. Actually, the cemetery constitutes the initial and only monument in the Park for well over a hundred years. In 1909, an Alabama veteran tried to purchase and preserve the small parcel. Owned by the daughter of a Union veteran at the time, she wouldn't sell but promised not to disturb the graves.

As we walked back to the trailhead, I was astonished to learn from Bill that the park now has over one hundred thousand visitors a year. There's no visitor's center yet, but plans are in the works. From the hilltop, looking down over the fields of green grass to the station, it's hard to imagine the scene after the battle, the ground covered with North Carolina boys. I couldn't find any photos or sketches of the gentle slope after the battle. Alfred Waud did a few sketches of the battle from the Union position. Dense lines of North Carolinians cover the hill as they charge forward. Today, families of Virginians walk the hill in a relaxing escape in a scene that couldn't be farther from the events a century and a half ago.

Bristoe Station Battlefield Heritage Park
10708 Bristow Rd.
Bristow, VA 20136
(703) 792-4754
http://www.pwcgov.org/government/dept/publicworks/hp/pages/bristoe-station-battlefield.aspx

CHAPTER 16

"Fighting Means Killing"

Fort Pillow, Tennessee

As I drove north out of Memphis on Highway 51, rolling up and down and through the alluvial floodplain of the Mississippi River and the Chickasaw Bluffs, I headed to one of the least tactically and strategically important battles of the War, but one whose ramifications were as gigantic as any fight in the Rebellion, and probably resulted in as much suffering and death as any event in the War.

Fort Pillow is located in the middle of nowhere, about seventy road miles north of Memphis. There's not even a sign on the turnoff from Highway 51, and then it's twenty miles down a one-way winding highway to the Fort Pillow State Historic Park opened in 1971 by the state of Tennessee, the only sign of civilization on the road, the West Tennessee State Prison. You won't go by this fort on the way to anywhere—certainly the most out-of-the-way stop on my journey.

To my disappointment, I couldn't even find any Elvis Presley on the radio to pass the time on the boring ride, my cell phone going dead past the prison. Fort Pillow, on a high bluff overlooking the river where it narrowed in a sharp turn, was built by Confederate general Gideon Pillow, later sacked for his conduct at Fort Donelson and Stones River, in early 1862. By the summer of '62, the Rebels abandoned the isolated fort, and it was then occupied by Union forces only to be later abandoned by the Yanks and then reoccupied—emphatically with a token force of second-tier troops. Who'd want the fort anyway, difficult to support and only watching over the upper Mississippi, already in Union hands? If anything, the ride out to the fort convinced me that any loss of life or treasure here had been a waste.

It was here in April of 1864, one of the War's most controversial and successful generals, Nathan Bedford Forrest, took the fort and massacred almost two-hundred Union colored troops—or that's what we've been told for a century and a half. The best evidence suggest that Forrest attacked the fort because locals complained about mistreatment from the fort's defenders, some batteries of lightly trained colored artillery, and the Union 13th Tennessee Cavalry, about six hundred men total, almost evenly split between black and white. Forrest called the fort a "nest of outlaws." The Unionists Tennesseans probably got Forrest's men as riled as the colored troops, if not more, especially since more than fifty were Confederate deserters.

Tennessee was the last state to secede, and probably the most polarized Confederate State during the War. Only Virginia hosted more battles, and by this time in the War, a brutal guerrilla war raged in west Tennessee, bleeding into all facets of society. Distasteful commanders, North and South, reverted to the sword to get almost anything done. At Fort Pillow, as the Union soldiers surrendered, a large portion of the colored and some of the white troops were gunned down in what has become known as the Fort Pillow Massacre.

Forrest has taken the brunt of the blame for the day's events. Forrest's reputation is further soiled by his status before the War, one of Memphis's largest slave owners and traders, and his involvement with the early Ku Klux Klan, he the first Grand Wizard, a name derived from his war-time nickname, the Wizard of the Saddle. Forrest's modern biographers have pretty well refuted the general as a homicidal bigot. He did disavow the Klan when it spun off solely into race bating, and at least for his day in the South, thought rarely liberally on race issues. But the fact remains that he was in charge on the fateful day, and as a veteran, I agree—the episode was one of the most unsavory in the nation's proud military history. To this day, opinions vary on the degree of the massacre.

What's not in dispute is Forrest's battlefield record. Fort Pillow is really his single blemish. The only man to rise from private to lieutenant general during the War, NPS's Chief Historian, Ed Bearss, called Forrest the "most colorful man in the War," and said he, "killed more men than any other general officer has, had more horses shot out from him than any other general officer." Robert E. Lee called him the best general of the War. One of Grant's aides said, "He was the only Confederate cavalryman of whom Grant stood in much dread." General Sherman declared him "the greatest cavalryman America ever produced." Historians Bruce Catton and Shelby Foote have called Forrest a "genius." I could go on and on with the tributes from the Civil War's greatest men.

There's no doubt Forrest was hot-blooded, and he summed up War pragmatically, "War means fighting, and fighting means killing." There wasn't much of a fight at Fort Pillow, but the battle is the one thing we know about. Forrest's men, outnumbering the Federals three-to-one, quickly took the inland approaches abandoned by the Tennessee cavalry with little resistance. This site contained a high ridge that looked down on the river batteries where the entire Federal force had retreated to. The clumsy General Pillow's fort was indefensible without fifteen thousand troops.

A Federal gunboat sat parked on the river, but the Rebels managed to run it off with concentrated fire. Surrounding the river batteries, Forrest twice offered surrender terms that guaranteed all Federal troops would be treated as prisoners of war, but adding one of his favorite conditions that often put his enemies in a more receptive mood, "Should my demand be refused, I cannot be responsible for the fate of your command."

The fort's commander, Maj. Lionel Booth, was killed by a sharp-shooter early in the battle. Maj. William Bradford, an officer of marginal repute and deficient skill, took over command and refused the surrender terms. Forrest then ordered the fort be stormed, and that's where the details get blurred.

I showed up at the park and met its manager, Robby Tidwell, at the park's museum, near the inner breastworks where the 13th Tennessee put up a meager defense before fleeing early in the battle. From here, Robby led me and several other visitors on a mile and a quarter hike to the fort's main battery positions (you can drive to within a quarter of a mile) where guns ranged the river and pointed inland. Here, some of the original earthworks remain, augmented with modern timbers. The earthworks sit atop a hundred-foot bluff that today looks over Cold Creek, but during the War, looked over the river, now two miles off to the west.

It was here, after the surrender, that the dead began to pile up, almost two-hundred colored and more than a dozen white soldiers. It didn't take

The Mississippi River from Fort Pillow State Park

me long to figure out the Tennesseans' opinion on the massacre. During the day, several corrected me, saying this was "maybe a massacre . . . not an ideal situation for sure, but exactly what happened is still a matter of debate." Confederate policy at the time did not allow colored troops to be treated as prisoners of war. White officers of colored troops were to be executed.

The stories you read and hear are wide, varied, and never-ending. Some of the Union troops picked up guns and shot after they surrendered; Forrest rode through ranks yelling, "shoot them down like dogs"; the Union soldiers never raised the white flag and drunk, they taunted the rebels; the Rebels were drunk and blood-thirsty; Forrest finally arrived to stop the murders. There's a never-ending list. Just do a little research. The accounts of Union soldiers, blacks, and Confederates both blame and pardon Forrest.

The only thing I'll believe for sure is they were all probably drunk and taunting, having been sent to this Godforsaken place to fight! It *is* known that Forrest captured the Union commander, William Bradford, alive, and kept him as a prisoner of war, at least for a few days. Allegedly, Rebel guards shot Major Bradford while he "attempted to escape!" It is documented that Forrest *wasn't* present for that. It's also been asserted that Forrest's men terminated the Unionist Tennesseans and deserters on their knees. They at least let the colored troops stand. Only soldiers received the privilege of standing to be executed.

Forrest provided few words on the matter, but he did later say that the fight proved, "Negro soldiers cannot cope with southerners," and "the river was dyed with blood for two-hundred yards." No matter, it was a heinous crime, and by any measure, a massacre. The degree of the slaughter, and who was responsible will never be known. Jack Hurst, one of Forrest's contemporary biographers, has surmised that the truth may be in the middle. His temper up, Forrest may have ordered it, but arriving on the scene and witnessing the carnage in person, then tried to curtail it. I guess the state of Tennessee's official opinion, inscribed on the historical marker, is, "Forrest lost control over his troops."

The Northern press went wild, embellishing and spinning the events into the means they sought, even publishing completely unfounded stories of women and children slain at the Fort. It's hard for me to believe the American press, in any century, would spin and embellish a story to get their point across. The *New York Herald's* headline read, "Capture of Fort Pillow by the Rebels. Reported Massacre of Black and White Troops. Women and Children Murdered in Cold Blood. The Dead and Wounded Negroes Burned."

Anyway, the after-effects were tragic and far exceed any cost here on the riverbank. In the remaining year of the War, mostly in the West, the call for no quarter became tragically ever-present, and all sides were guilty, North and South, black and white. Much worse, especially in its toll, after Fort Pillow, plans to reinitiate the prisoner-exchange policy were put on the back burner. There's no telling how many men who honorably surrendered eventually perished in the horrid conditions of Andersonville, or one of the other prison camps, North and South, none of which apparently displayed any real concern for the well-being of their captives. During the War, about thirty thousand bluecoats and twenty-six thousand men in gray died in captivity. If any good came from the massacre, it hardened Northern resolve, resulted in the massive recruitment of African American troops for the Union, and resulted in equal pay for colored troops.

Standing in front of the breastworks, looking off the bluff at the green blanket of trees, it's hard to sense that something epic happened on this ridge in the middle of nowhere. It's even difficult to envision the murders, but this is it, the spot where the Fort Pillow Massacre, in whatever form, happened.

We walked back to the museum, and Robby told me all the trees are post-war. During the battle, the fort's trees had been felled. I took a picture with the park staff and checked out a genuine Parrott cannon recovered from the battlefield and on display in the museum. Robby told me, amazingly, that the park, which has no admission fee, has about five hundred thousand visitors a year.

Pondering this, what I'd seen this morning, and still a little perplexed at the colossal events here, I hiked some of the park's twenty miles of trails, many that pass additional earthworks and some with excellent overlooks of the great river, the unspoiled views probably very similar to the haunted time in our history here. It's a peaceful walk.

Fort Pillow State Park
3122 Park Rd.
Henning, TN 38041
(731) 738-5581
http://tnstateparks.com/parks/about/fort-pillow

CHAPTER 17

"And May God Forgive Me for the Order"

New Market, Virginia

In early March of 1864, Ulysses S. Grant came east and took command of the army. Everybody knew this was the big show, the culmination, both countries' greatest generals going head to head. The opening battle of this great duel, the Battle of the Wilderness, pitted more than 150,000 Americans against each other, solving little, but keeping the undertakers swamped.

In May of 1864, the Shenandoah Valley had become a sideshow to the big war in the east. The small valley town of New Market had about seven hundred residents, and had largely avoided the War to date. Today, with about two thousand citizens, it's still a small, pretty valley town. Driving into New Market on the Valley Pike, I noticed the colorful pennants of the local high school attached to every light pole on main street: Stonewall Jackson High School—Go Generals.

If you've ever driven the dreadful, congested I-81 through the valley, you've driven through one of Virginia's most preserved battlefields, the Battle of New Market. In May of 1864, as General Grant pushed Lee's army back into Virginia, a Federal army under Gen. Franz Sigel again occupied the north Shenandoah Valley. A German immigrant and one-time officer in the German Revolution, Sigel's accomplishments thus far in the War had been mixed. Grant wanted the political general removed from command, but Lincoln held firm. Sigel was a hero to the masses of German immigrants filling the Union ranks.

Grant made the best of the situation, hoping Sigel might at least occupy the Rebel forces in the Valley. He lamented, "If Sigel can't skin himself, he can hold a leg whilst someone else skins."

Gen. John Breckenridge, once the vice president of the country he now fought and the runner-up to Lincoln in the 1860 election, commanded a small Confederate army in the south of the valley, but thought Sigel might move east to aid Grant, his best route through a pass in the Blue Ridge Mountains known as New Market Gap. Early in May, he gathered his scattered forces.

Sigel, with an army of about nine thousand, and at Grant's urging, moved south through the valley. In Woodstock, about twenty miles north of New Market, his troops surprised the Confederates, capturing the telegraph office and much of Breckenridge's recent correspondence. Sigel learned of Breckenridge's meager forces and concerns, but instead of attacking, he dallied, and worse, split his forces.

Breckenridge scrapped together about four thousand troops, almost all Virginians, which included 258 cadets from the Virginia Military Institute (VMI). Instead of waiting on Sigel, on May 14, Breckenridge's army, camped about eight miles south of the village of New Market, set out on a march about midnight to attack Sigel.

On a fateful spring day, the ground sopping from recent rains, Breckenridge's outnumbered Rebels routed Sigel, the German immigrant's army barely escaping. The day has lived on in celebration by Virginians and VMI for the critical role of the cadets in the battle, some as young as fifteen, intended by Breckenridge to only be in reserve at the battle, but forced into the center at its height.

In 1944, VMI graduate George Collins purchased the Bushong farm, the site of most of the battle, and in 1964 donated it to VMI. Subsequently, VMI created the New Market Battlefield and the Virginia Civil War Museum at the battlefield that the institution still operates today. New Market is the basis for the only major Civil War film that I know of made in the last few years, *The Field of Lost Shoes*, made in 2015 and starring Jason Isaacs, Keith David, and Tom Skerritt. The movie is a sanitized version of war that takes some liberties with some of the personal details, but it tells the story of the cadets, including the interesting tale of the VMI cook, a slave named Judge, who went on to serve the cadets after gaining his freedom.

I pulled into the museum one overcast July Friday. Warning, you first come to a museum on the left that has a sign that says New Market Battlefield Military Museum. This is a private museum, not VMI's or the battlefield's museum. I didn't go in, but heard it has some artifacts from the battle, and a lot of other stuff not related to the battle.

The parking lot at the battlefield was more than half full. I inspected the license plates, Pennsylvania, Texas, Virginia, Illinois. I pulled into a spot beside a replica of the General Lee, the famous car in the 1970's TV show, the *Dukes of Hazard*, painted like the Confederate Flag. On each side of the car, two attendees at the museum sported prominent bumper stickers announcing they were big supporters of President Obama. The Civil War is for everybody.

Inside, I met Sarah Mink, supervisor of historical interpretation for the museum. She told me that the museum's displays in the "Virginia Room," were the ones put together by the State for the Virginia Centennial Civil War Museum. Not only can you view the state's history in the War, you can do it from a fifty-year-old perspective.

The museum has a documentary of the battle and a remarkable gun collection, some only recently donated by Martin Kaminsky. It doesn't take long to figure out the museum, like *The Field of Lost Shoes*, is as much a grand celebration of VMI as it is the battle, which is fine with me.

Behind the museum sits the largely intact battlefield, about three hundred acres. I walked it all. At the Bushong house, still in existence, I followed the cadets up to the distant ridge, Bushong Hill. It's near the house and the apple orchard behind it, where, at the battle's apex, the Confederate center gave way. So short was Breckenridge on men that his only reserves were the 258 cadets.

As the Rebel center buckled, one of Breckenridge's staff officers, Charles Semple, suggested using the cadets to plug the hole.

Breckenridge replied, "No, Charley, this will not do. They are only children and I cannot expose them to such a fire as our center will receive."

Minutes later, the Rebel line no longer tenable, Breckenridge turned to Semple. "Major, order then up, and may God forgive me for the order."

The cadets' commander, Col. Scott Shipp, led the cadets around the Bushong House, through the apple orchard, still preserved by the museum, where they collided with the 34th Massachusetts. The Rebel line secured, the Virginians charged up Bushong Hill.

I walked on to the crest of the hill, today known as the *Field of Lost Shoes*. As the boys charged over the soggy wheat field, many lost their shoes, but the hill fell, the cadets capturing a federal gun.

So impressed with the charge, a Federal officer, Lieutenant Wyneken, wrote to Breckenridge after the War, "I never shall forget the magnificent aspect of your infantry attacking our left and centre, the triumphant yell and my cowardly comrades running back for their very life."

The assault had been costly. The cadets suffered more than fifty wounded, five who would die that day and five more who would later succumb to their wounds.

Sigel's front fell back in disarray. On the Federal left, a Confederate force led by Gen. John Imboden, one of his brigades commanded by George Patton's grandfather, Col. George Patton Sr., attempted to get behind Sigel unsuccessfully. Sigel had marched his men across a bridge on the North Fork of the Shenandoah River. If Imboden got the bridge, Breckenridge could bag the entire Federal Army. There's a tunnel under the interstate that will allow the twenty-first-century tourist to see where Pennsylvania boys fought off Imboden.

Before you go, check out one of the battlefield's overlooks. Below the two hundred foot, steep, rocky bluff, the placid North Fork of the Shenandoah River winds through the valley. It will give you some sense of how Sigel got trapped. These overlooks are great, especially if you're like me and from some place where everything is as flat as a board.

At the top of Bushong Hill, a sign tells the story of Federal Captain Henry du Pont (the museum's not all a celebration of Virginia). Du pont's artillery, and its fighting retreat, saved Sigel's army from complete destruction.

I walked back to the Bushong House, built in 1825 and home to the Bushong family during the battle. When the battle arrived on their doorstep, the Bushongs farmed wheat and built wagons. The family hid in the basement during the fighting, emerging to find the house and porch full of wounded men, including some of the cadets.

The house has survived several battles since May of 1864. A few months after the battle, as the Federal Army undertook the burning of the valley, Sheridan spared the farm. The best evidence suggests this was due to the fact the Bushongs, their house turned into a hospital during and after the battle, treated boys dressed in Blue and Gray. The second battle came a hundred years later during the construction of I-81 that bisects the site, the battlefield's only major scar. The intrastate makes a slight wiggle to avoid the house. I asked Sarah about this.

"We do know that powerful VMI alumni got involved," she said. "I'm just unsure as to their names."

After the nine-hour battle fought in intermittent rain and 1,400 dead, wounded, or missing Americans, the valley, the breadbasket of Virginia, at least for the time being, remained in Confederate hands. The cadet's valor energized and inspired war-weary Virginia. Ordered to Richmond, President Davis and the governor reviewed the corps of cadets, and the Confederate Congress passed a resolution commending their valor.

A few days after the battle, Lincoln and Grant sacked Sigel, but Breckenridge's victory, one of the last decisive Confederate victories, may have been a strategic loss. Grant put Gen. David Hunter in command of the Shenandoah. He promptly marched south, defeated a Rebel Army at Piedmont, and moved on to Lexington where he torched VMI, hauling off its statue of George Washington.

A year later, Sigel resigned from the army and became a prominent citizen in New York. There's a grand statue of him in New York City's Riverside Park. Breckenridge, a fierce fighter and one of the best of the War's political generals, became the Confederate secretary of war after the battle. At the outbreak of the War, he was a United States senator from Kentucky. He resigned to take up the mantle of the Confederacy, and is still today, the only Senator convicted of treason against the United States by the senate. Fearing for his safety after the War, he fled to Cuba, and then Britain. Finally assured he wouldn't be prosecuted, he returned in 1869 and entered into numerous private business ventures.

After touring the wonderful battlefield, I headed south, about seventy miles to Lexington. If you're in the area, stop by. It's worthwhile just to see the picturesque town, and VMI and Washington and Lee University.

Stonewall Jackson is buried here in a cemetery named for him, beside his family and two descendants who went on to be officers in the army he fought against. I stopped by the grave. Old Stonewall loved to suck on lemons. For more than a hundred years, as a tribute, admirers have placed lemons on his grave. The day I went, exactly 154 years and 4 months after his passing, three fresh lemons lay atop his grave.

Just down the street sits VMI and Washington and Lee University, sitting side by side, the well-manicured lawns and long lines of wonderful, symmetrical buildings gave a sense of discipline, age, institutionalized organization, like an army base. Though it was mid-summer, parking here might be a problem. I found some open spaces near the VMI parade grounds with serval signs posted that read "no parking." Several cars parked at the spot and two other cars pulled in. So much for all the rules and structure. I joined in on the disobedience.

I walked over to the Lee Chapel at Washington and Lee. The chapel is still used by the university for formal gatherings, but in the back sits a statue of Robert E. Lee, the university's president after the War. Downstairs, there's a museum to the general and a mausoleum holding

Lemons at Stonewall Jackson's Grave, Lexington, Virginia

Lee and seventeen of his family's crypts. Eleven spots in the mausoleum remain available.

I asked the museum's curator, "Are people still buried here?"

"Yes, if you're a direct descendant of the general and president, we'll take you. We had our last interment in 1994."

Wow, if you're a Civil War buff in Bobby's tree, this is the Holy Grail.

I asked the nice lady, "Is there somewhere around here I'm supposed to park?"

She pointed out the window to a parking lot with a big sign that read, "Visitor Parking for the Lee Chapel."

If the reader hasn't noticed, I'm bumbling my way through all this.

As I left the chapel, the lady pointed outside again. "And before you leave, don't forget to look at Traveller's grave just outside."

If you didn't know, Traveller was General Lee's horse during the War. Outside, beside the hedges, Traveller's tombstone lay surrounded by a square of cobblestones.

I walked the quarter-mile back to VMI across lovely Washington and Lee University, called only Washington University during the War. Hunter wanted to burn it too, but according to the story I got at the museum, the locals successfully pleaded with Hunter, citing the fact that the university was named after George Washington. Hunter moved on. He had bigger fish to char.

It didn't look like anybody was too worried about my car, so I went to the VMI museum. It's got everything you want to see about VMI, including a replica of Stonewall Jackson's horse, Little Sorrel, with the original hide, and the rain jacket he donned when the fatal bullet found him at Chancellorsville.

I also discovered that VMI loves guns, especially the old ones. I thought the collection at New Market was the most impressive I'd seen thus far, but it pales in comparison to the campus museum's display cases. If you're a gun enthusiast, you could view this collection for days, and I wandered it for thirty minutes. Jackson's house is also preserved at VMI, and outside on the parade grounds stands a statue of Stonewall, commanding over some cannons, instructing the cadets in the science of artillery just as he did in the 1850s.

Down the street in front of Nichols Engineering Building sits the Virginia Mourning Her Dead Monument, a sculpture done by famed VMI alumnus Sir Moses Ezekiel, the institute's first Jewish cadet, who fought in the battle. It honors the VMI cadets at New Market and looks over the remains of six of the young men who fell in the battle.

VMI survived General Hunter. Today it's one of the most revered military institutions in the world. The beautiful campus stands out in a country full of gorgeous plots dedicated to educating our reunited country's youth. The cadets still hold an annual ceremony honoring their fallen brothers at New Market.

Henry du Pont, whose bravery saved Sigel's Army on that rainy day a century and a half ago, went on to win the Congressional Medal of Honor, and fifty years later as a US senator from Delaware, passed legislation that compensated VMI for its destruction by the Union Army during the War.

If you've got time, there's one more Civil War site at VMI, George Washington's statue, given back to VMI after the War and rededicated. For you war tourists, Gen. George Marshall's museum is also on campus.

New Market Battlefield State Historical Park
8895 George Collins Pkwy.
New Market, VA 22844
(540) 740-3101
http://www.vmi.edu/museums-and-archives/virginia-museum-of-the-civil-war/

Lee Chapel
11-17 Letcher Ave.
Lexington, VA 24450
(540) 458-8768
https://www.wlu.edu/lee-chapel-and-museum

Jackson Memorial Hall–VMI Museum
Lecter, 415 Letcher Ave.
Lexington, VA 24450
(540) 464-7232
http://www.vmi.edu/museums-and-archives/vmi-museum/

CHAPTER 18

The Perfect Battle

Brice's Crossroads, Mississippi

By the summer of 1864, Nathan Bedford Forrest became the physical incarnation of evil in the Northern press. To the army leadership, he became the chief tactical adversary to the preservation of the Union.

Here is a typical description of Forrest from the *Chicago Tribune* under the title *The Butcher Forrest and his Family, All of Them Slave Drivers and Women Whippers*.

> *He is about 50 years of age, tall, gaunt, and sallow visage, with a long nose, deep set black, snaky eyes, and hair wore long. He usually wore, while in the "nigger" trade in Memphis, a stove pipe hat set on the back of his head at an angle of forty-five degrees. He was accounted mean, vindictive, cruel and unscrupulous. He had two wives-one white, the other colored (Catharine), by each of which he had two children. His "patriarchal" wife, Catharine, and his white wife, had frequent quarrels or domestic jars.*

Gen. William Tecumseh Sherman, on the ground and driven purely by military considerations, said, "Forrest must be hunted down and killed if it costs ten thousand lives and bankrupts the federal treasury." Uncle Billy, as his men called him, later admitted his worst nightmare as he approached Atlanta was Forrest turned loose on his supply line in Tennessee. Forrest and other Confederate commanders suggested this, but Jeff Davis, in another of his disastrous decisions, thought otherwise.

Just in case Mr. Davis wised up, Sherman decided he better do something, and in the summer of 1864, he sent an eight-thousand-man cavalry column, under the command of veteran Gen. Samuel Sturgis, to vanquish the feared cavalryman. If nothing else, they'd keep Forrest occupied in Mississippi. At a small crossroads in northern Mississippi, Forrest's fame and reputation reached its zenith.

Outnumbered more than two to one, Forrest, using his techniques of terrain, charging, and "keep the skeer (scare) on 'em," inflected more than 2,000 casualties, including more than 1,600 Union soldiers captured, with his losses of only 96 killed and less than 400 wounded. At Brice's Crossroads, even the Rebel artillery charged. In full retreat, General Sturgis confessed, "For God's sake, if Mr. Forrest will leave me alone, I'll leave him alone." Legendary German tank commander Erwin Rommel called Brice's Cross Roads "the most perfect battle in world history."

A month later, Sherman sent a second, larger column after the Confederate cavalryman, this time commanded by Gen. A. J. Smith. This one had a little better luck at the Battle of Tupelo. The Confederate leadership made another mistake. It put Forrest and his boys under the command of another general, West Pointer Stephen Lee.

Twenty years ago, there wasn't much left of the battlefield at Brice's Cross Roads, and there's little at Tupelo. Fifty years after the War, the Mississippians finally pestered Congress into action, and the federal government purchased two, one-acre plots at each battlefield, today administered by the NPS as National Battlefield Sites. There's not much at either site, a few monuments, no personnel. The one-acre Tupelo site doesn't even have a parking lot.

Otto came looking for Brice's Cross Roads back in the 1920s prior to the battlefield site's establishment. To find it, he located one of Forrest's old cavalry soldiers who lived in the area, Cavanaugh. Here's a paraphrased version of Otto's encounter:

A young boy appeared at the door, and I handed him a card.

A grin spread over the boy's face. "I'll find out if the old man wants to see you."

The old man appeared. He sat me down on his couch, and then promptly kicked me in the shin.

"Don't mind him," Cavanaugh's son said, "he just wants to see if you can take it."

"Out on a spying trip?" Cavanaugh asked.

"I thought the War was over," I said, cringing in pain.

"That so? Then why are you carrying them books under your arm."
Cavanaugh turned to his son. "Get me the latest copy of Confederate
Veteran.*"*

After I correctly identified several old Confederate generals in a picture, Cavanaugh took me to the battlefield for some real show–and–tell.
"Maybe Old Bedford didn't know how to spell strategy, but he could
handle it better than any of those West Pointers."

Cavanaugh showed me the battlefield. His body still quivered with
excitement as he told his tale. He then sent me out to look for some old
bullets. After a fruitless half hour, Cavanaugh laughed. "You'll never find
any bullets on that level ground where you are looking. Go over to that
little knoll and you may find some. I bet some Yanks were hiding behind
it and you can be sure we were shooting at them."

Later, Cavanaugh also gave Otto something he'd been in search of.
Though probably too old at the time to bring it to the appropriate pitch,
he had his son bellow the Rebel Yell. Otto described it as, "A yell like an
Indian. A most ungodly noise . . . HI-HI-HI."

Tupelo, nestled in the rolling hills of north Mississippi, is today best
known as the birthplace and childhood home of Elvis Presley. As you drive
north out of Tupelo, the landscape quickly transitions to rural, a patchwork
of row–crops and oak and pine thickets. On my way to Baldwyn, I passed
through the town with my favorite name in America, Guntown. That's
straight out of a Clint Eastwood western. It was here during the War. Brice's
Cross Roads sits at the old intersection of Baldwyn and Guntown Roads.

Today, there's still not much at Brice's Cross Roads, two or three
houses, and the Bethany Presbyterian Church. And I doubt you'll be able
to find any old Confederates to show you around, but no need. Until
the 1990s, the only meaningful tribute to Brice's Cross Roads was a log-
cabin museum in nearby Baldwyn owned and operated by native Claude
Gentry, born at the crossroads in 1902. A storm destroyed it in the 1990s.

Before going to Brice's Cross Roads, I stopped by the Mississippi
Final Stands Visitor and Interpretive Center in Baldwyn, which interprets

both the Brice's Cross Roads and Tupelo Battles. There's a theater with a nice movie. They've also got some of Mr. Gentry's artifacts. For six dollars, you can buy an audio disc for a driving tour of the battle.

I talked with the center's director, Edwina Carpenter, about the battlefield's preservation. Several local governments fund and operate the center, which opened in 1998, but the battlefield is operated and preserved by the nonprofit Brice's Crossroads National Battlefield Commission, formed by concerned local citizens in the 1990s. To date, with the aid of the Civil War Trust, the commission has preserved more than 1,400 acres of the battlefield.

Before heading out to the battlefield, I drove through downtown Baldwyn, population about three thousand, looking to grab a bite. It's got a clean, neat old downtown and square, nothing Civil War, but main street America. I didn't find a restaurant. I did find an old-school barber shop, advertising a special on "cut and shave." I didn't go in, but it looked like one of those places like my grandpa used to take me, full of old timers, where I'd probably get a wide range of opinions on the battle.

As you ride out to the battle-site, the audio tour begins, following a set of stone monuments placed along the side of the road in the 1950s by the state of Mississippi. It's easy to see how Forrest used the rolling hills, stands of black-jack oaks (kind of a scrub oak) to shield and deceive Sturgis. The key feature of the battle was a bridge over the raging Tishomingo River. Forrest let the union cavalry cross the bridge where he planned to initiate the battle. He figured the infantry would then be rushed, tired, and beat down over the muddy roads and under the merciless summer sun. He would trap a large part of the Union Army, or send them fleeing in a disorganized column across the bottleneck of the small bridge.

It played out about like Forrest figured. In addition to the human cost, Forrest captured sixteen cannons, three hundred thousand rounds of ammunition, and a trove of horses, wagons, and weapons.

As I arrived at the Cross Roads, a contemporary Mississippi cavalryman rode a horse on the shoulder of the road. At the Cross Roads, you can visualize how it all happened, the trepidation of the Illinois and Indiana boys, moving through the wild, foreign, and largely uninhabited backcountry of the famed Nathan Bedford Forrest and his cavalry, in route to Guntown! Unable to see much, the lead division soon heard and saw attacking Confederates from their front and rear. Despite being led by one of the Union's most accomplished cavalry raiders, Gen. Benjamin Grierson, all those factors trumped the fact that they actually, but not knowingly, outnumbered the Rebels more than two-to-one.

The rout was soon on, the disorganized Federals fleeing for their only escape, the tiny bridge.

Otto said the bridge was still around when he came almost a hundred years ago. The association has built a replica bridge. It's kind of replica anyway, but it has concrete abutments and handrails. There's some pictures of the old bridge on a nearby sign. If they'd rebuilt the old rickety bridge, they'd soon be in a lawsuit when it collapsed with a family on it, or somebody fell off. But the replica bridge gives a good sense of the trap Sturgis got into.

After the Federals retreated across the bridge, the only meaningful Union defense came from two regiments of US colored troops (USCT), most notably the 59th USCT. These troops guarded the wagon trains. Not subjected to Forrest's initial barrage, they still had some unit cohesion during the battle. They also had a bone to pick with Forrest from Fort Pillow. The colored troops were mauled and overwhelmed, their losses this day double their white counterparts, but their organized defense likely prevented an even bigger Union disaster. The Final Stands Center has a nice video about the USCTs in the area's battles. During the day, I saw African Americans touring the battlefield. It was a pretty Saturday when I visited, but I was surprised by the number of cars driving and pulling over to look at the battlefield.

I walked the battlefield's trails, maybe a mile, with signage. There's some other history around the Cross Roads. The Bethany Church is still there, though in a new building and at a little different location. The church's longtime reverend, Samuel Agnew, who died in 1902, kept a diary of the area for more than fifty years, including a detailed description of the battle. It's incorporated into the Southern Historical Collection at the University of North Carolina, but copies are available at the center. Much of the property the commission purchased belonged to the Agnews, still living in the area. The cemetery beside the NPS site is pre–Civil War and suffered significant damage during the battle. About thirty Rebel soldiers who fell are buried there in a mass grave. In 1990, individual headstones were installed at the mass grave for all the Confederate dead.

I drove on, following the audio tour. Forrest actually chased the Federal forces out of the area over six or seven counties in a running battle. I'm fast becoming an ardent Civil War preservationist, but it would be impossible to set aside all the battle. We've got to move on. You can't have half of northeast Mississippi set aside for Civil War buffs.

The most somber site on the audio tour was the grave of Alabama cavalryman Sergeant James Jourdan, who fell in the battle. James happened to die by the house of the Philips family, who buried him between two cedar trees right beside Ripley Road. There's only a few known graves on the battlefield. If James had not died near an occupied house, and by a distinctive natural marker, he'd probably be lying beside the road today, unmarked and unknown, just another missing from the great War. How many of these graves did I unknowingly walk or drive by today, the soldiers resting peacefully for more than a century and a half on this largely unaltered landscape, their locations likely never to be known?

Sergeant James Jourdan's grave near Brice's Crossroads

If you want to come check out Brice's Crossroads, here are the details:

Brices Cross Roads National Battlefield Site
28 MS-370
Baldwyn, MS 38824
(662) 680-4027
https://www.nps.gov/brcr/index.htm

Mississippi Final Stands Interpretive Center
607 Grisham St.
Baldwyn, MS 38824
(662) 365-3969
http://www.finalstands.com/

CHAPTER 19

"Get Down, You Damn Fool"

Washington, DC

A month after General Hunter and the Federal Army's burning of VMI, the strategic battle for Virginia reversed course. Bobby Lee, unable to tolerate the Northern occupation of his food source in the Shenandoah Valley, removed a full corps of Rebs from the lines around Richmond and Petersburg and sent them west, under Gen. Jubal Early, to reclaim the valley.

Early defeated Hunter at Lynchburg, sending the Yanks fleeing into West Virginia, and then marched north through the valley, again defeating Federal forces at the Battle of Monocacy, forty-five miles north of Washington. A little more than three weeks after Lynchburg, Early and his ten thousand men had marched more than 250 miles and approached Washington's northern defenses.

On July 11, 1864, Early's men scouted lightly manned Fort Stevens, a few acres of earthworks and artillery, five miles north of the White House, and decided to attack the next morning. A Rebel army advancing on the nation's lightly guarded capital sent Washington into a crazed frenzy. The Northern newspapers' headlines pronounced doom of all makings, and the terrified citizens scrambled, making plans to evacuate. A steamer waited on the Potomac to ferry Lincoln and his government out of harm's way if need be.

Henry Halleck, the army chief of staff, telegraphed Grant. "Considerable reinforcements must be sent here. If you can't send reinforcements it is doubtful I can hold the city."

Lincoln asked for Grant to come north himself. All three knew that most of the troops stationed at Washington had been stripped from the capital's defenses and sent to Grant's army, pushing for Richmond.

Grant had already sent some dismounted cavalry, and also rushed the 6th Corps under Gen. Horatio Wright by steamer up the Potomac, but he stayed around Richmond. Grant had Lee hemmed up, but he knew the political ramifications of Rebs plundering the streets of the capital. There would also be political consequences if the commanding general of the Army had to return to defend Washington. He wired Lincoln of the troop movements, but said, "If I come it will have a bad effect."

By the time Early readied for his attack on the morning of the twelfth, Grant's veterans arrived and manned the fort. A small skirmish ensued, and Early, his men nearing exhaustion from the days of heat and hiking, blinked and moved west away from the capital. The casualties for the two armies totaled less than nine hundred, but the battle is best known today as the only time in our history that the nation's chief executive came under fire.

On July 12, Abraham Lincoln arrived at Fort Stevens to view the happenings. He toured the big guns. A witness recalled the six-feet-four president wore a tall hat, making for quite a target. Lincoln mounted a parapet and inspected the Rebel lines through a field glass. Several soldiers warned the president that the Rebel sharpshooters were only two hundred yards away. Lincoln, unperturbed, continued his inspection. A surgeon came and stood beside Abe. A shot pierced the air. The surgeon buckled over, hit in the leg.

Somebody yelled in the president's direction, "Get down, you damn fool!"

Legend has it that the future Supreme Court Justice Oliver Wendell Homes uttered the words, but historians have found no evidence to who spit out the insult or words of wisdom, however you want to look at it.

A few Rebels later recalled the sight of a strange, tall, out-of-place figure dressed in long frock coat at the fort that day. After the raid, Old Jub proclaimed, "We haven't taken Washington, but we scared Abe Lincoln like hell!"

Fort Stevens, or part of it, is still there, about three acres of green grass, earthworks, and a few cannons as part of the NPS's Rock Creek Park on Georgia Avenue, on old 7th Street, one of Washington's main roads into town during the War. Fort Stevens, perched on a hill, doesn't have any personnel or parking, but there are a few signs. The Battleground National Cemetery with a monument to the battle sits four blocks up the road. Getting to Fort Stevens isn't easy. There's no subway station nearby. A car or cab through the dreadful DC traffic is about it.

The City of Alexandria has a museum at Fort Ward with some neat artifacts and maps of Washington's defenses during the War, including some great models. It's not easy to get to either, but worth the trip if you're in town. There's a great story of the guns at the capital's forts. During World War II, the munitions makers arrived in search of scrap metal, removing the guns from the carriages and readying them for their trip to the melting pot until somebody from the NPS showed up at the last minute to save them.

The forts are a nice stop, but I thought there had to be more of off-the-tourist-trail Civil War DC than I found. I reached out to Tom Schultz, a retired Naval officer who gives military tours of the nation's capital, and then went to see him in Alexandria. One of Thomas's assistants, Meredith Barber, gave me a brief walking tour of Old Town Alexandria, at least as charming as its name. She showed me the interesting spot where the first two combat casualties of the War occurred.

On May 24, 1861, Col. Elmer Ellsworth, a personal friend of Lincoln, raised a regiment, the famous New York Fire Zouaves, in response to the president's initial call for seventy-five thousand troops. After the Zouaves arrived in DC, Mr. Lincoln gave Ellsworth and his men a job. Across the Potomac, atop a tall pole on the Marshall House Inn in Alexandria, fluttered a large, defiant Confederate Flag in full view of the White House. Flying for almost a month, the flag became an insult to all of Washington.

With some of his men, Elmer took off to improve the president's view. The colonel and seven of his men entered the inn, and Ellsworth went upstairs, promptly cutting down the flag. Descending the stairs, the inn's owner, James Jackson, shot Ellsworth in the chest with a shotgun. One of the Fire Zouaves then shot Jackson. The twenty-four-year-old colonel whom Lincoln called, "the greatest little man I ever met," lay in state at the White House after his death, and "Remember Ellsworth" became an early rallying cry for the Unionists.

There's still a small war going on in Alexandria about this. A plaque at the site commemorates James Jackson. The New Yorkers and Unionists have tried to put up a monument to Ellsworth, but a Virginia law states that once a monument is up, another monument cannot be put near it. The Jackson plaque went up first. Alexandria stayed in Federal hands almost the entire War, but the Rebs won the battle to honor the first fallen!

While in Alexandria, Thomas told me about a new Civil War site that's becoming one of the most popular stops on his tours, the Cottage at the Soldiers' home. This was a house just outside of War-time Washington, owned by the federal government, where Lincoln spent much of his presidency, kind of a Camp David of its day.

I'd never even heard of it. "Where's it at?" I asked Thomas.

"Right up there by Fort Stevens. I think that's where Lincoln was when he went over there during the battle."

This sounded like something I wanted to see, but I sucked in a deep breath. It had just taken me almost two hours to drive the twelve miles from Fort Stevens to here. I grabbed some crab tacos at a chic restaurant in Alexandria and then got back into the maze of honking horns.

The cottage sits at the Soldier's Home, today known as the Armed Forces Retirement Home, a retirement community for veterans established before the Civil War. The almost three hundred acres, part veteran's cemetery, part retirement home is populated with grand nineteenth-century buildings and tall trees that combine for a marvelous sanctuary from the concrete jungle just outside the gates.

On these grounds, atop one of the tallest hills in DC, Lincoln found refuge from the pressure of the White House and War in a thirty-four room country cottage, built in the early gothic revival style. In 2008, the National Trust for Historic Preservation cleaned up and repaired the home, and opened it to the public.

During his presidency, Lincoln spent more than a quarter of his time at the cottage, especially during the temperate months, the breezes and air at the retirement home more refreshing and inspirational than the capital. During the War, more than 150 veterans also lived at the Soldier's Home, in the adjacent buildings. They're still there today, 1,100 of them in 2017, enjoying the open space, nine-hole golf course, and other amenities.

This was the country then, and most days the president made the forty-five-minute ride by horse or buggy to the White House, three miles away.

Walt Whitman passed the president often on his trips to and from the White House and left these words to posterity. "Mr. Lincoln generally rides a good-sized easy-going gray horse, is dressed in plain black, somewhat rusty and dusty; wears a black stiff hat, and looks about as ordinary in attire as the commonest man . . . I saw very plainly the President's dark brown face, with the deep cut lines, the eyes, always to me with a deep latent sadness in the expression."

The cottage is open to the public but requires a tour to see the interior. There's also a good museum at the cottage, generally about Lincoln, War-time DC, and the Emancipation Proclamation. The cottage's biggest historical contribution to the nation occurred in the summer and fall months of 1862. Lincoln spent most of these months at the cottage, and this is the timespan when he conceived the Proclamation, announcing it to the world on New Year's Day, 1863.

If you're looking for authentic items of Mr. Lincoln, War-time Washington, or even the house itself, the cottage is not the place to find them. There wasn't much left of Mr. Lincoln that's not housed and guarded somewhere else by the time of the restoration, but the house has been returned to the rustic, simple layout of its Civil War days. Touring it gives us some sense of the simplicity of our greatest President, at his greatest moments of peril and accomplishment.

Today, as from its inception, the Soldiers' Home is operated at no cost to the tax-payer, initially purchased with money pillaged during the Mexican War. In one of the War's great ironies, Jefferson Davis introduced the bill to create the home as a senator from Mississippi.

The cottage, the Soldiers' Home, and the museum are worth seeing for any fans of Lincoln, or anybody who wants to see a great slice of America's living history.

Fort Stevens
6001 13th St. NW
Washington, DC 20011

(202) 673-7647
https://www.nps.gov/places/fort-stevens.htm

Fort Ward Museum & Historic Site
4301 W Braddock Rd.
Alexandria, VA 22304
(703) 746-4848
https://www.alexandriava.gov/FortWard

President Lincoln's Cottage at the Soldiers' Home
140 Rock Creek Church Rd. NW
Washington, DC 20011
(202) 829-0436
http://www.lincolncottage.org/

CHAPTER 20

"Kill Every Son-of-a-Bitch"

Winchester, Virginia

Today, Winchester, Virginia, is a pleasant, pretty, affluent southern city of thirty-thousand people at the north end of the Shenandoah Valley, surrounded by apple orchards, the fantastic Blue Ridge, and Allegheny Mountains—an idyllic backdrop. It's one of the cutest cities of any size I've ever visited. It looks like the American dream, clean, filled with ship-shape shops and cafes, and dotted with old delicate neighborhoods filled with a hodgepodge of historic architecture, a mixture of old and older with a little new added in. Well-manicured parks and green lawns are around every corner. The smiling citizens stroll along the wonderful tree-lined boulevards seemingly without a care. Who wouldn't want to live here?

But 150 years ago, this was literally the crossroads of the Civil War. The town, only forty miles from four states, seventy miles from Washington, sat on several major roads. During the War, it changed hands seventy-two times, and hosted three major battles and numerous skirmishes, not to include the two major battles at Kernstown fought just out of town! The casualties at Winchester likely resemble or exceed some of the War's biggest battles.

Founded in 1752, the town also featured prominently in the Revolutionary War, and George Washington once lived here. For me, Winchester held a special meaning. There was nowhere in the War, outside my home state or possibly Gettysburg, where the Louisiana forces played a more pivotal role or displayed more skill and success than here.

Union forces first occupied the town in April of 1862 when a major Union Army under our old friend from Port Hudson and Kernstown, Gen. Nathaniel Banks, forced Stonewall Jackson to retreat out of town. Jackson would be back with sixteen thousand troops to retake the town and inflict more than two thousand Union casualties in what has become known as the First Battle of Winchester.

Over the next few years, the town seesawed back and forth. Every time one of the armies was ordered out of town to deal with some impending threat, the valuable crossroads would be occupied by one army or another. It was recaptured by the rebels in another major battle, the Second Battle of Winchester, by Richard Ewell in June of 1863, launching Robert E. Lee's invasion of Pennsylvania on the way to Gettysburg. Additionally, twice during the War, after the battles of Antietam and Gettysburg, Winchester served as a large hospital. Thousands of Confederates wounded from those battles were brought here to convalesce or die.

During the War, most of Winchester's fighting-age men marched off to battle, leaving the Southern belles of Winchester, their beauty exceptionally noted by many of the Yanks, to fend for themselves. Hardened by being pressed into service to treat the mangled soldiers, and repeatedly under the occupation of unsympathetic Federal Armies and generals, the girls turned openly hostile and disobedient. They made it a point to turn their backs to the Yanks, and paraded off the sidewalks and into the muddy streets to avoid brushing up against the occupiers or walking under the Stars and Stripes, sporting their Jeff Davis bonnets that hid their faces.

There are numerous accounts of the town's women shooting at, and even killing Federal soldiers during the Northern army's frequent retreats from the town, the ladies stepping out on their porches or leaning through their windows, pistols and muskets firing away with deadly accuracy. In some cases, with mortal results, the Yanks shot back.

Winchester native Laura Lee wrote: "We are glad to hear that they are very much disappointed in their reception here . . . They say they were never treated with such scorn as by the Winchester ladies." Mary Lee wrote: "My contempt of the Yankees is so great that I cannot fear them."

Union Secretary of War Edwin Stanton described Winchester's women more bluntly: "The women are the devil!" Union general Milroy had a plan for the bunch of insolent hostesses, "Hell is not full enough. There must be more of these Secession women of Winchester to fill it up."

Winchester fell into Federal hands for the final time in September of 1864 when Union general Philip Sheridan put an end to the rambunctious Rebels in the Shenandoah Valley and Winchester once and for all. It is said that before the battle, Sheridan's officers actually took a vote on whether to burn the town. The count: seventy-one in favor, one hundred against! Though the diminutive city at the crossroads avoided a complete razing, during the battle, Little Phil, as Sheridan's troops dubbed him, rallied his troops, yelling, "Kill every son-of-a-bitch!"

Winchester is a Civil War enthusiast's dream. As I arrived in town, I turned off I-81 onto Jubal Early Drive and pulled into the Best Western Lee-Jackson Inn and Conference Center. Having knowledge of the fighting spirit of the town's women, I made it a point, while in town, to speak with my most accentuated Southern drawl!

Earlier in the day, I met with Terence Heder, the director of interpretation for the Shenandoah Valley Battlefields National Historic District (SVBF), to find out what to see. Terence gave me a brief history of the district, a quasi private-government organization whose purpose is to preserve and showcase the battlefields in the Shenandoah Valley. Terence's office, built in 1808, had old Stonewall as a visitor once. He showed me the street corner at his front door where the general once stood to direct his passing troops.

With a list of sites in hand, I took off into the giant Civil War wonderland. My first stop was Stonewall Jackson's Headquarters Museum, where the general had been sent to raise his army in the Valley in 1861. The museum is the former home of Col. Lewis Moore, a commander in the Virginia Militia, who offered it to Jackson as his headquarters. Today, the old structure is largely intact.

Jackson's wife, Mary Anna, joined the general in the house that became both a headquarters and home for the Jacksons. The actress Mary Tyler Moore was a descendant of Colonel Moore, and she helped pay for the museum's restoration, including making annual visits and contributions.

I got a tour of the house from Brian Daly, one of the museum's historians. After twenty battlefields, some of this stuff can become redundant, but I was pleasantly surprised and highly recommend the house and tour. I got to see locks of hair from the general and his mount, Little

Sorrel, and dozens more of Jackson's personal artifacts, including one of the general's most cherished, his prayer book, owned by Time Life.

There's a giant, authentic Confederate battle flag that flew over some of the War's grandest battles, and an original Confederate flag that Jackson flew over Romney, West Virginia, only discovered in 1966 in the possession of the state of Indiana. The then governor researched the flag's origin and sent it to the museum. Brian also told me the interesting story of the Moore house's central heat, revolutionary for the time. Old Stonewall was a master of the battlefield, but the little hole in the floor that pumped heat into his bedroom perplexed the general. He even got down on the floor to investigate the mysterious hole.

I then proceeded to Winchester's inviting, historic downtown to see the Old Courthouse Civil War Museum. The old courthouse, built in 1840, sits next to the brick pedestrian mall, North Loudoun Street, flush with loveable restaurants and shops, like a Bourbon Street without the bourbon.

During the War, the courthouse served as both a hospital and a prison for North and South. The courthouse was renovated in 2003 and opened as a Civil War museum that is operated by the SVBF. The museum has a significant collection of artifacts, over three thousand, most donated by Harry and Trish Ridgeway, local residents. Harry and his dad collected most of the artifacts from the field during the 1960s, and the Ridgeways managed the museum until it was turned over to the SVBF recently. Most appealing to me was the old graffiti written on the walls by prisoners from both sides.

Today, for preservation purposes, the graffiti is cased in glass boxes on the walls throughout the museum. One disgruntled soldier scratched out a note to Jeff Davis, which has become known as the "Curse to Jefferson Davis," condemning him to be

swallowed by a shark
the shark swallowed by a whale
whale in the devils belly
the devil in hell
the gates locked
the key and lost

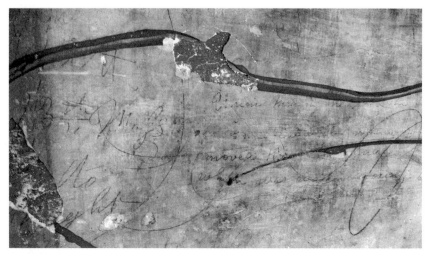

Graffiti written by prisoners of war in courthouse in Winchester, Virginia

The grammar's not perfect, but we get the point.

Eric Petitta, one of the museum's historians, told me they thought a Federal soldier wrote the curse, but there is plenty of graffiti from both sides that ranges from boasting to pouting. One that caught my eye was an exchange between both sides of the Mason-Dixon.

First Line: "Rebels, if you can hear, we will whip you . . ."

Second Line: "If you do, it will be the first time you impedent [*sic*] scoundrels."

Third Line: "You are cowards nothing but a thief the robbers of millions of women and children you good for nothing skunk."

The walls do, in fact, talk!

I took off to see what else I could find. There's not much left from the First Battle of Winchester, but it was Jackson's first major victory as an independent commander. The routing of the Yanks resulted in an outburst of festival-like celebration in town. Jackson himself later commented: "I do not remember having ever seen such rejoicing . . . the people seemed nearly frantic with joy . . . Our entrance into Winchester was one of the most stirring scenes of my life."

The battle's climax and culmination occurred when Jackson sent Gen. Richard Taylor's Louisiana Brigade on a flanking movement to charge up Bower's Hill, where the bulk of the Union guns were positioned. A Virginia veteran who fought through the entire war later wrote: "This charge of Taylor's was the grandest I saw during the war."

General Bank's forces fled north, leaving almost everything behind. Due to the booty of Union war supplies captured by Jackson's men, the Federal general garnered the nickname, Commissary Banks. As General Commissary tried to stem the stampede, he yelled at his men, "My God, men, don't you love your country?" It is claimed that a Union soldier replied, "Yes, and I am trying to get to it as fast as I can!"

I rode out to Bower's Hill to see what I might find. Today, it's occupied by John Handley High School (where Patsy Cline attended), and a very nice neighborhood on the heights. It didn't take me long to determine the Louisiana boys cleared off a spot for the town's future lawyers and investment bankers.

The second *major* battle for Winchester occurred in June of '63 when Robert E. Lee again headed to Pennsylvania, bound eventually for Gettysburg. To clear his way, he sent Gen. Richard Ewell, in his first action as a corps commander, to clean the Yanks out of Winchester. Without the leg he lost in a skirmish retreating from Bristoe, he marched nineteen thousand veterans back to take the town, now under the dominion of Gen. Robert H. Milroy. Milroy, commanding almost seven thousand troops, had been ordered to abandon the town, but he thought he could hold it, at least for a few days. To add to his problems, he had so mistreated the citizens of Winchester that even the local Unionists determined they'd be better off without him, and hence, his spy and scout network didn't make him aware of the huge Rebel force descending on the town.

Milroy's planned defense employed a series of forts northwest of town. Ewell started his conquest feigning an attack south of town and then sent Gen. Jubal Early with three brigades to take the most critical fort, West Fort. As Ewell watched the lead brigade, Gen. Harry Hays's Louisianans, storm the fort's ramparts, he shouted, "Hurrah for the Louisiana boys! There's Early. I hope the old fellow won't be hurt."

Seconds later, an out-of-gas Union slug hit Ewell, spinning him around, but only leaving a bad bruise! Ewell later renamed the West Fort hill the Louisiana Heights.

When West Fort fell, Milroy decided to hightail it out of Winchester, but it was too late. Mr. Lincoln's prediction that Milroy would be "gobbled up" if he remained in Winchester proved accurate. The Confederates captured more than 3,300 men and another bountiful basket of war supplies. Somehow, Col. Warren Keifer and his Ohioans who defended Fort West escaped to fight again. Confederate major Robert Stiles, a four year veteran of the War, called the flanking, feigning, charging, and well-coordinated battle of 2nd Winchester "one of the most perfect pieces of work the Army of Northern Virginia ever did." It announced Ewell as another competent Rebel commander for Mr. Lincoln to deal with.

There's little of the Second Battle of Winchester either, just a few historical markers around town, but one of the forts still remains, Star Fort. Though not critical at 2nd Winchester, it played a key role in probably the most significant battle in town, 3rd Winchester, or what is sometimes called the Battle of Opequon fought in the Fall of 1864, the precursor to the Battle of Cedar Creek, fought a month later that effectively ended Rebel-organized resistance in the valley. The NPS has a national battlefield at Cedar Creek, fifteen miles up the valley. It is 3rd Winchester where the SVBF is currently putting most of its restoration efforts around Winchester, and this battle holds the most significance to the outcome of the War. It seems nowadays that the only new preservation efforts revolve around Yankee successes!

Anybody, of any merit, who has studied the Civil War knows that the Confederacy lost the War not on the battlefield, but on the ballot when the nation reelected Abraham Lincoln in the fall of 1864. Yeah, there were more battles and bloodshed to come, mere formalities. But the dye had been cast. The surrender of Atlanta in the summer of '64 gets most of the credit for reelecting Lincoln, but much nearer to home, and closer to the First Tuesday in November, was the Valley Campaign of October of '64.

General Early's recent victory at Monocacy and raid on Fort Stevens had been the straw that broke the back, literally threatening Lincoln's control of the nation, both physically and psychologically. Union general David Hunter had burned not only VMI but also houses of important Virginia citizens. In tit-for-tat reprisals, Early burned the homes of the Maryland governor and postmaster, as well as torching Chambersburg, Pennsylvania. Things were spinning out of control. Something had to be done before the conciliatory Democrats strolled into the White House and let the South go.

Grant got the message. The valley, its only strategic value its annual harvest that fed Virginia, was no longer a sideshow, a distraction from the War's ultimate goals. It had to be brought to heel, and he needed a man for the dirty job. Someone not afraid to strike hard, keep up relentless pressure, and mercilessly wage a total war not only on the soldiers, but society at large and all its components, i.e., killing, torching, and freeing. He chose one of his old subordinates from the West, the thirty-three-year-old, five-foot, five-inch Gen. Phil Sheridan.

At this time in the War, Sheridan was mostly known for his cavalry's curtailing and killing of Confederate cavalry legend J. E. B. Stuart at Yellow Tavern three months earlier. Little Phil requested permission to go after Stuart. General Meade was leery, but Grant intervened. "Well, he generally knows what he is talking about. Let him start right out and do it."

Grant told Sheridan to go after Early, not mincing words, "Follow him to the death," and he gave Little Phil some of the army's best troops, forty thousand hardened veterans without exception. Grant reiterated his intentions to Sheridan. "Do all the damage to railroads and crops you can. Carry off stock of all descriptions, and Negroes, so as to prevent further planting. If the war is to last another year, we want the Shenandoah Valley to remain a barren waste." He later said that he wanted the valley so destroyed "that crows flying over it for the balance of the season will have to carry their own provender with them."

To his credit, Mr. Lincoln, at least later in the War, rarely meddled with his generals, generally letting them succeed or fail on their own, and handling them based on their results. Growing impatient with the political situation and knowing the consequences of Early's Army running free in the valley, he sent a note to Grant on September 11: "Sheridan and Early are facing each other at a deadlock. Could we not pick up a regiment here and there to the number of say 10,000 men and quietly, but suddenly concentrate them at Sheridan's camp, and enable him to make a strike. This is but a suggestion."

Mr. Lincoln had little to fear. Little Phil readied to strike the decisive blow. Through a network of spies, he knew that Early had just lost one of his major commands, a division and some artillery, under Gen. Richard Anderson who had been sent back to Richmond to aid Lee. His spy in town was the daughter of a Union officer imprisoned in Richmond, his courier, Thomas Laws, a slave owned by a prominent local family that freely moved about selling vegetables.

On September 19, Little Phil attacked. He outnumbered the Confederates more than two to one.

I drove over to the SVBF's recently opened Third Battle of Winchester Battlefield Park that preserves more than six hundred acres of the battle with a new visitors' center and five miles of trails with interpretive signs. The park is so new that the visitors center hadn't even opened as of the summer of 2017. It's a lovely walk in and around Reb Bud Creek, some of the topography hidden but steep. Here, in his first independent command, Little Phil employed his lightning war that incorporated massed cavalry, not merely as scouts or skirmishers but integrated in the attack with deadly mobility and efficiency. Still, the battle waned in doubt as Rebel guns ripped a hole in Sheridan's center. Gen. Robert Rodes, who held off Meade at South Mountain, rushed in and threatened to split the Federal force.

Sheridan sent a division under Gen. David Russell to stem the tide. Russell reestablished the battle line, but both he and Rodes perished in the desperate fight for survival. Most somber for me on the stroll was the Middle Field, maybe the bloodiest spot in the entire valley. Here, John Gordon's Virginia, Georgia, and Louisiana regiments outflanked Union general Cuvier Grover's 2nd Division, inflicting 1,500 casualties in just minutes. Grover lost all of his regimental commanders in only minutes, the New Yorkers suffering the most. As the Federals fell back in the "grandest disorder," to the First Field, the massacre continued. Union general William Emory bellowed, "My God! . . . This is a perfect slaughterhouse."

The Federals regrouped, and soon the greatly outnumbered Confederates began to flee, but they too rallied. Early regrouped and readied the Rebs at a stone wall along Hackwood Lane. But Sheridan's advantage was too great, and the Rebels took to foot "Whirling through Winchester," as Little Phil later said, the catchy phrase filling newspaper headlines for weeks. Artist James Taylor summed up the Rebel retreat as a "whirling mass of Gray madly pouring through the streets of Winchester amid shells shrieking and moaning their death cry."

My somber morning at the killing fields over, I had a few more stops to make. The first was Star Fort, one of the two major Confederate defenses of Winchester that Sheridan took in a parallel attack on the nineteenth.

Star Fort sits right in the center of a nice, middle-class neighborhood. Only the earthworks remain today, managed by the SVBF. The fort's grown up and covered in trees, but if you drive just past it, at the corner of Sentinel and Fortress Drives, you look down on Winchester and recognize the prominent position of the citadel. Of note, Gen. William Averell, the Union cavalry officer who provided the apocalyptic description of Malvern Hill the day after the battle, led a division that took part in the capture of Star Fort.

Fort Collier, the other major defensive position in the battle, sits a half mile to the southeast. There's a Civil War Center there. Here, Gens. George Armstrong Custer and Thomas Devin, who infamously started the hostilities at Gettysburg, participated in the largest cavalry attack in American history, seven thousand horses, swept the Rebel left to take the Fort. Col. George Patton fell resisting this charge.

The 3rd Battle of Winchester resulted in the bloodiest battle in the Shenandoah, with the Union losses exceeding the Rebels, but it was the major Union victory Lincoln needed. The President later told Sheridan, "I thought a cavalryman should be at least six feet four inches high, but I have changed my mind. Five feet, four will do in a pinch!" Sheridan was a sharp instrument of war, like a sword, which could now be wielded by Lincoln and Grant, the North's version of General Forrest.

A few months later, Lee summoned most of Early's men back to Richmond, and Early's fighting days essentially ended. After the War, Old Jub resurrected his name, becoming one of the leading voices for the

Lost Cause, its themes of Southern honor and valor dominating the historical narrative of the War well into the next century.

Before I departed the amazing Civil War Disney Land of Winchester, I had one final stop, two cemeteries. The first was the Winchester National Cemetery replete with unit monuments and over 5,500 Union interments. Even more breathtaking is the fifty-five acre Mount Hebron Cemetery beside it that houses the Stonewall Confederate Cemetery. I don't know if I've ever been to a more humbling place. The long lines of aged tombstones, monuments, green grass, and tall trees gave me goosebumps. Mount Hebron is the final resting place for Revolutionary general Daniel Morgan, and Founding Father Daniel Roberdeau.

The Stonewall Confederate Cemetery, part of the bigger plot, holds almost 2,600 Confederate dead from the War, to include Turner Ashby, Stonewall Jackson's cavalry commander. I was told that when his body was re-interred here from Port Republic, it was the largest funeral in the history of Winchester, more than ten thousand in attendance. Col. George Patton, who died late in the day on the nineteenth, is also here, as are three other Confederate generals. And yes, while there, I found the Louisiana boys who fought so fiercely here over four years, partitioned away in their own section, under a monument dedicated to their service. The tombstones, the engravings almost weathered away and unreadable, rest peacefully far from home and under a large oak tree beneath the perfect blanket of green grass.

I talked to the cemetery's superintendent, Donald Shade, about the huge Louisiana monument adjacent to the Louisiana tombstones. I instantly liked Donald, a man not afraid to convey his opinions. He asked my thoughts on New Orleans's monuments, whose removal still made national news. Donald didn't have any details on the Louisiana addition but turned me to another gentleman, Ben Ritter, whom I contacted.

Ben said he had some old newspaper clippings.

"Can you email them to me?" I asked.

Ben came from the old school. "I don't email, but give me your address and I'll mail them."

Sure enough, the clippings arrived in a few weeks, and I made it a point to go by and see Ben when I was back in Winchester. I did. He's a

The author with the Louisiana Boys at Winchester's Mt. Hebron Cemetery

classic and drove me around town pointing out all the Civil War structures not yet ripped down for new subdivisions or retail areas.

Anyway, the Louisiana monument's dedication on July 4, 1896, turned out to be a rather big happening, both in Virginia and Louisiana. According to the paper, a third of Winchester's citizens greeted the Louisiana delegation at the train station, and the town opened its arms for a grand celebration.

I'm no expert, and I'm sure somebody will write to tell me I'm wrong, but the eighteen-foot-tall obelisk, carved of Georgia granite, might be the most significant Louisiana Confederate monument outside the state. There's a big one at Gettysburg, but it went up in the 1970s. On one side of the Winchester monument, "Remember their Valor," is engraved. Whether you like these monuments or not, I'm certain that today, almost nobody in Louisiana even knows, much less cares, that this monument is here.

Third Winchester Battlefield
541 Redbud Rd.
Winchester, VA 22603

(540) 667-2754
http://www.visitwinchesterva.com/third-winchester-battlefield

Old Court House Civil War Museum
20 N Loudoun St.
Winchester, VA 22601
(540) 542-1145
http://civilwarmuseum.org/

Thomas J. Jackson Headquarters
415 N Braddock St.
Winchester, VA 22601
(540) 667-5505
http://winchesterhistory.org/stonewall-jacksons-headquarters/

Mount Hebron Cemetery
305 E Boscawen St.
Winchester, VA 22601
(540) 662-4868
http://www.mthebroncemetery.org/

CHAPTER 21

The Lost Battle

Mine Creek, Kansas

No state was more divided during the War than Missouri. It had a star on both countries' flags, had duel governments, and outfitted armies in both blue and gray. One of the Show-Me state's favorite sons, ex-governor and Mexican War hero Gen. Sterling Price, who sided with the South, had some early success in Missouri. But by September of 1861, the capital and most of the major towns in Missouri fell under Union military control. Confederate ruffians and bushwhackers still ruled and terrorized the countryside, requiring Lincoln to keep large troop concentrations in the state.

Policing Missouri and the guerrilla bands was a difficult task for the Union army. The notorious outlaws, Bill Quantrill and Bloody Bill Anderson to name only two, struck hard and then disappeared.

In the fall of 1864, Sterling Price gathered up twelve thousand men and Gens. James Fagan, John Marmaduke, and the steady Joe Shelby, and marched back into Missouri in hopes of reclaiming the state. Even if he failed, he'd pillage the state for badly needed supplies and replenish his ranks with fresh troops, or so he hoped. He planned on the assistance of six thousand pro-Confederate guerrillas. Price brought Confederate governor Thomas Reynolds in hopes of re-installing him in the state capital.

Price, fifty-five years old, was no longer the soldier of earlier days. Now over three hundred pounds, he was forced to ride into Missouri not on horseback, but in a buggy. Arriving in his home state, Price met with Bloody Bill Anderson's raiders—on October 6. Bill brought Price some war trophies, scalps. Price declined the scalps but sent Anderson to raid the railroads. This resulted in the Centralia Massacre, where more than a hundred unarmed and off-duty Federal soldiers were murdered, some of their bodies mutilated. The affair turned into a national media sensation.

To say things in Missouri at this time were a little out of hand would be an understatement. In fact, the fighting along the Kansas–Missouri border in the 1850s started the conflict that evolved into the War. Raiders and soldiers on both sides burnt, stole, and murdered, settling old scores. Kansans and Missourians didn't like each other much then. Some say that hasn't changed much in a century and a half. After pro-Confederate bushwhackers sacked Lawrence, Kansas, in August of 1863, Union general Thomas Ewing issued the famous Order 11 that depopulated four Missouri counties. The order, though not directly, gave the Kansas Jayhawkers and other pro-Union guerillas a free hand to torch the counties, still called the Burnt District today.

The War had gotten barbaric here, literally an eye for an eye, civilians not exempt. Many of the deeds in Missouri, some sanctioned by both armies, exceeded anything that happened at Fort Pillow. George Caleb Bingham, one of the nation's preeminent painters of the time and a Unionist Missourian, painted his famous Order 11 in an attempt to smear Ewing and the army. So mistreated were the Missourians by the army that Harry Truman's mother, just a young girl at the time, refused to sleep in the Whitehouse's Lincoln Bedroom in her nineties.

Hoping to redeem Missouri, Price marched on, but decided against an attack on Jefferson City, the capital too fortified. Still, a month after he crossed the state line, he neared Kansas City, trailed by five hundred wagons of pillaged supplies, stolen from everybody, blue and gray.

Gen. Samuel Curtis commanded the Union garrison in Kansas City. As the Rebels neared, he tried to raise additional men, calling on Kansas Governor Thomas Carney. Carney had no desire or intention of sending his boys to protect the hated Missourians, but they would fight to save Kansas. Curtis and Carney compromised, the line would be held at the state line, fifteen miles south of Kansas City in the town of Westport.

To buy time, Curtis sent two thousand troops and Gen. James Blunt to Lexington, sixty miles east of Kansas City, to check Price's advance. I drove into Lexington one Saturday morning to look around, and tour the Battle of Lexington State Historic Site. To my disappointment, most, if not all of the site, is dedicated to an earlier battle at Lexington in 1861 between Sterling Price and Union general James Mulligan. Mulligan would be wounded and captured in the battle, but later paroled, and would die in the Pritchard House at Kernstown three years later.

There's not much in Lexington left from the second battle, but it's a neat place. There's still a cannonball lodged into one of the columns of the courthouse downtown, and the State Historic Site, dedicated to the first battle, sometimes called the Battle of the Hemp Bales, is a great site.

In the Battle of the Hemp Bales, General Price, with fifteen thousand Confederates, surrounded and defeated three thousand Illinois and Missouri boys. Price employed soaked hemp bales that were slowly pushed forward to break the siege. The museum has a good movie about Lexington's history and the early War in Missouri, and the Anderson House, a large Greek Revival and plantation home that served as a hospital during the battle is on the grounds. It still has plenty of bullet and canister holes.

Blunt didn't have much luck delaying Price in Lexington, who marched on to Kansas City, and there I went in search of the battle, one of the biggest west of the Mississippi. Westport is sometimes called the

Cannonball lodged in courthouse in Lexington, Missouri

Gettysburg of the West. Several battles make that claim, a few that probably deserve it more, but Westport essentially ended major organized hostilities in Missouri.

There's only one problem: You can't hardly find the Battle of Westport today. It's almost all been covered with concrete. There's a visitor's center in wonderful Swope Park that contains artifacts and information on the battle. There's also a driving tour that I didn't take. I'm no fan of big-city traffic.

The only sizable portion of the battle left is a fifty-acre tract around Byram's Ford acquired by the local Monnett Battle of Westport Fund in the 1980s. I drove down to the ford. Not much there, just a stand of trees around the Big Blue River in an industrial area. There's no parking or signs that I saw. I heard the old road to the ford is there, but I didn't venture into the overgrown brush to look for it.

The Battle of Westport was fought throughout this general area, but it was here at Byram's Ford where Union general Alfred Pleasonton, in heavy fighting with Marmaduke, fought his way across the Big Blue River to get into Price's rear. This forced Price and his five hundred wagons of loot to retreat south. Due to the running nature of the battle, the casualties of both sides were never accurately quantified, but the best estimates are over a thousand for each side. Only a determined effort by Shelby and his Iron Brigade, fighting a rear-guard action, allowed Price to escape.

Curtis made it a point that when his cavalry finally got into action, his forces tracked down many of the notorious Missouri ruffians. The border outlaws had murdered his son, Maj. Henry Smith, a year earlier at Baxter Springs. Three days after the battle, they got Bloody Bill and some of his ruffians, parading his body through Richmond, Missouri.

I visited with Daniel Smith, a local attorney and the chairman of the fund. He described their struggle, preserving and restoring a battlefield in a major industrial area. The fund has given their tracts to Kansas City and developed a master plan. They're attempting to purchase additional tracts and pursue funding mechanisms, but it's an uphill battle. For now, Civil War buffs have to wait for more of Westport.

There had to be more to such a big battle, somewhere. I met a friend of mine for lunch in Kansas City, Max McCoy. Max is an author, journalist, and professor at nearby Emporia State University in east Kansas. He told me that another battle, Mine Creek, actually undid Price for good, and it's still around, fifty miles south of Kansas City. This is where Curtis and Blount finally caught up with Price's column in one of the largest cavalry engagements of the War. He also pointed me to Arnold Schofield, the retired historian at Fort Scott National Historic Site.

"Nobody knows more about the War around here than Arnold," Max said. "Give him a call."

I did a little research on Mine Creek. The state of Kansas has preserved the battlefield, complete with a museum. Kansas started acquiring land in the 1970s, and since, the Mine Creek Battlefield Foundation has raised about a million dollars for the site. The museum opened in 1998. Actually, in 2004, the History Channel did an hour-long documentary on Westport and Mine Creek, called *The Lost Battle of the Civil War*.

I drove down to Pleasanton, Kansas, population about a thousand, named after General Pleasonton. It's a nice drive through the rolling prairie. The modern, uncongested freeway slicing through the slow-moving country, the sky big and blue, the air clean, the natives friendly—something that looks like an idyllic setting for a postcard from the heartland. But this is where it all started, the border between Missouri and Kansas, and the cross-border violence to determine if Kansas would be a free or slave state in the 1850s.

Just outside of Pleasanton is another significant site, the Marais des Cygnes Massacre State Historic Site. Here, in 1858, proslavery ruffian Charles Hamilton massacred eleven Kansas free-staters. The event caused a national outcry, and John Brown came to the Massacre site, built a cabin, and raided into Missouri.

There are no employees at the site, but there is a stone building, built beside Brown's cabin, and interpretive signs. Warning, make sure it hasn't rained if you go to Marais des Cygnes. You have to drive over three miles of gravel roads through rural Kansas. This is Americana, nothing but picturesque amber fields of grain, the deer grazing along the road. The nearby community of Trading Post also has a museum with information on these bloody years, and a monument to the Marais des Cygnes Massacre.

I drove on out to Mine Creek, rolling pasture beside the trickling creek. Here, two days after the Battle of Westport, Price's column of wagons got bogged down crossing a ford on the creek. Curtis had sent his cavalry in hot pursuit, leaving his militia behind. His two divisions of cavalry, about 2,500 troopers, under Pleasonton and Gen. James Blunt, were outnumbered three to one but charged with a veracity that caught Price's disorganized men by surprise.

It had the makings of a real fight, but the fresh Bluecoats had the fighting spirit, charged downhill, and more importantly, carried Spencer repeaters, lever-action rifles with seven preloaded rounds. Confederate soldiers moaned that the rifle could be "loaded on Sunday and fired all week." The line of Federal cavalry didn't employ any fancy flanking movements, just an old-fashioned charge. William Forse Scott of the 4th Iowa later wrote, we "struck the enemy's line like a thunder- bolt, and broke it wholly away. The other companies struck it in succession from left to right, and it all fell away like a row of bricks. . . . The rebels were so confused and at so short range that they could not well use the muzzle-loading guns with which most of them were armed."

In thirty minutes, it was all over. Confederate losses totaled more than 1,200, a thousand of whom were taken prisoners including Confederate generals Marmaduke and William Cabell, and most of Price's war booty. The Federals lost about a hundred men, wounded or killed.

Mine Creek may have been one of the largest battles of the conflict not to have a reporter present anywhere nearby. None of the major Northern or Southern papers ran stories on the battle, all too busy covering the presidential election exactly two weeks later, hence the battle's obscurity, even in 1864.

There are probably few battlefields more intact. Arnold told me, "The best archaeology tells us the battle occurred over about 1,000 acres, and we've got about 900 of those preserved."

I walked the site's trails, probably more than a mile. This is still the wild west. I plucked a tick off of me later. On the fateful October day, the Federal cavalry commenced a one-thousand-yard cavalry charge over the grounds.

Much of Pleasonton's cavalry was composed of the Missouri State Militia, raised to fight the guerrillas. These, by all accounts, were an undisciplined lot, with plenty of blood and a few massacres on their resume. They had standing orders to kill any Confederates in blue, and though they knew many of the Southern boys donned stolen Union uniforms out of necessity, they carried out their orders.

I asked Arnold about this.

"Well," he said, "we don't really know. We think probably a hundred to 150 Confederates may have been killed before the officers got control of the situation. You have to understand, this was Missourians fighting Missourians, and they didn't like each other very much."

As we all know, family affairs get personal quickly, and typically in these matters, we don't think rules apply . . . At least that's how it works with my clan.

Shelby again saved Price, or what was left of his army, his cavalry rallying to save the day, but not before six hundred Rebels were killed and wounded, and another six hundred captured. Shelby recounted it. "It was a fearful hour. The long and weary days of marching and fighting were culminating, and the narrow issue of life or death stood out all dark and barren as a rainy sea. . . . Slowly, slowly my old brigade was melting away."

The battle moved on with no flag of truce to collect the dead. Many of the boys are still on the battlefield, under the almost incessant Kansas wind and grass.

The War in Missouri and Kansas was over. Price would continue his retreat into the Indian Territories and then Arkansas, never to take up the sword again. He is best known today—not for glory on the battlefield, but for leading a group of Confederates to Mexico after the War, his antics the inspiration for the 1969 classic starring John Wayne and Rock Hudson, *The Undefeated*.

Marmaduke would go on to be governor of Missouri—Marmaduke, Arkansas, is named after him. We drive through these towns every day, at least unknown to me, named after Civil War heroes. Shelby, one of the best soldiers west of the Mississippi, joined Price after the War in Mexico, and allegedly was the inspiration for the post-War song, "The

Unreconstructed Rebel." Shelby, a pre-War slave owner, came back into the Union family later in life and was appointed US Marshal in Missouri in 1893.

If you're in the area, come see Mine Creek and eastern Kansas. These fields of grass are where it all started and where it ended west of the Mississippi.

Battle of Westport Visitor Center
6601 Swope Pkwy.
Kansas City, MO 64132
(913) 345-2000
http://www.battleofwestport.org/VisitorCenter.htm

Mine Creek Battlefield State Historic Site
20485 Kansas 52 Scenic
Pleasanton, KS 66075
(913) 352-8890
http://www.kshs.org/mine_creek

CHAPTER 22

"Let Us Die Like Men"

Franklin, Tennessee

It is the blackest page in the history of the war of the Lost Cause. It was the bloodiest battle of modern times in any war. It was the finishing stroke to the independence of the Southern Confederacy. I was there. I saw it. My flesh trembles, and creeps, and crawls when I think of it today. My heart almost ceases to beat at the horrid recollection. Would to God that I had never witnessed such a scene! I cannot describe it. It beggars description. I will not attempt to describe it. I could not. The death-angel was there to gather its last harvest. It was the grand coronation of death.

So was the battle of Franklin described by Sam Watkins, one of only seven men to start and finish the War with the 1st Tennessee.

If there's a Civil War battle that almost all historians agree should be on the list of battles that every American can count on their fingers that's not there, it took place in this small town twenty miles south of Nashville. Nowhere is a battle more a microcosm of the War.

A few weeks before the battle, the United States reelected Lincoln. There would be no political solution that left the Confederacy in place. After Franklin, most of the War's leaders realized the South, at least militarily, would not win the War. There remained battles to fight, better terms for the South gained, Southern honor preserved, but there would be no victory.

The battle emphasized the Confederacy's terrible civilian leadership, emblematic of one of its major shortcomings compared to the Union. Franklin has also become the poster-child for modern Civil War preservation. Once lost, the battlefield now laces a modern American city, its restoration ongoing around us. We can go shopping or out to dinner on the sacred, hallowed grounds, and tens of thousands of Americans drive through it daily. Through preservation, maybe it will finally be given the prominence in history that it is entitled.

I'll confess to my readers, of all the places I visited, this is the one I studied the most. The battle, the events surrounding it, and its preservation fascinated me. It's been called the greatest story of the Civil War, and I believe it. It was the most costly in flesh, proportionally to duration and men engaged.

Franklin's destiny was set five months earlier with Sherman at Atlanta's doorstep. Jeff Davis, not happy with Gen. Joe Johnstone's performance at the head of the army of Tennessee, replaced him with Gen. John Bell Hood, a much more aggressive fighter, and a dogged hero of many battles with the Armies of Northern Virginia and Tennessee. Hood had an arm mangled at Gettysburg, and he lost a leg at Chickamauga. At this stage in the War, he had to be strapped to his saddle to ride. For certain, Hood, at least physically, was not the soldier of his earlier days. With Robert E. Lee bottled up around Richmond, Hood's army constituted the last major Confederate force free in the field.

Robert E. Lee once said, "Hood is a bold fighter. I am doubtful as to other qualities necessary." Veteran Confederate Corps Cdr. Gen. William Hardee, not wanting any part of Hood's reckless charges and heavy casualties, asked for and received a transfer out of the army of Tennessee upon Hood's promotion.

Hood concocted a new strategy after the fall of Atlanta. Instead of contesting Sherman's march to the sea, he marched his army north, hoping to retake the giant Federal supply bastion of Nashville, in Union hands most of the War, but not the military juggernaut of Sherman's army. His plan had merit, at least on paper. He intended to catch up with Gen. John Schofield's army of Ohio, falling back to Nashville where thirty thousand additional Yanks were garrisoned. Hood hoped to get the numbers on his side and destroy each army before they joined forces.

In late November, Hood almost caught and surrounded Schofield's army at Columbia, Tennessee, on the Duck River. Only a few days later, on November 29, Hood again managed to maneuver his army into a perfect position near Spring Hill, Tennessee. The Rebs caught Schofield's army split in two, half of it cut off and primed to be devoured. Due to a calamity of Confederate errors, Schofield managed to escape, arriving in Franklin, thirteen miles away, at dawn.

In Franklin, the Federals discovered all the bridges over the Harpeth River destroyed. Schofield, knowing he had to fight, ordered his engineers to go to work repairing the bridges and his troops to dig in. Schofield's back was to the river, but fortunately, Franklin sat on a hill, and as a result of a small battle in town a year earlier, entrenchments existed that could be occupied.

When Hood got up on the thirtieth, discovering the Yanks gone, his blood stirred. He angrily chastised his subordinates and made for Franklin in all haste to make amends. In hot pursuit, he left most of his artillery behind.

Later that day, Hood and his generals viewed the Federal lines south of Franklin, wrapped around a hill that constituted the Fountain Carter's home and farm. Hood's generals recommended against a frontal attack.

Nathan Bedford Forrest asked Hood to give him a division of infantry, and he would outflank the Federals. Forrest, never afraid to speak his mind, once told Braxton Bragg, "If you ever again try to interfere with me or cross my path it will be at the peril of your life." Forrest, angered with Hood, had earlier confronted him. "If you were a whole man I'd whip you to within an inch of your life."

Hood would have nothing of it. He meant to fight, and fight here, saying, "We shall make the fight."

As Gen. Patrick Cleburne inspected the Federal lines and the long hill ahead of Hood's army, one of his generals, Daniel Govan, said, "Well, General, there will not be many of us that will get back to Arkansas." Cleburne, looking through a field glass, despondently replied, "Well Govan, if we are to die, let us die like men."

By day's end, in five hours, the Rebels lost six generals dead or mortally wounded, seven more wounded, one captured. In all, they lost eight thousand men and fifty-four brigade or regimental commanders. That's just the Confederate losses. More than two thousand Yanks fell. Nothing in American military history compares to Franklin.

Gen. Isaac Sherwood of the 111th Ohio Infantry later said, "The Battle of Franklin, fought Nov. 30, 1864, was the most destructive of human life in proportion to the number engaged of any battle in the four years of war . . . at midnight on the battlefield of Franklin, the finger of destiny was lifted pointing the open road to Appomattox."

I drove south out of Nashville to find this place, only recently recognized as one of the War's major battles. The urban sprawl of one of the country's fastest-growing major cities wedged into every nook and cranny of the rolling hills. Nashville traffic, crammed onto the six- and eight-lane freeways, was as bad as any I'd ever experienced, but gave me a sense of the blanket of concrete threatening the battlefield.

Franklin, Tennessee, just a few decades ago, a rural town of ten thousand, has experienced an economic boom, its population now over seventy thousand, almost all affluent American suburbanites. Teslas and SUVs motored through the crowded streets. I pulled into the Lotz House, one of two structures around the Carter farm during the battle still standing, to meet with Thomas Cartwright.

Thomas was the curator and executive director of the Carter House for more than twenty years before moving to the Lotz House. He's still involved in the preservation of the battle, often lecturing, appearing in documentaries, and giving walking tours of the battleground. Before I looked around, I wanted to ask Thomas about the battle's preservation. With the aid of numerous organizations to include the Heritage Foundation of Franklin, Save the Franklin Battlefield, the Battle of Franklin Trust, City of Franklin, and the Civil War Trust strides have been made.

In 2006, essentially all that remained of the battle were Winstead Hill (Hood's headquarters), the Carter House, Fort Granger, and Carnton Plantation, all islands in a sea of neighborhoods and strip malls. Since, numerous tracts have been purchased, including a Pizza Hut and Dominos that were recently removed. My global positioning system (GPS) unit still plotted the Dominos. The latest purchase, 2.8 acres for $2.8 million, just south of the Carter House is so recent that the final house on the property only came down a few months before I arrived.

I drove down to Spring Hill, to the Rippavilla Plantation where Hood conceived his battle plans. Thomas told me it was only a dozen miles outside of town, but the drive took almost an hour, through stop and go traffic and a never-ending landscape of new restaurants, subdivisions, and shopping plazas. The plantation is a grand old house and symbolic of what Thomas and Franklin face. Outside the huge Greek revival house, rows of corn dot the landscape between a modern freeway and General Motors' massive Saturn Plant almost in the front yard. It's a strange contrast of old and new.

I drove back up to the Carter House, on the top of the hill and at the center of the battle. Here, the Federals, left under the command of Gen. Jacob Cox who had commanded the fierce battle at Turner's Gap two years earlier, formed their defensive line.

From here, you can look to the south (most of the distant view blocked with development) where Hood's army charged. I got a tour of the site from Mike Eaton, one of the Franklin Trust's guides. The red-brick Carter House sat at the epicenter of the battle, atop the hill where the Rebels broke through. The house and two remaining structures, kitchen and office, have more than one thousand bullet holes. The back wall of the office, facing the Rebel Charge, maybe only twenty feet wide, has over three hundred bullet holes. It's said to be the most damaged structure remaining from the War.

Carter owned twenty-eight slaves at the start of the War and had three sons fight for the Confederacy. The seven slave-quarters on the plantation were torn down by the Federal soldiers, the wood used for entrenchments. Mike showed me the Federal lines, only recently discovered with the removal of two houses and by an archeological exploration, where the Illinois and Ohio boys put up a fierce fight. In fact, the two or three acres around the Carter House may be the bloodiest turf of the entire War—the site of savage hand to hand fighting.

Dozens of soldiers were killed on the steps of the Carter House. The Carters, and the nearby citizens and slaves, weathered the fight in the house's basement. After the battle, the Carter grounds were literally covered with dead and wounded, stacked in piles and occupying almost every inch of ground. Todd Carter, son of Fountain and a captain in

Bullet holes in the Carter office, Franklin, Tennessee

the Confederate army, fell in the assault. Located the next morning by his sister, Todd made it back to his home only to die in the care of his family. Somehow, after the War, the Carters went about their business in the house.

North of the Carter House, a gym has recently been removed, and now we can view downtown Franklin from the hill, where a division of Wisconsin boys, under Col. Emerson Opdycke, and in reserve, stormed up the hill to plug the breached Federal lines. The "Boy Colonel," Arthur McArthur, the father of Douglas McArthur, was wounded three times in this charge.

Though five or six acres have been cleared around the Carter House, everything else is modern city: houses, businesses, condos, streets, etc. The preservation efforts *have* finally provided enough space around the Carter House that today's visitor gets a sense that this is a commanding hilltop. From the Carter House, the spires of Franklin poke up to the north. To the south, the long sight lines, commercial districts, and streets fall off and stretch out for miles from the hilltop in all directions, helping comprehend the Johnnies' impossible charge.

Mike walked down the street to show me where General Cleburne fell near Carter's cotton gin, today Cleburne Park, where the Pizza Hut once sat. The gin is no longer there, but according to Mike, the trust has plans to build a replica. Here, Cleburne had a horse shot out from under him, tried to mount a second horse that also fell, and then took off on foot, waving his kepi, before a minié ball struck him in the chest.

Cleburne had become known as the Stonewall of the West, his men almost single-handily saving the army of Tennessee at Chattanooga, amongst other heroic deeds. But Cleburne only commanded a division. His sin: He formally proposed to enlist slaves into the Southern army and grant them their freedom for their service. Jeff Davis shelved any talk of this, ordering that no word of Cleburne's proposal even be discussed. The Irish immigrant became an outcast in his own army.

Mike showed me several other tracts the trust has made bids on. The dollar values he mentioned were astronomical. This is where preservation meets capitalism, market forces in play. Mike casually pointed to a marker where Gen. Hiram Granbury fell. Leading his Texans up Columbia Pike, he turned to his troops: "Forward men; never let it be said that Texans lag in a fight." Seconds later, a musket ball struck him in the head. Granbury fell to his knees, his hands clasping his cheeks. He was found in this position after the battle.

I could go on and on with the valiant deeds of the epic struggle, North and South, but that would take a book unto itself. If you're interested in these stories, come take one of Thomas's tours. I read one more story, maybe the most courageous I discovered on my journey, that I wanted to see.

I asked Mike, "Where did General John Adams die?"

Mike pointed down Cleburne Street, sided by green lawns and cute southern houses. "Down there, somewhere near the end of the street. It's doubtful we'll ever get that property."

Adams, leading a brigade of Mississippians on horseback, rallied his men late in the day, the bullets whizzing around him. One Yankee recalled, "We looked to see him fall every minute, but luck seemed to be with him." Other accounts say the Federals, taken with Adam's bravery, yelled, "Don't shoot him. He's too brave to die." Adams, a West Point graduate, finally rode up to the Federal line and tried to grab the Union colors. This was too much for the Southern general's Yankee admirers, and a blanket of Northern lead instantly collided with his body.

Hollywood couldn't make this stuff up.

Col. Edward Baker, of the 65th Indiana infantry, later wrote,

General Adams rode up to our works and, cheering his men, made an attempt to leap his horse over them . . . As soon as the charge was repulsed, our men sprang over the works and lifted the horse, while others dragged the general from under him. He was perfectly conscious and knew his fate. He asked for water, as all dying men do in battle as the life-blood drips from the body. One of my men gave him a canteen of water, while another brought an armful of cotton from an old gin nearby and made him a pillow. The general gallantly thanked them, and in answer to our expressions of sorrow at his sad fate, he said, "It is the fate of a soldier to die for his country," and expired.

I drove down Columbia Avenue to Winstead Hill, where Hood set up his headquarters. In 1948, Walter Robers gave a portion of the Hill to the United Daughters of the Confederacy, and today the City of Franklin and the Sons of the Confederacy still maintain this hill as a park. It has a great lookout of the Rebel charge of Franklin. The day I visited, a stand of trees partially inhibited the view. I've got a suggestion for the City of Franklin. You're spending those tens of millions to reclaim the battlefield, send a tree trimming crew to Winstead Park.

The view of Hood's charge, the scene of such epic folly and valor, is today marred by a large commercial and residential area. Under the concrete, the Southern soldiers marched to their deaths. Like a funeral, and very rare during the War, the Confederate bands played as the Southern boys marched off to their doom.

I'll leave the reader with one final description of the trepidation the boys felt as they marched toward Franklin, atop a distant hill, by Lycurgus Sallee of the 1st Arkansas.

I fully understood and realized the fearful sacrifice our grand old division was called upon to make. They never once faltered or hesitated, but here made the grandest effort in their splendid history. I paused to observe and admire the line as it moved forward under heavy fire . . .

*the slowness of the step forcibly suggested to my mind the idea of a
body of pallbearers marching to their own funeral, causing involun-
tary tears to flow down my cheeks.*

One of the questions I had when I came to Franklin was, "why?" Why did
these officers and men do this? There were other suicidal charges in the
War, the Yanks at Cold Harbor, Pickett's at Gettysburg, neither of this
scale or so knowingly doomed in advance. The best answer I got: They
were ordered to do it. They believed in the cause. From Winstead Hill,
it's easy to see how this War spun out of control. Wars are mostly fought
either between bad guys or by good guys against bad guys. There's not
many instances in history, if any, where two democracies fought. For that
to happen, these men, their societies, not their deranged leaders, chose
to fight.

I had a few more things to see but went down to one of the shopping
areas below the Carter House and grabbed a piece of pizza, the natives
going about their business like they were in suburban Seattle. Maybe it's
normal to them. Strange to me.

I then drove over to Carnton Plantation, like the Carter House,
managed by the Franklin Trust. Beside Carnton, in what was once the
Franklin Country Club and Golf Course, is the city of Franklin's recently
opened 111-acre Eastern Flank Battlefield Park, where the Rebels
attacked the far Union left.

Carnton's main house, an eleven-room, Federal-style red-brick home
built in 1826 served as the biggest of forty-four hospitals in Franklin
during and after the battle. Almost unique in the War, most of the battle
occurred after dark, and it was not until the next morning when citizens
and soldiers awoke to the hellish scene. Owned by John McGavock, four
Confederate generals lay stretched out on the porch of Carnton. Three
hundred more wounded were crammed into the house, half of whom died
the first night. Hundreds more were spread around the grounds. You can
take a tour of the house.

Like the Carter and Lotz houses, plenty of blood still stains the floors.
John and Carrie McGavock and their two children, both under ten, stayed
in the house, caring for the wounded. A few months after the battle, the

McGavocks donated two acres. At a price of five dollars per soldier, the Confederate dead were removed from the shallow graves around town and buried in the McGavock Confederate Cemetery, more than 1,500 total. Almost eight hundred are identified, the remainder unknown.

Carrie McGavock managed the cemetery until her death in 1905. Since then, it has been run by the Franklin Chapter of the United Daughters of the Confederacy. Until modern preservation efforts got underway after World War II, the cemetery constituted the major memorial to the battle. Carrie's story has in recent years come to the American public through Robert Hick's bestselling novel about her, *The Widow of the South*.

It's a short walk over to the cemetery from Carnton. I recommend it. It's a solemn place. Soldiers from every Confederate state except Virginia are buried here, organized by states. The Mississippi boys paid the heaviest price. There's only nineteen Louisiana boys here. Bringing up the rear, they were largely spared—at least for a couple of weeks.

Hood actually won the battle, at least tactically. Schofield evacuated Franklin during the night and made it to Nashville to join up with Gen. George Thomas, their combined forces numbering over fifty thousand.

McGavock Cemetery, Franklin, Tennessee

Despite losing a quarter of his army, Hood pressed on. Outnumbered almost two-to-one, he attacked Nashville two weeks later, the results almost as devastating as Franklin, with more than 4,500 Rebels taken prisoner. There's little to nothing left of the battlefield in Nashville, but in these weeks, the army of Tennessee, the last major Confederate army in the field, destroyed itself. A month later, Hood resigned and never fought again.

Federal general Jacob Cox, commanding at the Carter House, survived the battle. After the War, he went on to be governor of Ohio and later secretary of the interior.

Franklin is a great stop on any Civil War Tour. You could spend days here seeing everything. In the early twenty-first century, Franklin is the headquarters of Civil War preservation. You can't understand the War, at least through a modern prism, without coming to Franklin. It's essential.

Carter House
1140 Columbia Ave.
Franklin, TN 37064
(615) 791-1861
http://boft.org/visit/

Carnton
1345 Eastern Flank Circle
Franklin, TN 37064
(615) 794-0903
http://boft.org/carnton/

Lotz House
1111 Columbia Ave.
Franklin, TN 37064
(615) 790-7190
https://www.lotzhouse.com/

CHAPTER 23

"You and Your Garrison Are to Be Sacrificed!"

Fort Fisher, North Carolina

I drove south out of Wilmington, North Carolina, through the urban sprawl, golf courses, middle-class neighborhoods, scattered commercial establishments, and into the affluent beach towns of Carolina and Kure Beach. Here, fifteen miles south of Wilmington's historic downtown, State Highway 421 transitioned to Fort Fisher Blvd., and the two-lane stretch of asphalt moved adjacent to the vast sheet of blue water stretching endlessly to the east.

Past the beach houses and condominiums, the land fell off to the salt marshes and a little sliver of land wedged between the great ocean and the Cape Fear River. A mile south of Kure Beach, I turned into the Fort Fisher State Historic Site, operated by the North Carolina Division of State Historic Sites and Properties.

I got out and whiffed the salty air. The wind howled. The sun warmed my cheeks. Overhead, seagulls effortlessly glided over the white, sandy beach. The trees and salt grass fluttered wonderfully over the half-mile-wide peninsula. The beautiful, peaceful setting looked like something out of a Nicholas Sparks novel and gave no hint to the violent struggle that took place here a century and a half earlier.

In January of 1865, Wilmington was the last Southern port open on the East Coast and one of the only remaining Confederate railroads connected it to Richmond where Generals Lee and Grant were locked in the climactic struggle of the War, the Siege of Petersburg, which would decide the fate of the Confederacy.

All that sat between the Union Navy and General Lee's lifeline was Fort Fisher and its two thousand defenders, commanded by Col. William Lamb. The fort's 44 big guns and more than 120 pieces of smaller artillery covered both the coastal approaches and the Cape Fear River leading to Wilmington.

So important was Wilmington to General Lee that when he got word that the Federals might be planning to attack it, he pulled Gen. Robert Hoke and his division of proven veterans from the besieged line in Petersburg and sent them by train to Wilmington.

On Christmas Day, 1864, the Union Army and Navy made a failed attempt to take the fort. The Navy, commanded by Adm. David Dixon Porter, bombarded the fort with more than ten thousand shells. And the army, under the command of another of its bumbling political generals, Benjamin Butler, stormed the ramparts. Or so was the plan. To aid the attack, Butler came up with the crazy idea of towing a ship, the *USS Louisiana*, laden with 235 tons of gunpowder and disguised as a blockade runner, to the fort's shore and exploding it.

But when Billy Yank inspected Fort Fisher's steep palisades the next day, they discovered that the Navy's bombardment and Butler's powder-ship inflicted little damage.

The fort's defenders were ready for a brawl, and Butler lost his nerve, balked, and decided to retreat and reevaluate.

Learning from Fort Sumter, where its masonry defenses had been shelled to rubble, Johnny Reb constructed Fort Fisher's ramparts of twenty-five feet thick embankment, twenty-feet high, and over a wood frame. Called the Southern Gibraltar, the fort's mounds of sand, breastworks, and fortified artillery were a formidable defense against artillery or assault. Additionally, the Rebs laced the approaches with mines, torpedoes with ignition wires stretching into the fort.

After the Christmas debacle, President Lincoln got involved. Having been recently reelected, he no longer needed his political generals. Butler had been popular with the radical Republicans. His first executive order of 1865 sacked General Butler.

General Grant told Porter he would "be back again with an increased force and without the former commander" and, subsequently, sent Gen.

Alfred Terry, who later gained fame as an Indian fighter, and whose column found Custer after the Battle of Little Big Horn, to the fort with orders to close Bobby Lee's last supply line.

Terry and Porter's second plan involved landing three divisions, one composed of two brigades of colored infantry, north of the fort, and assault the Southern Gibraltar with the support of the Navy's guns. This was risky and required the fort be taken quickly. If Hoke's recently arrived veterans attacked from Wilmington, the Federal Army would be caught between two Confederate forces.

Two weeks after the Union's first attempt, Fort Fisher's commander, Col. William Lamb, saw the huge Union flotilla gathering offshore. Little did he know that the almost sixty ships would constitute the War's largest amphibious operation. He sounded the ready and immediately sent word to the Confederate district commander in Wilmington, Gen. Braxton Bragg, to send Hoke's Division.

On January 13, Terry landed eight thousand men a few miles north of Fort Fisher, immediately going to work on a large set of breastworks to guard against an attack from Hoke. The same day, the largest naval bombardment of the War began as Porter's fleet began to hammer Fort Fisher. During the bombardment, Confederate general William Whiting arrived at the fort from Wilmington with bad news. Bragg, who somebody for some reason put back in the field, worried about his own hide. Hoke had been ordered to stay outside of Wilmington. There was no rescue party coming.

Whiting bluntly told Lamb, "My boy, I have come to share your fate. You and your garrison are to be sacrificed!"

Two days later, Terry left a division of United States colored troops at the breastworks to protect his rear and moved toward Fort Fisher. On the eve of the battle, Admiral Porter, a reckless fighter, but also a notorious showoff, decided he wanted in on more of the glory. He solicited 2,261 of his Marines and sailors to join the attack and assault the fort's ocean front simultaneously with Terry's offensive. The only problem . . . they were armed with only revolvers and cutlasses! Nevertheless, the naval landing party came ashore unopposed, and the Union ground assault commenced.

Midday on January 15, after two days of shelling, the sailors and Marines moved down the beach and stormed the fort's northeast corner.

Lamb's troops, mostly native North Carolinians, emerged from their bombproofs, shaken from the constant shelling, but ready to spar. They unleashed withering fire on the approaching sailors, tearing them to shreds. Only one Federal soldier gained the crest of the fort's parapet, James Tallentine, with only sword in hand. His glory fleeting, he was quickly mowed down by Rebel fire.

With almost four hundred killed or wounded, the sailors and Marines retreated, having accomplished little. They did succeed in distracting the fort's defenders. As the Confederates celebrated, Terry's troops moved forward toward the fort's northwest gate, many armed with the new Spencer repeating rifles, shovels for digging in, and axes to chop down the large wooden spikes and breastworks.

Even more important, Admiral Porter's fleet honed their skills. By midafternoon, only a few of the fort's big guns remained operable. The cannonading also splintered some of the parapets, filled some of the ditches, and severed the lines to the Confederate mines.

Still, the fort was a daunting task. The next eight hours and little plot of land on the north ramparts of the fort in front of me became the setting for one of the War's bloodiest, and probably lengthiest, assaults on fixed fortifications. Colonel Lamb and his 1,200 remaining defenders would not be "sacrificed" without a fight.

Led by Col. Newton Curtis, the Federals pushed forward through the ditches and over the parapets. Then they entered the fort.

As the battle got hot, Whiting sent repeated messages to General Bragg in Wilmington to send reinforcements. Trying to repel the Federals that had breached the fort, Whiting led a counterattack, removing an American flag placed atop one of the traverses. "Go to hell. You Yankee bastards!" he yelled but soon crumpled over, the victim of Union sharpshooters.

As the Union push stalled, Curtis came forward to encourage his men. He met a unit taking cover from the Rebel fire, urging them to continue the advance.

A Yankee officer told the Colonel, "Keep down, or you'll see why we don't advance."

Curtis peered over the bombproofs and breastworks. Seconds later, a shell exploded. The colonel became one of the battle's casualties.

Over the next few hours, Terry fed two more brigades into the fight, the Federals having breached the fort's northwest gate. All afternoon, the Union Army made a slow advance, stepping over their comrades "piled up a dozen deep," most of the brigade commanders killed or wounded in the fight.

Union Captain Adrian Terry recounted the mayhem, stating the Confederates guns poured "into them a tremendous fire of musketry . . . The enemy contesting every foot of ground with a gallantry worthy of a better cause," as the fire from the Union fleet shook "the solid earth, and threw huge clouds of sand high in the air from every part of the fort."

The battle still in doubt, the Navy's canons continued to tear into the fort with deadly accuracy, sweeping the ground in front of the Union advance.

Later in the day, again counterattacking, Colonel Lamb fell, wounded in the desperate struggle.

As the sun set, the battle still hung in the balance. The Rebels put up a stubborn defense, much of it devolving into a hand-to-hand fight. Terry sent his last brigade of reserves forward into the storm of battle, now a bizarre mass of confusion. Red muzzle bursts and the thunderous snap of fire filled the Southern night in all directions.

I walked behind the fort's museum to inspect what remained of the massive Confederate earthworks, by far the grandest I'd seen anywhere. Over the last century and a half, much of the fort has been consumed by the sea, the endless waves eating away the entire coast and with it, the east fortifications including the Mound Battery, a sixty-foot high man-made hill that took the Rebels six months to construct. Only in the 1990s did the US Army Corps of Engineers complete a revetment project on the beach that has stabilized the shoreline and saved the remains of Fort Fisher.

A large portion of the powerful mounds and parapets remain on the fort's north wall, including the northwest gate area abutting the Cape

Fort Fisher Earthworks

Fear River where Terry's troops entered the Fort. Here, I climbed up on the mounds. To the east, the sand and scrub fell away to black and green marsh, then the Cape Fear River stretching miles to the tree-covered mainland. To my right, on the fort's northern approaches, sat thicker brush and sand where so many American boys fell.

Fifty-one Congressional Medals of Honor were awarded for heroic service here in one day. They bear testament to the violence of the assault. Only about eight thousand Union troops were engaged. At Gettysburg, where over one hundred thousand troops fought a three-day battle, only sixty-four medals were awarded. Of the seventeen Marines awarded the nation's highest honor in the War, six were earned here. It was also here, just in front of these ramparts, that Galusha Pennypacker, commanding one of Terry's brigades and later the Union's youngest general of the War at only twenty, became a casualty of the battle.

A half-mile trail circles what's left of the fort's fixed defenses. Several replicas of the Confederate artillery are on display, including the Armstrong Gun, which fired 150-pound projectiles accurately up to five miles and commanded the seafront. After the fall of the fort, the Armstrong Gun became a war trophy. Shipped to West Point, it has overlooked the Hudson River for a century and a half. It remains a popular attraction today.

I went inside the fort's museum to meet the battlefield's historian, Ray Flowers, quickly learning that Fort Fisher has over six hundred thousand visitors a year. As early as 1906, North Carolinians tried to get Congress to make the fort a National Monument without any luck. Finally, in 1928, Congress appropriated money for a memorial to the battle, completed in 1931. In the 1960s, the state of North Carolina established the Fort Fisher State Historic Site.

The battlefield's museum has numerous displays, a large interpretive model, and dozens of great photographs. Noted photographer Timothy O'Sullivan came to the fort shortly after its fall. The museum's best attraction, at least for me, was the twelve-pounder Whitworth rifle on display. These cannons, employed at Fort Fisher, fired a deadly accurate projectile up to five and a half miles and were a constant menace for Federal warships blockading.

I asked if and when Fort Fisher might get its Armstrong gun back.

"It's never coming back," someone lamented. "They'll never let us have it."

In fact, the fort's guns seemed to be a sour subject at the park. Ray told me that the Whitworth on display does not belong to the park. It's just on temporary loan from the Navy Yard in Washington, DC. "The gun belongs to the Navy Yard," Ray said. "They could easily make the Whitworth on permanent loan to Fort Fisher."

I thought the War ended a hundred and fifty-two years ago! The only permanent, authentic cannon at the fort is a thirty-two-pounder salvaged off a sunken Federal Warship in 1963.

"Is there a cemetery here?" I asked.

"No, the soldiers have all been reinterred. Most of the Confederates were right where the museum sits. The undertakers that moved them were paid by the body, so they probably got them all."

I watched the museum's fifteen-minute film on the battle and then strolled back outside to take in some of the park's remaining components. I ambled through the battlefield, down the beach, and to the Fort Fisher Memorial. The walk is pleasant under the majestic oaks, over the green grass, and down the promenade along the ocean. Families played, couples strolled along hands clasp, and senior citizens sat on the park's benches. The tranquil, lovely scene gave no hint of the tremendous human drama that had unfolded here, deciding the fate of two nations and thousands of men.

The memorial, a tall column, sits almost on the beach. A plaque states that an unknown Confederate soldier is buried beneath. Ray earlier told me that the soldier's remains had been discovered during the construction of the monument. A note at the bottom of the monument states: Erected by the North Carolina Division of the United Daughters of the Confederacy. Standing in front of the monument, I looked over my shoulder to the public beach, filled with modern Confederate beauties sunbathing. Did any of them even know what this monument was?

If you're interested in hiking, the Fort Fisher Recreation Area, just south of the battlefield, has dozens of miles of trails along the beaches, marshes, and sand dunes. It's supposed to be a birdwatcher's paradise and also contains the North Carolina State Aquarium.

Before I left, I drove about a mile south to the battlefield's other main attraction, Battery Buchanan, where the road ends at Federal Point. A ferry here can take you back to the mainland. I highly recommend the ferry. It crosses the stunning Cape Fear River, a mile wide sheet of water, marshes, islands, and wildlife, more of an estuary than a river, to Southport.

Even if you don't like ferries, I recommend it if you're coming or going from the south or west. Coming to Fort Fisher through Wilmington and Carolina Beach is a step back in time. It's got to be the largest metropolitan area in the States without a freeway through the City. I-40 ends before you get to Wilmington! The traffic is terrible, especially during the warmer months when everybody's headed to the beach. You putter along for thirty miles from red light to red light, kind of like you do on the interstate in Dallas, but that's big-city madness.

Here at Battery Buchanan, an inlet to the Cape Fear River existed during the Civil War. After the War, the army corps of engineers closed the inlet with a more than three-mile rock apron called "the rocks" that is still in place today. Here, you can marvel at the work of the engineers who built the country, and I noticed as many people viewing the remarkable public works as the Civil War ruins. Early in the twentieth century, the corps completed Snow's Cut, a three-and-half mile long man-made channel that connects the Cape Fear River to the Atlantic north of Carolina Beach. Today, ocean-bound cargo can easily avoid Fort Fisher. Maybe the army got worried that the natives of Wilmington might again get full of themselves.

All that remains today of Battery Buchanan are some historical plaques and a twenty-foot-high mound of sand. General Whiting and Colonel Lamb were evacuated to here as the battle for the fort ebbed back and forth late into the day and after dark on January 15. At about 10:00 p.m., after more than nine hours of fighting, Union soldiers arrived at the battery and found Lamb and Whiting lying on stretchers. Knowing all was lost, General Whiting called for General Terry.

When Terry arrived, Whiting, from his stretcher, said, "Here is the fort. I surrender it to you. I don't care what becomes of me."

Colonel Lamb, shot in the thigh, would survive the War. General Whiting had no such luck. Wounded twice during the day, he would die two months later as a prisoner of war on Governor's Island in New York.

The day after the battle, a powder compartment at the fort blew up, killing and wounding two hundred Union soldiers and Confederate prisoners. Terry initially thought it was Southern sabotage, or possibly an attempt to retake the fort, but an investigation revealed that the most likely culprit was an accident, possibly some Marines overserved during the celebration. Imagine that!

Fort Fisher was in the hands of the Union Army. A month later, Fort Anderson and Wilmington would fall to the Union Army. To no avail, Jefferson Davis spent the spring of 1865 trying to find another seaport for the Confederacy. And three months after the fort's fall, as we shall see, the Confederacy surrendered.

Ft. Fisher
1610 Ft. Fisher Blvd. South
Kure Beach, NC 28449
(910) 458-5538
http://www.nchistoricsites.org/fisher/

CHAPTER 24

The Last Grand Charge

Bentonville, North Carolina

Driving north from Wilmington on I-40, I looked over the pleasant North Carolina countryside—gently rolling stands of timber in the Cape Fear River valley. There's almost nothing of significance on the ninety-mile drive north. Fill up with gas before you head out. Services are sparse. The largest town along this modern highway is Warsaw, population about three thousand. It was here, a month after the fall of Wilmington, that the Confederate army undertook its last offensive of the War, around the village of Bentonville, fifty miles south of Raleigh and six miles east of Interstate 40.

I read that the largely forgotten battlefield opened by North Carolina in the 1960s, which essentially ended the War in the East outside of Virginia, had changed little in a century and a half. From the interstate, little proof existed of a great battle that claimed more than four thousand killed, missing, or wounded. Only a small, official sign indicated that anything of consequence sat just off the road. I tapped the brake and put on my blinker, escaping the hundreds of cars and trucks roaring to and fro trying to get somewhere, to see what I might find.

As I slowed to exit, a big black Ford truck rushed around me. A two-foot-wide American flag was pasted on the back windshield and also the image of a cut-off shotgun above the words, "Come and get it." North Carolina still has plenty of fighters left!

Early in 1865, General Sherman and his sixty-thousand-man Grand Army of the West marched north from South Carolina, through here, en route to Virginia to support Grant in the conquest of the Confederate capital of Richmond. All knew, if Sherman reached Virginia, any hope for Lee's army would be squashed.

In late February, at General Lee's request, Jeff Davis reinstated Gen. Joseph Johnston as the commander of the army of Tennessee. Johnston, known as the "great retreater," part a slight and part a testament to his defensive abilities, was ordered by Lee to, "concentrate all available forces and drive back Sherman."

Johnston was pessimistic about his chances for success. Known as "Old Joe," Johnston had been the army's most senior officer to defect to the Confederacy at the commencement of the War, and he knew Sherman well. Johnston stymied Sherman's march on Atlanta until his dismissal seven months earlier, and had high praise for Sherman's army, saying: "There had been no such army in existence since the days of Julius Caesar."

Making matters worse for the Rebel commander, many of his troops were young boys, old men, or militia, and even his veterans were ill-equipped. But he did have some of the South's finest commanders still in the field at his disposal, most notably Generals D. H. Hill, Virginia veteran Lafayette McLaws, Hoke's division retiring from Wilmington, the army of Tennessee's most accomplished remaining corps commander, William Hardee, and two of its best cavalry commanders, Gens. Wade Hampton and Joseph Wheeler.

The situation around the Rebel capital growing less tenable by the day, Lee cabled Johnston on March 11: "You must judge what the possibilities will be of arresting Sherman . . . a bold and unexpected attack might relieve us."

"Old Joe" scraped together every man available, almost twenty thousand, and began to look for a suitable place to strike. Sherman's army approached on two fronts, each with about thirty thousand troops. Johnston thought his old adversary might be headed for the rail town of Goldsboro to be resupplied after weeks living on the land. If he guessed right, he might pull off one of his old tricks—attack one of the columns with a line of cavalry, and trick them into unknowingly attacking his infantry concentrations, concealed and on favorable ground.

Sherman, hearing of Johnston's return and familiar with his tactics, warned his commanders to be vigilant, especially on the flanks.

On March 18, Johnston ordered his men to converge on Cole's Plantation, two miles south of the little town of Bentonville, for the trap.

The next day, Yankee general Jefferson Davis took the bait, chasing the Rebel cavalry up the road. Davis, commanding one of Sherman's corps, was a hot-tempered fighter. He's the general who killed William "Bull" Nelson after the Battle of Richmond.

One of Davis's officers later recalled what happened next: "They came down on us like an avalanche."

And so the die was cast for the last major Confederate offensive of the War, and Sherman's last fight. By midafternoon, ten thousand bluecoats were on the verge of being swept from the field by a twenty-thousand-man gray-line. Uncle Billy later wrote that his March to the Sea had been "child's play" compared to the Carolinas campaign, and over the next few days, both armies came perilously close to disaster.

The Bentonville Battlefield today is much like it was during the War. The state of North Carolina has purchased about 2,200 acres, but much of the more than 6,000 acres that comprise the battlefield is still being cultivated by local farmers, and by my inspection, fifteen or twenty families still lived within the battlefield.

If you're coming from I-40 and drive the Harper House Road to the site's museum, you're on the old Goldsboro Road that Sherman's lead elements marched up on March 19, 1865. I suggest stopping at the museum first. The museum has some artifacts, displays, and a dynamic light map that describes the battle and will give you some sense of events before you head out to look around.

Behind the museum sits the Harper House that became a Union hospital during the battle and treated both Federal and Confederate soldiers. Built in 1855, in the Greek Revival style, I highly recommend the tour of the house. The surgeons' rooms have been restored, complete will their tools to sever arms and legs. I found the story of the Harpers very interesting. Confederate farmers with nine children and three slaves, the War stumbled on them when the Union Army commandeered their house. The slaves, two women and a man, took the Harper surname after the War and settled a few miles away.

Also adjacent to the museum are about a mile of trails that tour the hasty earthen breastworks constructed by the 1st Michigan Engineers and Mechanics during the battle. By this time in the War, the days of charges and armies butting heads in open fields was long over. Both sides developed the ability to quickly entrench themselves, digging trenches and felling trees to build breastworks. This is why, late in the War, few battles were decisive, and capturing occupied ground got expensive as at Fort Fisher. A Union soldier from the 22nd Wisconsin at Bentonville stated that in forty minutes, his company constructed defenses that would have been extremely costly to take.

Though some erosion has occurred, the Michigan trenches still look formidable. The little two-foot-tall by three-foot-wide mounds of dirt, urgently constructed, are excellent examples of hasty Civil War earthworks. The trails are an easy walk. Take your insect repellent and lookout for snakes. I stumbled on a big, ugly reptile, but unlike the snakes in Louisiana that stand their ground, he quickly slid off into a hole off the trail!

The park has a driving tour of the battlefield, with an audio tour that can be dialed up on your phone. I recommend driving up Harper House Road about a mile and a half to its intersection with Bass Road. This short trip is over the road where Rebel cavalry Gen. Wade Hampton skirmished with lead elements of Sherman's west wing, led by William Carlin's division.

You can pull over at Harper House Road's intersection with Bass Road. General Bragg's rebels hid in the woods to your right. To your left up the gentle hill is where General Hardee lay in wait as Carlin's division chased Hampton up Harper House Road. The field to the left of Bass Road constituted Cole's Plantation, where at about 2:45 p.m. on March, 19, General Hardee came storming down out of the woods in the last Confederate charge of the War. In the midst of the Rebel yells, Hardee led the charge on horseback and smashed Carlin's Division that soon took flight.

Over the next few hours, Johnston hurled his troops forward, nearly encircling ten thousand troops as Sherman and his subordinates struggled first to come to grips with the scope of events, and then to get more troops forward to stabilize the Union lines.

A Union officer said, "The onward sweep of the Rebel lines was like the waves of the ocean, resistless." One of Carlin's brigade commanders later stated, "Half minute's delay and General Carlin, myself and most of the brigade would have been captured."

During the afternoon, the fighting got testy. A Confederate veteran later stated, "If there was a spot as hot as this at Gettysburg, I did not see it."

Late in the day, additional Union forces arrived, and equally as important, they brought their artillery to bear; most decisive were the twelve-pound Napoleons that by this time in the War were best utilized as giant shotguns fired into oncoming ranks.

The sun setting, Johnston made one final push to carry the day with five separate frontal attacks. Many of the seasoned troops, both blue and gray, later claimed that the afternoon fighting was some of the most desperate of the entire War.

As darkness fell, the Rebels, unable to penetrate the reinforced Union lines, retired back to their initial, fortified positions, and the two armies spent the next day cautiously observing each other.

From here, I drove the rest of the audio tour that has ten stops. If you drive this, buckle up. As you mosey along, looking over the battle, the crazy Tar Heels storm by you wide open, dashing off to somewhere in a hell-of-a-hurry, probably annoyed at the throwbacks inspecting the fields of wheat and chicken houses.

At one place where I stopped to get out, not on the tour, but just somewhere I wanted to get out and look around, an old Confederate dog got after me. I tried to explain to him that I had Southern blood to no avail. Maybe it was the Red Cross/US Army T-shirt I wore?

I drove up to the area of Johnston's headquarters during the battle, near the once thriving village of Bentonville—not much more than a crossroads today. Two days after the Reb's last charge, both armies still sat on the battlefield, eyeing each other warily.

Maj. Gen. Joseph Mower, one of Sherman's division commanders, got permission for a reconnaissance-in-force on the Rebel's thin left flank. He soon found himself in the Rebel rear, nearing Johnston's headquarters, and ordered a full attack. A desperate fight ensued as Mower's offensive threatened to cut Johnston's only avenue of retreat, a single bridge over Mill Creek at the Rebel's back.

In the pelting afternoon rain, Johnston and Hardee summoned all available forces. It was a touch-and-go thing, but when Mower asked for more troops, Sherman declined, wanting to avoid another general engagement. Later, after gathering all the details, he admitted that this was a mistake, as he probably could have captured or destroyed one of the two remaining Rebel armies of any magnitude still in the field. Union soldiers actually made off with General Johnston's sword and sash.

General Hardee later commented on the near disaster. "This was nip and tuck, and for a time I thought tuck had it."

Earlier in the day, Hardee reluctantly allowed his sixteen-year-old son, Willie, to ride with the 8th Texas Calvary. Unfortunately, he was shot dead in his saddle during the contest to repel Mower. In a strange twist, the Union commander of Sherman's right wing, Gen. Oliver Howard, who arrived on the battlefield the day before, tutored Willie when Hardee served as the commandant of West Point, and Howard, as a math professor.

The close-run battle with Mower convinced Johnston it was time to skedaddle. He moved his army across the now swollen Mill Creek via only a single bridge.

The Confederate cavalry under Hampton and Gen. Joseph Wheeler weren't in such a hurry to depart. The latter, "Fighting" Joseph Wheeler, had sixteen horses shot from beneath him and bears the distinction of being one of the only Confederate soldiers buried in Arlington National Cemetery. This is due to his later service in the Spanish American War. Readers may know him from the 1997 movie, the *Rough Riders*. He was played by Gary Busey. In the movie, he told President McKinley, "Don't worry too much about them people in the South. There's nothing they like better than a good fight."

I don't know if he actually ever said that, but it is rumored that during the Battle of Las Guasimas, the thrill got the best of Fighting Joe, and he yelled out, "Let's go, boys! We've got the damn Yankees on the run again!"

Wheeler and Hampton, covering the Confederate rear, wanted another shot at the Union cavalry commander, Judson Kilpatrick. Kilpatrick took Sherman's orders to make the South "howl" rather liberally, and Uncle

Billy had even commented once, "I know that Kilpatrick is a hell of a damned fool."

Needless to say, the skirmishes to keep the Mill Creek Bridge open were not gentlemanly. In fact, when Johnston's army did finally surrender a month later, Confederate Cavalry general Wade Hampton refused to shake Kilpatrick's hand, and the two almost got in a fight.

Having seen most of the battlefield, I went back to the museum to meet with Sharon Laboda, a park guide. What I wanted to find was someone who lived in the battlefield, who went to bed every night on such sacred ground. Could they still hear the echoes of the cannons, the terrible shrieks of pain, the Rebel yells? What was it like? I succeeded. He was a Yankee from Garden City, New York. Larry Laboda was Sharon's husband. I asked if she'd call him and see if I could go by and visit.

Larry was one of the most interesting people I've ever met. He lives on a few acres in the battlefield. He actually once owned more but has sold everything but his house site to the state.

"How the hell did you end up here?" I asked.

"My brother and I liked to go look for Civil War artifacts, and then somebody told me about some land for sale in the Bentonville Battlefield. I bought in and moved on down. I love it! I met my wife after I moved down."

Larry showed me some of his collection of historical artifacts. He's also moved several houses from the 1860s onto his property and completely restored them. He lives less than a hundred yards from the statue of General Johnston, and says, "I never get tired of digging around and finding something, either on the ground or in the record of the battle."

I could have talked to Larry all day and would have loved to go on a driving tour around the battlefield with him, but the sun hung just over the western horizon. It had been a long, wonderful day at Bentonville. It probably would have been dark-thirty before I got out of there if I'd jumped in the truck with Larry!

Before I departed Bentonville, I pulled into the small monuments area. Little Rebel flags fluttered over the two dozen Confederate tombstones in the park's cemetery. Beside the cemetery stands the first monument erected at Bentonville in 1895, a granite column with a broad trapezoidal base. Wade Hampton, then the governor of South Carolina, presided over its dedication. There's also a monument to the North Carolina Junior Reserves at the intersection of Harper House and Bass Roads dedicated in 1937.

Throughout the battlefield, there are a few more fixtures put up before it became a public historic site, most notable are the white signs put up by the North Carolina Highway Historical Marker Program, probably prior to the 1950s. These markers and the older monuments recall an earlier time and mindset. I noticed many of them cited the battle as the spot where General Johnston "checked" General Sherman's advance. Hell, only three or four days after the battle's commencement, Sherman marched on north!

After Bentonville, the fighting ended for both Sherman and Johnston. They became friends after the War. Johnston managed to outlive Sherman, but only by a few weeks. An honorary pallbearer at Uncle Billy's funeral, he kept his hat off out of respect on a cold February day twenty-six years later, and hence caught pneumonia and died a month later.

Before you leave Bentonville, listen to the last stop on the audio tour. It deals with the Confederate surrender of Raleigh, three weeks after the

Confederate Cemetery, Bentonville Battlefield

Battle of Bentonville. Interesting stuff. Raleigh was almost sacked by mistake. Sherman gave written assurance to the North Carolina governor that the state's capital would be spared if the Rebels would not defend it. As the Union Army entered Raleigh, a lone rebel, a Texan no doubt, fired at Sherman's men. Confederate forces quickly apprehended and hung the Rebel, saving Raleigh. If you're heading north, check out the last stop on the audio tour.

Bentonville Battlefield
5466 Harper House Rd.
Four Oaks, N.C. 27524
(910) 594-0789
http://www.nchistoricsites.org/bentonvi/

CHAPTER 25

"The Confederacy Goes Up"

The Breakthrough, Petersburg, Virginia

Even amateur Civil War enthusiasts are familiar with Robert E. Lee and the army of Northern Virginia's bloody forty-day retreat to Petersburg, Gen. Ulysses Grant in constant pursuit—the epic battles of the Wilderness, Spotsylvania, and Cold Harbor to name just a few etched into the American psyche. Grant's ten-month siege of Petersburg followed. The NPS's Petersburg National Battlefield entertains hundreds of thousands of visitors a year to the sacred ground of The Crater, Five Forks, and Fort Stedman, among others. But not near as well-known is the small plot of Virginia where Grant, on April 2, made his actual breakthrough of Lee's entrenchments, some of the strongest in the world at that time, in what is often called The Breakthrough.

The more than four hundred acres where the 5th Vermont stormed through the lead and earthworks along the Boydton Plank Road that started what many historians consider the most important eight days in American history belongs to the Pamplin Historical Park. The park, created by successful local businessman and philanthropist, Robert B. Pamplin, a former president of Georgia-Pacific, and his son, Robert B. Pamplin Jr., opened to the public in 1991. I'd never heard of it, but Bob Krick with the NPS, whom I visited with back at Malvern Hill, told me about it.

I talked to the park historian Edward Alexander about the Pamplins. He told me they were direct descendants of the Boisseaus, whose farm was the setting for much of the battle. When development in the 1990s threatened the battlefield, the Pamplins stepped in to save the land. Though Ed wouldn't give me details, my research determined that the Pamplin Foundation has contributed more than $40 million.

To get some sense of the importance of this sacred ground, we have to put ourselves back in April of 1865. Lee and his men, against all odds, besieged in trenches, held off Grant and his huge army that outnumbered them more than two to one for ten months at the gates of Richmond. To date, all Federal attempts to take Petersburg, the rail hub for Richmond, had failed, most with miserable results. In one instance, the 1st Maine made an ill-fated charge on Petersburg's defenses. In one day, the Federal regiment lost six hundred of its nine hundred men, the single-highest casualty count of any regiment in the War in a single day. The Confederate losses were one dead and twenty-four wounded.

On April 1, at the Battle of Five Forks, Grant managed to flank Lee's beleaguered right. Under fiery Gen. Philip Sheridan and his army, freshly arrived from the Shenandoah, the battle had been the first Union success of any significance in months. As the battle hung in the balance, Sheridan rode into the lines yelling, "Where is my battle-flag?" As musket balls whizzed and shells exploded, he carried the staff through the ranks, rallying his men. On the heels of the Union success at Five Forks, Grant ordered a general assault along the entire line, hoping to gain a foothold inside the defenses and initiate the climactic battle of the War.

As you approach the Pamplin Historical Park today on the Boydton Plank Road, an old Virginia historical marker on its shoulder, placed in 1920, marks the spot where Gen. A. P. Hill was killed, and announces the importance of the ground around the road. Hill, who had been with Lee from the start and risen to corps commander, rode out to check the lines early on April 2, not knowing the Federals had broken through, and ran into advancing Bluecoats. Pennsylvania Corporal John Mauk shot Hill through the heart. Lee later said, "He is now at rest, and we who are left are the ones to suffer."

I pulled in to the Pamplin Historical Park, toured the excellent museum, and then walked the two-mile Breakthrough Trail that slithers through 3,300 feet of Confederate earthworks constructed by South Carolinians in the fall of 1864. By this time in the War, trench warfare dominated the battlefield, foreshadowing the killing fields fifty years later in World War I. Even the besiegers quickly entrenched themselves. It should be noted that today, the breastworks and the area to the south toward the Federal lines is covered in trees, but during the siege this area, like much of the area around Petersburg, was a battle-scarred wasteland— all the trees felled for fuel, parapets, or to remove any cover for the Yanks.

At Pamplin, like most Civil War Battlefields, the earthworks are all that remain. But the park's trail leads the modern time-traveler through the elaborate defenses: rifle pits in front of the main defenses that replaced pickets, moats, man-made swamps, and abatis, the latter long, sharp wooden poles. The trenches themselves evolved, now supported by vertical wood timbers, not easily scalable and with traverses and zigzags to protect the troops from enfilade or artillery. The park's museum has plenty of excellent pictures and models. It's easy to see why most of the fights around Petersburg were inconclusive.

On the park grounds, the VI Corps, under the command of Horatio Wright who had arrived to save Washington at Fort Stevens, made one of the most famous charges of the War, larger than Pickett's up Cemetery Ridge.

I walked the trail with keen interest. One stop highlights the remains of a dam used to flood an area in front of the defenses, and another, the pickets' rifle pits. Grant ordered the attack here, undertaken by three

Earthworks at Pamplin Park, Petersburg, Virginia

divisions, under the commands of Gens. George Getty, Frank Wheaton, and Truman Seymour, to commence at daylight.

The attack was one of the boldest and most ingenious of the War. Over the preceding weeks, the Yanks studied the defenses and mapped a couple of gaps in the breastworks where the pickets entered and egressed the defenses. Additionally, pioneers, or what would be called combat engineers today, led the attack to chop down the abatis.

Every facet of the attack had been planned out, but still, most of the Union boys thought the attack on the fixed defenses would turn out like the numerous others over the last ten months, a suicide mission. One commander told his troops, "We are going to have a hell of a fight at early daylight . . . if any of you have anything to say to your folks, wives or sweethearts make your story short and get what sleep you can for hell will be tapped in the morning."

The Yanks moved forward in the night, guided by a ravine (a stop on the trail) and were forced to lie on the wet, cold ground for hours to conceal themselves with unarmed weapons so not to fire and lend any hint to the North Carolinians, manning the defenses, of their pending attack. The Rebels fired into the dark commotion, hitting scores, killing two regimental commanders, and wounding Gen. Lewis Grant, commanding the lead brigade of Vermonters. Somehow, the Northern boys' discipline held.

Following a massive artillery bombardment along the entire front that commenced before midnight, the attack began at 4:40 a.m. and the Northern boys started their death run. So great was the trepidation of the Yanks, Captain Darious Safford of the 1st Vermont, said, "I never had to strike men with my saber before to make them advance but that day I did strike a great many of them and in earnest too, as hard as I could with the flat of my sword."

Within an hour, the ground in front of the Rebel breastworks lay strewn with the bodies of nearly a thousand Yanks, but the Stars and Stripes flew over the defenses, the Federal forces pouring into Lee's rear along the Boydton Plank Road. It was at this time that Gen. A. P. Hill rode forward in an attempt to rally his men. Hill had said he had no desire to live to see the collapse of the Confederacy. In the cold, early morning of April 2, the sky in the east transitioning from scarlet to blue, he got his wish. Sergeant Albert Harrison of the 14th New Jersey summed up the battle: "The Confederacy is gone up."

I also discussed one of the longest-running debates in Civil War history with Ed Alexander—what soldier first breached the Petersburg defenses here at Pamplin Park? He stated that the best evidence suggest this was Captain Charles Gould of the 5th Vermont, who received the Medal of Honor for his service that day. Gould received three wounds, a bayonet through the mouth, a sword slash to the skull, and another bayonet to the back, all testaments to the brutality of the fighting. Gould's men pulled him to safety, throwing him in a ditch, and he survived.

Of course, there's quite a few other versions. I quote one by the commander of the 6th Maryland, "I have made a full investigation as to who was, in fact, the first man from this brigade to enter the works and am fully satisfied that Sergeant John E. Buffington, Co. C 6th Maryland Volunteers, was the first man to pass over the works." Sergeant Buffington was also awarded the Medal of Honor.

Ed told me that war of words for the credit for being the first to breach the line has led to a great understanding of the Breakthrough because it resulted in a disproportionally high number of written battle accounts. Everybody wanted to make their case that their man first breached the vaunted Rebel defenses.

Along the entire thirty miles of the Union's general assault around Petersburg that morning, the defenses at the Pamplin Historical Park were all that gave way. But that was enough. Before noon, Gen. Robert E. Lee ordered the abandonment of not only Petersburg but also the Confederate capital, recommending the Confederate government relocate to Danville that night. The Confederacy had "gone up." The government's move was really a moot point. Lee's army was, for all intents and purposes, the Confederacy at this point in the War, and it still had fight in it.

Pamplin Historical Park
6125 Boydton Plank Rd.
Petersburg, VA 23803
(804) 861-2408
http://pamplinpark.org/

CHAPTER 26

"My God, Has the Army Dissolved?"

Sailor's Creek, Virginia

As Richmond burned on April 3, panic-stricken citizens scrambling for trains and buggies . . . any way to escape, General Lee and his army slipped out of Petersburg under the cover of darkness. Lee's escape plan was complicated and had been in the works for months. He had to disengage more than thirty miles of defensive lines and move thirty-five thousand men, one thousand supply wagons, two hundred heavy guns, and four thousand horses and mules. He hoped to eventually reach Danville, the new Confederate capital, on the border with North Carolina, where his forces would join up with Joe Johnston's army now around Raleigh.

Despite the long odds, Bobby Lee pulled another rabbit out of his hat. His army, almost intact, fled north out of Petersburg, over the Appomattox River, burning the bridges behind them, the last troops pulling out under the fluid light of the flames engulfing Richmond and Petersburg. Was this the endgame for the Confederacy? Lee managed to escape to the West with a day's lead over the pursuing Federal Army.

As I drove west on Highway 360, through the largely empty rolling hills, I passed Amelia Court House, a quiet little town of a thousand residents forty miles west of Richmond. On April 5, Lee's now famished army arrived at Amelia Court House wedged into the rural patchwork of farms and timber. The three-day march had been taxing. Sheridan's pesky cavalry chased hotly, constantly harassing the long line of Rebels. Lee ordered his men to evacuate with only a day's rations.

To Lee and his army's grave disappointment, an administrative mistake resulted in the train cars at Amelia Court House stuffed only with guns and ammo. What they needed desperately was food. What they lost was precious time. The need for food now superseded any tactical or strategic goals. Cruelly, Lee ordered his men to march on west, toward Farmville, where he hoped to find rations.

The dislodging of Lee's army and the chase took a toll on Grant's men too, their losses almost eight thousand for the week. Not wanting to let the Southern army slip away, Sheridan begged Grant to let him go get Lee. Grant consented, essentially putting most of the army currently commanded by the timid General Meade at the direction of the ever-pressing Sheridan. On April 5, sensing something big in the works, Grant threw caution to the wind. With only a small party, he made a hazardous sixteen-mile night ride through Rebel-held territory to meet with Little Phil.

The next day, Sheridan's constant cavalry raiding, most notably by Custer, Crook, and Devin who had taken the forts back at Winchester, created some gaps in Lee's long column. As Union troops poured into these gaps, three Confederate corps got trapped between the cavalry and the Federal II and VI Corps, hot on the tails of the Rebel rear. At Sailor's Creek, Grant finally forced the issue. April 6 came to be known as Black Thursday for the Confederates.

I pulled up at the Sailor's Creek Battlefield State Park, operated by the state of Virginia to meet with Chris Calkins, the park manager. Chris is another Civil War lifer. He's a retired chief of interpretation at the NPS's Petersburg National Battlefield where he was instrumental in the preservation of the Five Forks Battlefield. He's been featured on numerous national TV shows and has written several books on the 1865 war in Virginia. Chris told me the story of the park, only recently established after Virginia passed a tax in the early 2000s for the establishment of the park. The director of the Virginia State Parks sought out Chris to put the park together, and when you pull in, you get the sense that the park's paint is still drying.

I've taken the reader to a lot of battlefields, but nowhere, except maybe Franklin, do the factors of newness and importance collide more meaningfully in the story of Civil War preservation than here. Here, two indomitable men who each built one of the greatest armies in the history of the world, each in his own image, squared off. One saw all his blood, sweat, and tears fall apart. The other experienced the ultimate fulfillment, conquest. Tragically, this battle, probably Lee's worst defeat, its scale in both losses and consequences one of the most momentous of the War, has been almost lost to history mainly because major events rushed onto the stage in the two subsequent weeks, dominating the press and pushing the event that triggered it all to the back pages of the papers and forgotten in the Republic's history . . . Appomattox, Lincoln's assassination, Johnstone's surrender, the hunts for Booth and Jeff Davis. I could go on and on.

As Chris tells it, the state actually tried to create a federal park here back in the 1930s, but apparently, the local congressman hailed from Appomattox, and they got the national park. The site wasn't even nominated for the National Register until the 1980s. Until then, a single roadside monument, two old houses present at the battle, and a few signs put up by the Virginia Conservation Commission in the '30s or '40s were all that marked the battlefield. It was only in the 1970s that historians started to piece together where the actual components of the battle occurred.

The new park encompasses the main battlefield at Sailor's Creek around the Hillsman House, one of three engagements fought in close proximity late that fateful day. As you walk into the park's new visitor center, a huge, wonderful painting portrays the late-afternoon events of the unfolding human drama with consequences around the world. I got a tour of the park from Jim Godburn, one of the park's historians, accompanied by a group of US Army medical personnel also looking and listening with interest.

Stepping out of the visitor center, I looked north, down along, gradual hill to Little Sailor's Creek, probably waist-deep and fifteen feet wide, and over to the next hilltop to the Hillsman House. Here, Richard Ewell's men, without artillery and now at the edge of human endurance, having gone three days without a meal, or meaningful sleep, and having marched over sixty miles over rough terrain and through cold and rainy weather, were forced into a fight for survival. Events soon spiraled into a major battle. In less than two hours, the once almost invincible army of Northern Virginia fell apart.

On the hill behind the visitor center, the Federal forces attacked the hastily entrenched Rebels. The Northern boys ambled up the hill waving

Sailor's Creek education specialist, Jim Godburn, giving a tour, Sailor's Creek Battlefield State Park

white flags in an attempt to induce a surrender. Johnny Reb answered with a perfect volley of musket balls that initiated the fight. The well-fed Yanks fell back, regrouped, and came on again, but were repulsed a second time. Confederate Marines and Georgians swept the Yanks off the field again. According to Sheridan aid Fredrick Newhall, the starving Rebs attacked "with an elan that has never been surpassed."

By all accounts, the discipline in both armies soon gave way, and a savage battle ensued where men shot, stabbed, and clubbed each other as all military order degenerated—a street fight for life and death. One thirsty Rebel soldier noted that during the battle, he tried to take a drink from the Creek, but the water, running high with the spring rains, was red with blood. John Gordon and Richard Anderson's corps, just north and south of the Hillsman House, each surrounded, suffered similar fates.

Confederate major Robert Stiles said, "The battle degenerated into a butchery of brutal personal conflicts. I saw . . . men kill each other with bayonets and the butts of muskets, and even bite each other's throats and ears and noses, rolling on the ground like wild beasts."

As the shadows grew longer, more and more Union troops poured onto the battlefield. Before this day ended, fifty Confederate battle flags had been arrested, and eight thousand Rebels, almost a quarter of Lee's army, had been killed or captured. Among them were Gens. Richard Ewell, Joseph Kershaw, and Montgomery Corse, all who had been there since the beginning; Eppa Hunton, who broke President Lincoln's heart at Ball's Bluff; and four other generals to include Custis Lee, Robert E. Lee's eldest son.

As the fight waned, an exasperated General Lee arrived on the scene trying to rally his troops. Seeing the total disorder, he asked Little Billy Mahome, who had made the disastrous charge up Malvern Hill three years earlier, "My God, has the Army dissolved?"

Little Billy replied, "No, General, here are troops ready to do their duty."

Among those who narrowly escaped were Gen. Richard Anderson, who had stormed Fort Pickens four years earlier, and George Pickett, each of whom Lee removed from command that night for fleeing the battle. Lee said, "A few more Sailor's Creeks and it will all be over."

It was already over, the army of Northern Virginia routed and falling apart. After the battle, Sheridan wired Grant: "If the thing is pressed, I think Lee will surrender." President Lincoln, monitoring the telegraphs, wrote back: "Let the thing be pressed."

The next day, General Grant sent a messenger through the lines with an offer to discuss surrender terms, and after some correspondence, two days later, Robert E. Lee surrendered the army of Northern Virginia at Appomattox Court House ending the Civil War in Virginia.

The Hillsman House is still at the park, built in 1780 and restored to its 1865 condition under Chris's watchful eye. It's open for tours. From here, the entire battle lies before you, and just outside this house, Gen. Philip Sheridan arrived that fateful day, to the roar of his men, to inspire his troops. On this high perch, simple stands of trees, varying in hues of green and brown, are all that envelop the little open plot around Sailor's Creek. This is it, just a little pleasant valley, but also the culmination of Mr. Lincoln's will and all the nation's resources and sacrifices. I couldn't help but ponder what the Union commanders thought, witnessing the end, the culminating event, the focus of the nation if not of the world unfold, in this little valley in the middle of nowhere that had been untouched by

Hillsman House, Sailor's Creek Battlefield State Park

the War because it lacked anything of value. They had to feel the eyes of the world watching.

Chris told me to drive over to the Lockett House, two miles down the creek where General Humphreys II Corp surrounded Gen. John Gordon. Though Gordon escaped, a similar disaster transpired. The Lockett House is still filled with bullet holes. Outside it sits the original and sole monument to the battlefield for almost a hundred years, placed here in 1925 by a local chapter of the United Daughters of the Confederacy.

There was more to Bobby Lee's undoing than just Sailor's Creek. Just a few miles down the road is High Bridge Trail State Park, also run by the state of Virginia. On April 6, two bridges here were the only route back across the Appomattox, one a half-mile long, thirteen-story high rail-bridge, the other a smaller wagon bridge.

Both armies raced to the bridges, one intent on saving them, the other on destroying them. Union general Edward Ord sent a brigade of eight hundred men under Col. Theodore Read to burn the bridge. The only problem, they were going to a gun fight with a knife. James Longstreet's entire corps had been sent to take the bridges. Aside from the numerical advantage, the Rebs just wanted it more. Read and Confederate colonel

Original monument to the Battle of Sailor's Creek, placed by a local chapter of the United Daughters of the Confederacy at the Lockett House

James Dearing killed each other in a pistol duel at the bridge. All of Read's men were killed or captured.

After Lee's army crossed the bridge, the Rebels attempted to burn it, but Union infantry arrived to stomp out the flames. The Rebs put the rail-bridge out of action, three of its four spans destroyed, but the wagon bridge survived, and Grant's II Corps soon crossed the river in hot pursuit of Lee.

The rail-bridge was later rebuilt, and in 2004, Norfolk Southern sent its last train across the bridge. In 2012, the state of Virginia opened an $11 million hiking trail and pedestrian bridge adjacent to the old bridge, and of the same length and height.

I found the trail and bridge, though my GPS couldn't find it. I stumbled on it. You can drive to within a half mile of the bridge and walk across it. The piers of the old one are right beside the new one. Remember, this bridge is a half-mile long and thirteen stories above the river. Wow. I'm not really that scared of heights, but walking across this pedestrian bridge will make your knees weak. You step easy only leerily letting go of the handrail.

Piers to the old High Bridge over the Appomattox River

Walk out to the middle, stop, and stand, and then imagine rushing tens of thousands of men, horses, wagons, and cannons across this. It will give you some sense of the awe-inspiring scale of Lee's retreat. His army stretched out for miles and miles, and Grant's army was three times as big!

After his eventual surrender, General Lee is alleged to have told the engineers who burned the bridge, "to go home and start its rebuilding."

Sailor's Creek Battlefield Historical State Park
6541 Sayler's Creek Rd.
Rice, VA 23966
(804) 561-7510
http://www.dcr.virginia.gov/state-parks/sailors-creek#general_
information

High Bridge Trail State Park
6888 Green Bay Rd.
Green Bay, VA 23942
(434) 315-0457
http://www.dcr.virginia.gov/state-parks/high-bridge-trail#general_
information

CHAPTER 27

The Last Battle

Fort Blakeley, Alabama

With Robert E. Lee's surrender, and Joe Johnstone's army of Tennessee cowering in North Carolina, only one meaningful piece of the Confederacy remained unconquered. This included Mobile, the second largest Southern port and fourth-biggest city; Montgomery, the first Confederate capital; and Selma, the last leading center of war armaments production, all in southern Alabama.

David Farragut's fleet had entered Mobile Bay late in the summer of '64, the Union Army taking Forts Gaines and Powell. Fort Morgan was more troublesome, but it eventually fell after a two-week siege and bombardment. Forts Gaines and Morgan are still there. Hurricanes long ago swept away Powell, but Morgan and Gaines are really cool and open to the public. The state operates Morgan, its most visited Civil War attraction, and Fort Gaines is owned by Mobile County.

Farragut hurtled his fleet between the two forts, tying his ships together in case some lost power. The old fighter, sixty-four at the time, climbed up into the rigging of his flagship, the *Harford*, lashed himself to the rigging, and directed the battle from his perch! His fleet stormed the heavily mined bay, losing one ironclad, and then took on the Confederate Navy's most formidable vessel, the *Tennessee*, manned by the Confederate navy's only admiral, Franklin Buchanan, an old comrade of Farragut and the first superintendent of the Naval Academy.

When Farragut saw Franklin and the *Tennessee* approaching his fleet, he said, "I did not think Old Buck was such a fool!" After a fight, Farragut captured the mammoth *Tennessee*, wounding Buchanan. Despite switching sides, Buchanan survived the War, and the Navy has since named several ships after him. The superintendent's house at the Naval

Academy is named the Buchanan House. After capturing the *Tennessee*, Farragut put it to work, shelling Fort Morgan.

You have to take a ferry to get to the brick fortress of Morgan, at least from Mobile, but if you're into it, the fort's got a good collection of authentic cannons, twenty-four pound Flank Howitzers, some thirty-two and hundred pounders, and one of the deadly seven inch Brooke Rifles. There's also visible damage from Farragut's bombardment. It's where the bricks are new. Fort Gaines is on Dauphin Island, another masonry fort, but also with some authentic cannons. It was taken by land. At both forts, the concrete is all twentieth century.

Old Otto came to Fort Morgan in the '20s. According to him, just getting to the fort was a hell of an adventure. In Foley, Alabama, as he filled up his ford, the attendant warned him that no road led to the fort, just, twenty-eight miles of, "swamps and thickets," that were once a military road. Otto responded, "This sounds attractive," and he took off for Morgan. In 2017, that stretch looks like Hollywood Boulevard, high rises and strip malls. Otto found the fort. According to him, "Old newspapers, all dated 1917, lay strewn over the floors. The town gave on an eerie feeling, like the city of the dead. The ground was overgrown with semitropical vegetation!"

Fort Morgan, Alabama

Alabama has cleaned up the fort, but in 1864, the Union's occupation of Mobile Bay and Mobile were two different things. For one, the forts were forty miles from the city, largely regarded as one of the most fortified in the War. Second, the Rebs mined the bay. In the eight months after Farragut first sailed into the bay, he lost about half of his fifteen vessels to the hazards.

By March of 1865, General Grant's patience with the Federal commander around Mobile, Gen. Edward Canby, grew short. He had recently sent him an additional corps of veterans. In all, Canby's force now topped forty-five thousand troops. He sent Canby a telegraph: "I expected your movements to have been cooperative with Sherman's last. This has now entirely failed. I wrote to you long ago urging you to push forward promptly and to live upon the country and destroy rail-roads, machine shops and not to build them. Take Mobile and hold it and push your forces to the interior to Montgomery & Selma."

Canby got moving, but his problem was the two forts guarding the eastern shore of Mobile Bay, Spanish Fort, and Blakeley. And here I headed, to the largest battle in Alabama and the last major battle of the War.

The author with a thirty-two-pound cannon at Fort Morgan

Driving across Mobile Bay on the traffic-snarled I-10, one of Mobile's favorite sons, Jimmy Buffett, crooning on my radio, I looked out across the second biggest delta in the United States, blue, brown, and green water spotted with vast stands of trees and marsh. Off to the left, opposite Mobile, a string of small, green hills poked up above the water. Here, Confederate general Dabney H. Maury, who had led the charge on Battery Robinette at Corinth two and a half years earlier, commanded, 6,500 men and more than seventy canons entrenched and ready for a fight.

Canby first invested Spanish Fort and it six batteries. After a thirteen-day siege, on April 8, the Confederates abandoned the fort, most escaping safely. Canby then turned to the biggest entrenchments, Fort Blakeley, manned by 3,500 Rebs and commanded by Gen. John Richardson Liddell.

Late in the day on April 9, only a few hours after General Lee surrendered (of course nobody in Alabama knew this), Canby formed a three-and-a-half-mile line of sixteen thousand troops 1,500 feet from the fort, and in one of the War's great charges, the Yanks pushed forward at a full run, over the mines, trip wires, and through the sharpened wood stakes, musketry, and grape. Notable in the attack was a full division of USCT commanded by Gen. John Hawkins.

The shadow of Fort Pillow clouded the battle, with neither side expecting quarter. In fact, to motivate the colored troops, they were told, incorrectly, that some of Blakeley's defenders had been at Fort Pillow. As Yanks collided with the defenses, yells of "The damn niggers are coming," and "Remember Fort Pillow" came from both lines. Though initially no quarter was given by either side, the Yanks' rapid and complete envelopment of the fort allowed officers on both sides to curtail their men. More than 3,400 Rebels surrendered. Three days later, Mobile fell into Lincoln's hands.

Eight years later, General Canby, as part of a peace commission, was shot twice and had his throat sliced by the Modoc Chief Captain Jack in California.

Early one morning, I pulled up at the Historic Blakeley State Park, only established in 1981, which preserves the battle. Most of the park is owned by the Historic Blakeley Foundation and operated by the state. The park, on undeveloped land, has changed little in 150 years, except its once barren grounds are now overrun with dense trees. Twenty-five miles of trails and more than ten miles of almost pristine earthworks constructed by both armies lace the park.

I thought about walking the trails, but after more than twenty-five battlefields, I've walked enough earthworks and been bitten by enough mosquitoes and red bugs for a lifetime. Further discouraging me, insects buzzed and hissed everywhere in the wilderness. I met Mike Bunn, the park's director of operations, at the site's boat dock. We took a ride on the park tour boat and discussed the park and battle.

From the bay, you can see the commanding points of the forts. We also boated to the Huger and Tracey batteries, little islands on the Blakeley River that kept out the Federal gunboats. At low tide, some of the Rebel pilings can still be seen. Mike showed me a portion of the old telegraph line that linked Blakeley to Mobile—how the poles have survived the hurricanes I don't know. We motored all the way down to the World War II battleship, *USS Alabama*, moored in downtown Mobile. The only adventure on the boat ride was when Captain Steve Day pointed out an alligator. I thought the boat might tip over when the twenty or so tourists rushed to starboard to "uuh and ooh." I can see bigger gators from my backyard.

Mike told me the park is still a work in progress. They are still putting up the interpretive signage. One thing I wanted to see were a set of genuine Union zigzag trenches I had heard were in the park. These are the trenches the soldiers dug, weaving back and forth at angles to enfilade themselves and move closer to the fort. There's not many of these left, and I had never seen any. They've got them at Blakeley. I recommend taking a look if you're at the Park. What remains of the old river town of Blakeley is still in the park if you like that type of stuff, including the foundation of the county's first courthouse.

Mike had a request for me. He wanted a picture of Confederate general John Liddell's grave. Liddle commanded Blakeley during the battle. The general was both from Louisiana and is buried there. I'd never even heard of him until I went to Perryville. Liddell, a hard-fighting commander, led brigades not only at Perryville, but also Murfreesboro, and a division at Chickamauga. He was an outspoken proponent of Southern emancipation in return for the service of the slaves in the Confederate army. Robert E. Lee commented on Liddell's proposal, "He could make soldiers out of any human being that had arms and legs."

After the War, Liddell returned to Louisiana and wrote a memoir that was critical of the Confederate leadership. In 1870, he was murdered by an ex-Confederate colonel after a long-running feud. He was buried on his plantation somewhere in North Louisiana.

"I'll find him," I assured Mike, and later did, in an unmaintained little cemetery, in a grown-up grove of trees thirty yards off a state highway in rural Catahoula Parish, deep in the heart of the Mississippi Delta.

After the boat ride, I drove to Confederate Redoubt 4. Here, the park has cleared the trees between the Federal and Confederate entrenchments abutted with six and seven foot high mounds surrounded by abatis wood stakes protruding from the earthworks so we can visualize the charge. These five hundred yards are where the Illinois, Iowa, Indiana, and Ohio boys made their valiant charge, colliding with General Cockrell's famed Missourians. The best zigzags sit in front of Redoubt 4. Just north of Redoubt 4 is where Hawkins Colored Division and Mississippi boys fought it out.

Earthworks of Fort Blakeley, Alabama

Looking over the ground, we can today only ponder the waste . . . a battle for naught, almost one thousand killed or wounded Americans in the fight for Mobile. Still, with the last breaths of the Confederacy, a desperate life-or-death struggle took place here, the ground beneath my feet once blood-soaked to preserve the country we live in today. Here at Redoubt 4, Captain Henry Miller of the 8th Illinois Infantry captured the Blakeley garrison flag, for which he received the Medal of Honor.

On a map, Mike showed me how to get to two more sites in the area, what's left of Spanish Fort, and its strongest battery, Fort McDermott. I drove into the nice neighborhood of Spanish Fort Estates. Historical markers dot the neighborhood, the streets named after the battle's participants. At a cul-de-sac at the end of Cora Slocomb Drive sits what's left of Spanish Fort. I found an old marker. Behind it, the grown-up knoll is laced with earthworks and entrenchments.

In front of Spanish Fort, the Navy lost three vessels to mines and Canby took up a land siege, thirteen days of hell. Phillip Stevenson of the Washington Artillery described the scene:

We could hardly hear each other speak. The cracking of musketry, the unbroken roaring of artillery, the yelling, the shrieking and exploding of the shells, the bellowing boom of the mortars, the dense shroud of sulphurous smoke thickening around us. It was though "The Pit" had yawned and the uproar of the damned was about us. Men hopped about, raving, blood bursting from ears and nostrils, driven crazy by concussion.

After thirteen days, the 8th Iowa, led by the salty veteran, Gen. James Geddes, threatened Spanish Fort's left. The Confederate commander, Gen. Randall Gibson, who later became a US senator from Louisiana, snuck his men out of the fort using a hidden land bridge into the bay, almost a mile to the Huger Battery. The bridge was a marshy embankment, parts of it only barely visible at low tide.

Mike told me what's left of Spanish Fort is owned by the town, but nothing's been done to develop it. I drove by and stopped. It looks like it would make a fine park. Commanding over the bay and cute neighborhood, the hallowed grounds where our forefathers paid such a dear price is grown up in trees, hidden from passersby. I drove on through the neighborhood to Fort McDermott, owned and preserved by the Sons of the Confederacy. It's got huge earthworks, trails, and markers. Atop the fort's mounds, massive Mobile Bay expands to the west, a wonderful sheet of glistening brown water and green wetlands.

This was the sturdiest position at Spanish Fort, and storming McDermott put fear into even the Bluecoats' most veteran commanders. Gen. John McArthur, a veteran of Donelson, Shiloh, Corinth, Vicksburg, and Nashville, said, "My division will go in there if ordered, but if the Rebels stay by their guns, it will cost the lives of half my men. It won't pay." McDermott's defenders slipped out over the water bridge, and useless Armageddon was avoided.

The last major city in the Confederacy belonged to Lincoln. Three days later, John Wilkes Booth snuck into Ford's Theater, and two days after that, Joe Johnstone opened surrender talks with General Sheridan. Nathan Bedford Forrest and the Red River Valley still held out, and a few other estranged bands of Rebels roamed the countryside, but this was the end of the War where more Americans perished than in any war, before or since.

It was time for me to go back home, to my own corner of the defunct Confederacy, the piney hills, swamps, and cotton fields of Louisiana.

Fort Morgan
10 AL-180
Gulf Shores, AL 36542
(251) 540-7127
http://www.fort-morgan.org/

Historic Blakeley State Park
4745 State Hwy. 225
Spanish Fort, AL 36527
(251) 626-0798
http://www.blakeleypark.com/

CHAPTER 28

"One Damn Blunder from Beginning to End"

The Red River Campaign, Louisiana and Arkansas

On my trip into the nation's tumultuous history, I left out a couple of battles, very important ones, and an entire campaign for that matter. The campaign was the 1864 Red River Campaign, the third largest in 1864 after Grant's move on Richmond and Sherman's on Atlanta, and the only major Federal offensive of the critical year of 1864 that Lincoln lost. The grand campaign was General Banks's last attempt at glory, to reclaim his name, and entailed marching and sailing an army and a navy up the Red River to the Confederate capital of Louisiana, Shreveport. Another army, ten thousand strong and under the command of Frederick Steele, marched south from Little Rock to attack Shreveport.

The campaign had been largely forgotten until the War's centennial, and only recently has it grabbed the attention of historians and preservationists due to its strategic significance. The campaign's climax occurred at the Battle of Mansfield, today a Louisiana State Historic Site. On my journey, many of the Civil War enthusiasts I met told me that, in recent years, they'd come down to discover the campaign.

I've often wondered why the Feds wanted the yellow-fever infested swamp where anybody of any means fled during the temperate months. Actually, it wasn't Louisiana Lincoln wanted, but Texas. More than 150 years later, Louisiana's roads are still crammed full, mostly with people heading to and from Texas.

For me, this campaign had a special meaning and accentuated why all this is so important. I went looking for my own ancestors and found them. In my aid, my little sister, Karen, has spent the recent years tracking down our forefathers and mothers in great detail. She's into that and had already located all my kin who were around during the War. I just had to find out which ones fought.

Earlier, I mentioned to the reader that I'm four generations pure Southern. That may have been an understatement. Fifteen of my sixteen third grandparents were born in the South, and all sixteen are buried in Louisiana or Arkansas. Of my thirty-two third great-grandparents, twenty-nine of the thirty known resting places are in the South, all but seven buried in Louisiana or Arkansas. We Denmons could probably use the injection of some outside blood!

I was here, or we were here, and suffered through the War's hardships. Of my thirty-two third great-grandparents, six died during the War years . . . that's just under 20 percent!

I found four third or fourth grandfathers with documented Civil War records. All four fought in the Red River Campaign, three for the South and one for the North. Holly molly, looks like I may not be pure Confederate after all! None of these four signed up early in the War, but all enlisted between 1863 and 1864 with local units, and then, only after the Yanks started to move into north Louisiana. Like many Confederate veterans of the War, not interested in running off to fight in some faraway place for rich farmers, "they would fight to protect their homes and families." These men didn't hail from the gentry. They all enlisted as privates.

In the spring of 1864, General Banks put his plan in motion. He had twenty-six thousand of his own troops and was augmented with another ten thousand veterans from Sherman's army. In support, more than a hundred Navy boats and ships sailed upriver under the command of our old friend, David Dixon Porter. All forces were to rendezvous in Alexandria, Louisiana, and then they'd move up the river, the troops marching and the Navy escorting them along the way.

The Navy and Sherman's hearty veterans, under Gen. A. J. Smith, who chased Price across Missouri and made the best showing against Forrest at Tupelo, moved out from Vicksburg down the Mississippi and then up the Red to Alexandria. It's here that Smith's troops had their initial fight, at a small fort on the Red River, DeRussy, occupied by a couple of hundred Confederates and several big guns that commanded the Red River.

One of my third great-grandfathers, William Spencer, happened to be one of the unfortunate and outnumbered Rebs at DeRussy. William had already been captured and paroled once. William is my only direct ancestor to perish in the War as a result of combat. Luckily, he bore my second great-grandfather, Joseph Spencer, in 1861. William's story became a mystery for me. He's on the Federal prisoners-of-war rolls as captured at Fort DeRussy, March 14, 1864, but then he was admitted to a Confederate hospital in Shreveport on July 24, and died the next day. How did he go from Union hands to a Confederate hospital almost two hundred miles away in three and a half months? How did he die?

There wasn't much of a fight at DeRussy, General Mower, whom we met at both Corinth and Bentonville, surprised the fort, surrounding it with a large part of Smith's army. The Federals suffered about fifty casualties, the Rebs about ten, but 317 Confederates were taken prisoners, including William.

I took off for Fort DeRussy, today the Fort DeRussy State Historic Site, just outside of the town of Marksville. There, I met Steven Mayeux, the president of the nonprofit, Friends of Fort DeRussy. Steven wrote a book on the Fort, *Earthen Walls, Iron Men.*

I quickly determined Steven and I would hit it off. As he got in my Ford Escape, he said, "I forgot my pistol. You don't mind?"

"Hell no," I said, as he got a pistol out of his truck and put the holster on his hip. "I believe in shooting back."

Were we headed into the wild west? Of course not. It was a terrific, Southern day, everybody friendly, but we did bump into one snake.

Maybe Steven had some hints about William's fate? He had the Federal prisoners-of-war rolls from Fort DeRussy. Sure enough, there was William Spencer. Steven had followed William's record until he was admitted to the St. Louis Hospital in New Orleans forty days later.

"William likely died of disease," Steven said. "The captured boys were exchanged and put on a steamer on July 21. He died three days later. To be that sick, and still make that journey, he wanted to get home bad."

Later, I read the chapter in Steven's book about hospital life in New Orleans. Conditions were deplorable, infested with typhoid, pneumonia, diarrhea, and smallpox. One prisoner stated, "Three and four die every day."

We drove out to Fort DeRussy, its exact location and earthworks only confirmed and surveyed in the 1970s. The local historical society bought the first eighty acres in 1999 and then transferred the property to the state, which then established the historic site. There's a sign, but that's about it. The state appropriated some money to develop the site in 2005, but then Katrina hit, sucking it away like it did a lot of the state itself.

"We get the local prisoners to mow the grass," Steven said, as we went through the mandatory dosing of insect repellent before walking onto the site.

As we toured the site, Steven pointed to some recent holes dug in the ground.

I looked down at the fresh dirt and holes.

"Treasure hunters," Steven moaned. "We've got to come up with a better plan for this until we get a permanent presence here."

Steven then showed me two interesting things onsite. One is a monument the nonprofit put up to memorialize the slaves who built the fort. "I don't think there's another one of these anywhere . . . a Confederate monument to slaves. And it's got the individual names of the slaves."

"How did you get those?"

Steve Mayeux, Friends of Fort DeRussy, at the Fort DeRussy State Historic Site

"We searched the state archives. The owners were compensated for the use of their slaves."

The other site of interest is a small water hole in the fort, believed to be where the Federal forces blew up the Rebel powder magazine. The detonation went awry, killing two Yanks and injuring dozens more.

I looked over the impressive earthworks. By this time, I'd seen a lot of earthworks, but DeRussy's are as thick and tall as any I'd visited except Fort Fisher's. During the War, they were so tall that the Yanks had to stand on each other's shoulders to climb them. If you visit, don't go looking for the Red River. It's moved a mile or so from the fort in the century and a half since the War.

The biggest Yankee prize of the fight was the eight big field guns at the fort. There's one of these still in existence, a thirty-pound rifled cannon, No. 289 Columbia Foundry in Georgetown. It's at the Naval Yard in Washington, DC. The Friends of Fort DeRussy want it back, and they're not bashful about it. They've let the Navy and their congressman know their displeasure with the current situation. They've got a long list of reasons for the cannon's return on their webpage, one of which is: "Louisiana is no longer at war with the United States!"

Old Abe and the 8th Wisconsin arrived here the day after the battle. I wonder if William saw him? Two days later, with Mr. Spencer disarmed and sent off to his fate, General Smith and Old Abe headed up river to Alexandria to rendezvous with General Banks.

I too said goodbye and thanks to Steven and took off upriver following General Banks.

From Alexandria, Banks planned to consolidate all his forces and head for Shreveport. He had some obstacles. The first, many of his men, especially the sailors, spent their time robbing cotton, its price now tenfold what it had been at the start of the War. This portion of Louisiana had yet to see much fighting, and due to the blockade, the warehouses along the river were stocked full. His second problem was the terrain, extremely rough and rural, infested with mosquitoes and reptiles of every sort.

Mr. Banks's biggest hindrance was his adversary, Gen. Richard Taylor, one of the finest Confederate commanders of the War. Taylor had fought under Jackson in the east. It was he and his men who made the magnificent charge up Bower's Hill to carry the day at First Winchester. A Yale graduate, brother-in-law of Jeff Davis and son of President Zachary Taylor, the general lived in Louisiana, and so did a lot of his men, about fourteen thousand, fighting on their turf to protect their homes and families. But Taylor had another motivator. The Yanks had plundered his plantation outside of New Orleans, hanging his dead livestock in his house to rot. This, years before the Union took up its scorched-earth policy, required to bring about the War's end. The house is still there. Somehow, they've gotten rid of the stench.

Taylor and his fourteen thousand men let Porter and Banks come north to the only town of any size, Natchitoches, and its river port, Grand Ecore. On the rough terrain, Banks's column, laced with almost a thousand wagons, stretched out on twenty miles of narrow roads through the hills, swamps, and thick pines, described by one Federal soldier as a "howling wilderness." At this point, historians are still debating why possibly led by a Taylor spy, Banks moved his column away from the river and marched on north. Near Mansfield, Taylor sprung his trap.

Taylor's boys, all Louisianans and Texans, routed Banks, sending his army in a disorganized eighteen-mile retreat. At Mansfield, Louisiana has the second of its major Civil War parks. It's also here that another of my third grandfathers, G. B. Denmon, with the 28th Louisiana, called the Grays, ran into the Yankee army. G. B enlisted in Company B in my hometown of Monroe, Louisiana, on June 10, 1863.

I pulled into the Mansfield State Historic Site on a sunny, hot summer morning to meet Michael Mumaugh, one of the site's interpretive rangers. The site has over four hundred acres of the battle, but currently only preserves about forty acres. At Mansfield, Taylor selected Louisianan, Gen. Alfred Mouton, to lead the attack on the Federal center. Mouton had two brigades: the Louisianans commanded by Henry Gray, and some Texans commanded by Prince Polecat—yep, Camille Armand Jules Marie, the Prince de Polignac. In the fight, some Yanks who had surrendered shot and killed Mouton. The prince rode forward and led the now furious Rebels.

Banks, unable to get all his men into the fight because his long wagon train blocked the road, soon let the Texans sweep around both his flanks.

By nightfall, the three-hour battle ended, and Taylor captured almost 1,500 Yanks, not to include another 700 dead or wounded. The Park area encompasses the area where the Prince and Gray's Louisianans made their charge.

The museum has some neat items, a nice film, and some walking trails. I discussed the battle and G. B. with Michael for almost an hour. He told me where I could get the records for the Confederate hospital in Shreveport. I later chased this lead down. I found William Spencer in the hospital records. He died of measles.

Michael showed me a few old pictures from reunions. I looked over the rows of long-bearded men, wondering if one had my blood. I learned from Michael that the battlefield's preservation began with a local association in 1907. In 1919, six years after his death, the prince's wife came to Mansfield from France. Appalled that there was nothing left of the battlefield, she donated some money. Five years later, two monuments, one of which is dedicated to the prince and Mouton, and a one-acre tract was purchased. In 1954, the state established its first Civil War battlefield park at Mansfield.

The author at the monument to General Mouton and the Prince de Polignac, Mansfield State Historic Site

More needs to be done at Mansfield. It's lacking for signage and has over 350 acres that are currently undeveloped. The Civil War Trust has recently purchased the Allen House, a Yankee Hospital during the battle, but it's yet to be opened to the public. Of course, there's a bunch of streets in Louisiana named after Taylor and Mouton. Probably almost nobody knows where the names originated.

The day after Mansfield, Taylor, still outnumbered, attacked again at Pleasant Hill in a bloody fight. Even Sherman's veterans commented that the brutality of the fight surpassed anything they'd experienced. Pleasant Hill started out as another Taylor victory, but when the Yanks finally got organized, it ended as basically a draw.

G. B. Denmon is my only Civil War ancestor whom there is still a living connection to. My grandfather died in 2000, but some of his brothers, sisters, and cousins are still around, and I rang up a few relatives. Fortunately, according to family lore, G. B. got assigned to the Rebel undertaker crew mopping up after Mansfield instead of marching on to Pleasant Hill. He survived the War, and in 1878, fathered my great-grand-father, Green Denmon. If you're wondering, the Pleasant Hill Battlefield is still around, but on private lands and undeveloped.

After the War, according to family legend, G. B., illiterate during the War, was given two hundred acres of land in Webster Parish for swearing an oath of allegiance to the United States. This is allegedly what got the Denmons going, brought them into the middle class.

Skeptical, I researched this. G. B. did acquire two tracks of about two hundred acres after the War. Though not a direct conveyance from the Federal Government, it was land owned by a deceased gentleman, administered by the local probate court. I asked a couple of local recon-struction historians about this story, generally told that after the War, "a lot of things were done that weren't written down or talked about." Maybe the two hundred acres belonged to a vanquished plantation boss? Maybe the Denmons got in bed with the carpetbagger reconstruction government.

Whatever happened, we moved into the middle class. The record is clear. G. B. went on to buy nine more tracts in later decades, and my grandfather, James Denmon, born in 1914, graduated from college.

Let's get back to General Banks. Dazed and confused after the two battles, he wondered what else lay in the hostile, harsh, empty hills and considered his options. He had another problem, a big one. Though it was the spring, Porter had been noticing for days that for some reason the Red River was dropping rapidly. His fleet made it to Mansfield, but there the Rebels had sunk a steamer blocking the river. A sign attached to the steamer invited Porter to come to Shreveport. The city was throwing a ball in his honor. The invitation humored Porter, but his angst rose with the falling river threatening to strand his fleet.

Actually, the Rebels had rerouted the river upstream, choking off its flow. They planned to catch the Navy high and dry, and destroy it! Putting everything together, Banks had seen enough. It was time to retreat and in a hurry. Porter had two hundred river miles to cover to get back to Alexandria. As Banks fell back, most of Taylor's men were pulled from his command to stop another prong of the Red River Campaign, Federal general Frederick Steele's march on Shreveport from Little Rock. In case you're interested, this didn't pan out any better than Banks's foray.

Banks's retreat wasn't gentlemanly. His men, especially Sherman's boys, left a charred trail, burning and looting, leaving nothing in their wake. To give you some sense, here are the words of Elias Pellet of the 114th New York. "Destruction and desolation followed on the trail of the retreating column. At night, the burning buildings mark our pathway. As far as the eye can reach, we see in front new fires breaking out, and in the rear the dying embers tell the tale of war. Hardly a building is left unharmed. . . . The wanton and useless destruction of property has well-earned A. J. Smith's command a lasting disgrace."

I drove on down the river, following Banks and Porter, Taylor chasing the thirty thousand Bluecoats with only five thousand men. The Rebs had their eye on Porter's Navy, especially if it got stuck in the mud. And they almost bagged Porter. Twenty miles south of Natchitoches at the confluence of the Red and Cane Rivers, I found another of my third great-grandfathers, James Palmore, and the 3rd Battery, Louisiana Light Artillery (Benton's Battery), also organized in Monroe, La. They had been in reserve at Mansfield and Pleasant Hill, but now they posted their battery, along with three thousand other Confederates, on a high bluff along the river, Deloges Bluff.

A Rebel mine had already disabled one of Porter's gunboats, the *Eastport*, which blocked passage down the river. The Navy tried to salvage it but eventually settled for just getting it out of their way. As the Yankee flotilla passed the bluff, the Rebel artillery and sharpshooters went to work. Rebel artillery struck Porter's boat, the *Cricket*, thirty times, killing the vessel's gun crews. Disabled, the *Cricket* ran aground. The Rebs probably could have sunk the boat and got Porter, but they thought they had already killed the admiral and turned their attention to the other tinclads.

Porter rallied some of the freed slaves the flotilla had collected to man the guns and hold on until nightfall, where they could then limp on down the river. Porter, not afraid to blow his own horn, confessed, "the passage from Grand Ecore down could not be called a success," and stated the battle was "the heaviest fire I ever witnessed." The Navy escaped by the skin of its teeth, but not without the loss of eight boats, and a couple of hundred men.

James survived Deloges Bluff and went on to fight in several more skirmishes. He lived through the War, rearing my second great-grandmother, Julia Palmore, in 1868.

Porter finally made it to Alexandria, but here, one of the strangest events of the War transpired. The water still falling, Porter got really nervous. The river had fallen so much that a limestone outcropping in Alexandria blocked his boats. The Rebs had him trapped, and he came to grips with the situation. The Navy, its material value $2 million in 1864, might not get out. Here, Illinois officer and engineer, Lt. Col. Joseph Bailey, stepped in to save the day. He proposed building a dam to raise the water enough to run the shallow chute. Banks and Porter thought the idea crazy, but out of options, they let him get to work.

It took three thousand men and a thousand horses and mules and three weeks to build the dam, and after several failures and the building of some secondary dams, the boats, forced to leave their stolen cotton and cannons, managed to slip out, running the man-made rapids. May 13 was one of the darkest days in Louisiana history. As Banks retreated, his troops burned 90 percent of Alexandria. The city survived, due largely to the number of US military bases later established around the town (maybe this was supposed to be some sort of restitution). Today, there's more than 150,000 people in the Alexandria metropolitan area.

I made one final stop on the campaign's exploration. I drove back down to Alexandria. Across the river, at the spot of Bailey's Dam, there's a new state historic site dedicated to the Red River Campaign at Forts Randolph and Buhlow, two old Civil War forts that surrendered without a fight, opened in 2010. Bailey's Dam was still visible until the 1990s when the US Army Corps of Engineers built a set of locks on the river that raised the pool stage. The NPS did an excellent survey of the dam in 1984 prior to its inundation, including some great pictures. It's amazing how much of the dam survived more than a hundred years of raging waters. The site has a viewing stand over the site of the dam, but there's nothing to see but water. But I'll say, without the locks, seeing the old dam would have been one of the coolest things on my journey.

I walked over to the new museum dedicated to the Red River Campaign. It has all kinds of pictures, sketches, and old headlines of Alexandria and the dam during David Dixon Porter's drama and near doom . . . it must have been a massive news story. The museum has a model of the dam, and also a cotton bale with the letters C.S.A. and U.S.N. painted on it. A plaque tells the great story of the bale and the letters. During the campaign, the Navy thieves would paint the letters C.S.A. on the bales, thus allowing them to confiscate the loot, and then paint U.S.N., short for United States Navy. At the time, North, South, the press, everybody joked that C.S.A. U.S.N. stood for Cotton Steeling Association of the United States Navy.!

Getting a chuckle, I looked over some of Fort Randolph's maps on the wall. As Banks fled further south, Taylor wanted to make one last go of destroying Banks's army. Fifty miles southeast of Alexandria, near the little river town of Simmesport, his army had to cross the bridgeless Atchafalaya River. As Banks tried to bridge the river, Taylor attacked along the banks of a little stream, Yellow Bayou, hoping to trap the Yanks in Louisiana.

Even these small, seemingly insignificant battles turned deadly in the blink of an eye. In an afternoon, the two armies suffered almost a thousand, killed, wounded, or missing. At Yellow Bayou, my final third great-grandfather, Mark Reed, fought, not for Taylor but for the bluecoats with the First Louisiana Cavalry Scouts, put together by Banks of Louisiana Unionists. Mark survived the battle where Banks managed to hold off the Rebs until his troops built a bridge by lashing their transport boats together. There's a small city park at Yellow Bayou with one historical sign.

Mark Reed stayed in Louisiana after the War. He bore my third grandmother, Georgia Ann Reed, a year before the War. We have to imagine life wasn't that much fun for a scallywag. Mark died in 1878 in Morehouse Parish. It's no wonder that I couldn't find his obituary. To the contrary, G. B.'s passing in 1920 was celebratory. His obituary made the front page of the paper, giving a record of his life and Civil War Service.

General Taylor went on to be a lieutenant general, his command the last major command east of the Mississippi to surrender. After the War, he split time between homes in Winchester, Virginia, and New Orleans, Louisiana, and wrote what many historians consider one of the best histories of the War, *Destruction and Reconstruction*. Porter had glory ahead of him at Fort Fisher and eventually as admiral of the Navy. Banks never fought again. His terrible record as a general undermined his dreams of the Presidency, but after the War, Massachusetts voters sent him back to Congress, where he should have stayed all along.

I walked outside and up on the forts' earthworks. Across the river, stood downtown Alexandria, a dense jungle of concrete and glass. The site and park is top-notch, funded in part by the Federal government as part of the lock and dam project. Looks like the Feds came in and spread a bunch of money around to pacify the natives for the project's impact.

From the top of the earthworks, everything around me is a function of the War: Emancipation, me, the town across the river that's all post–Civil War, even the damned-up river, the park, and I-49 in the distance are derived from the War. Lincoln, Grant, and Sherman ended the country's ninety-year debate on who called the shots. The Federal government instead of the states would be in charge.

Fort DeRussy State Historic Site
Fort Derussy Rd.
Marksville, LA 71351, USA
http://www.fortderussy.org/

Mansfield State Historic Site
5149 LA-175
Mansfield, LA 71052
(318) 872-1474
https://www.crt.state.la.us/louisiana-state-parks/historic-sites/
mansfield-state-historic-site/index

Forts Randolph & Buhlow State Historic Site
135 Riverfront St.
Pineville, LA 71360
(318) 484-2390
https://www.crt.state.la.us/louisiana-state-parks/historic-sites/forts-
randolph-buhlow-state-historic-site/index

CHAPTER 29

I Found the Trophies

The Navy Yard, Washington, DC

While I was in our nation's capital to see its Civil War sites, I decided I'd go over and see if I could find the captured cannon from Fort DeRussy. I called ahead to the Navy Yard, and it's a good thing I did. The historian I finally got in touch with told me that before he could talk to me, I had to be cleared by the Navy.

I rang up the number he gave me, talked to an officer, and was emailed several forms to be filled out before I could meet with someone at the yard. I submitted these, with my book contract (the latter required), and a few days later was emailed a time and person to meet at the Naval Yard.

Early one morning, Thomas Frezza, the director of education for the National Museum of the US Navy, met me at the Navy Yard's visitor center and took me to his office within the museum. As we walked through the yard, I asked Thomas about the DeRussy cannon.

In his office, Thomas opened a book, *The Iron Guns of Willard Park* by John Reilly, written for the Navy. Scanning the book and a map, he said, "It's just outside, across the street on the left." He then pointed out the window of his office. "Those are the guns Farragut captured off the *CSS Tennessee* in Mobile Bay."

I went out to look, first at the guns from the Tennessee. These are rare, big six- and seven-inch cannons produced at the Tredegar Iron Works in Richmond. We then walked across the street. I found the DeRussy gun! More than a century and a half ago, along a great river, in the middle of nowhere, and almost 1,500 miles from here, Americans, including William Spencer, fought in a perilous struggle and gave their lives for this piece of steel. Today it looks docile, harmless, aimed out over the Anacostia River. The cannon is marked with a stamped inscription, Trophy No. 10, with a description of where and when it was captured. Thomas and I took some great pictures, and I told him the story of how Louisiana wanted the cannon back.

"I've been told and I've heard," I told Thomas, "we're going to have to get some better politicians if we're ever going to get this gun back."

"An interesting note," Thomas said, "Lincoln spent his last day here, right here where the cannons are. He left here about 5:00 P.M., went to the White House and then Ford's Theater."

I walked the wonderful yard, the uniformed sailors walking promptly and with a purpose, looking at all the guns, sitting peacefully on the manicured green lawns and below the old, exquisite buildings. Unfortunately, very few have descriptions of where they were captured, but according to Reilly's book, many have interesting stories. I found a Fort Fisher gun. Just outside the museum sit two pieces of thick iron, pierced with cannonballs. Thomas told me these are left over from the Civil War. Adm. John Dahlgren, in charge of the yard during the War and founder of the Navy's Bureau of Ordnance, tested his cannons' effectiveness against these iron plates.

The author with a cannon captured at Fort DeRussy, Navy Yard, Washington, DC

Thomas gave me Reilly's book, but it can be bought online for a few dollars.

I then toured the museum. It's a treasure. The Civil War section has the wheel and fife rail off Farragut's flagship, the *Hartford*, and a piece of the hull from the famed Swoop-of-war, *Kearsarge*, which haunted the Confederate Navy. A Rebel cannonball is still lodged in it. Most interesting were the ship models. They've got a bunch of models, big ones, in great detail, both Confederate and Federal, the *Hartford*, *Tennessee*, and *Monitor* just to name a few. Thomas told me the Navy actually has a model-building program that ensures all the models are accurate and to scale.

The museum is huge, housed in a six-hundred-foot-long old naval gun factory. It's got almost everything from start to present, models, planes, artifacts, pictures, you name it. If this museum sat on the National Mall, it would have millions of visitors a year, and Thomas told me there is some talk of moving the museum out from behind the secure walls of the Navy Yard.

To visit the museum requires proper identification and a security check at the yard's visitor center that typically takes about fifteen minutes, but it can be as much as an hour. If you're with a group, you can call ahead and get precleared. Either way, I recommend the museum and the yard's guns to Civil War fans or anybody interested in the history of the world's greatest Navy. And maybe, like me, you've got some of your own story here.

National Museum of the United States Navy
736 Sicard St. SE
Washington, DC 20374
(202) 433-2651
https://www.history.navy.mil/content/history/museums/nmusn.html

CHAPTER 30

Let Us Have Peace

New York City, New York

The War's preservation, at least today, is largely a Southern thing. That's where most of it transpired. Above the Mason-Dixon, there's Gettysburg, Monocacy, and Antietam, some of the nation's most visited national parks, but past that, there is not much living, interpretive history of the War. New York sent more men to fight than any state, and the Big Apple sent more troops than any city. To my knowledge, neither has a museum dedicated to the Civil War.

Pennsylvania sent the second most troops. They have a museum, the National Civil War Museum in Harrisburg, but it only opened in 2004. The Sons of Union Veterans of the Civil War call the museum home. The Civil War Museum of Philadelphia was the oldest Civil War museum in America, but it closed in 2008 and transferred most of its collection to Gettysburg.

But once upon a time, New York City was the largest Civil War museum in the world. Not that it had a collection of forts, battlefields, or museums, the city itself was, and is, a memorial to the War, the home to more monuments and notable tombstones than anywhere in the world. Until World War I, Grant's Tomb was the biggest tourist attraction in the city, even surpassing the Statue of Liberty, and people, by the tens of thousands, flocked to New York to see its Civil War sites.

Those monuments and memorials are still there, hidden between the lines of honking cabs and skyscrapers. The nation that the men the monuments honor grew into something much more imposing. Dozens of statues, circles, and monuments to Civil War generals and politicians dot the city, but there are a half-dozen sites that are of significance to the nation, and I took off one day to discover them.

New York City is the polar opposite of the South. I like New York. People are to the point. Hopping in a cab, I said to the driver, "Take me to Cooper Union. Straight down Broadway. No tourist side tour."

"Hey, no problem," the cab driver said, storming off into the traffic.

In the South, a statement so blunt and direct would be considered an insult, likely resulting in drawn-out drama, moaning, apologies, and maybe even the utterer asked to excuse himself from the cab, all in a process that may take longer than the cab ride!

The Cooper Union Great Hall, downtown, around East Village, was the Madison Square Garden of its day, and it was here that Abraham Lincoln, just a country lawyer from Illinois, gave his biggest speech when running for president in 1860, clarifying his views on Federalism and slavery. Lincoln later confided that this speech, covered and praised by the national press, got him elected. Seven other presidents have spoken here. I guess, even then, "if you made it in New York, you could make it anywhere."

The Great Hall is still there and functioning. I don't know if they give tours. I just walked in and asked the security guard if I could take a look around. The venerable walls feel important. On a snowy night on February 20, 1860, Lincoln stood on the wood stage and faced a packed house of 1,500. This speech started the political levers that led to the secession ten months later. Artifacts and interpretive signs line the walls outside the hall, telling its story of over 150 years.

From Cooper Union, I hiked seven blocks up 4th Avenue to Union Square, itself the site of several momentous Civil War events, not the least of which occurred on April 20, 1861. The Great Sumter Rally hosted as many as 250,000 people, the largest public gathering in America at the time, in support of Lincoln's initial call for seventy-five thousand troops to beat the Southern rascals back into line. The rally hosted Maj. Robert Anderson, the commander of Fort Sumter, and Sumter's flag hung over the large statue of George Washington in the square.

I have my own funny story about how New York's monuments have fallen by the collective wayside in the City. I have a friend who lives right around the corner from the square and has lived there for decades.

Meeting him for lunch one day, I suggested by phone we meet under George Washington in the square.

"Where?" he asked.

"Under the statue of George Washington in Union Square," I said plainly and slowly. Was my Southern accent too much for him?

"There's a statue of George Washington in Union Square?"

I won't throw the gentleman under the bus by giving you his name, but hopefully, you get the point.

What I didn't know until recently was that on the other end of Union Square sits the first outdoor statue of Abraham Lincoln, dedicated in 1870. In my defense, I might note that I *do* live 1,300 miles from here. I walked over to view Honest Abe.

I strolled on, up Broadway, six more blocks, a lively walk through the melting pot of the world, to wonderful Madison Square Park. Here, on a block of black granite, I found a statue of Adm. David Farragut. He's been standing here since 1881, perched on the bow of his flagship, *Hartford*, standing against the wind as he leads his fleet into Mobile Bay. The admiral also has a grand statue and entire square in DC dedicated one month before New Yorkers stood him up here for eternity.

Up 5th Avenue, at the southeast corner of Central Park, stands a memorial to William Tecumseh Sherman in the Grand Army Plaza. New Yorkers hired famed sculptor Augustus Saint-Gaudens to craft the monument, dedicated on May 30, 1903. The twenty-four-foot-high equestrian monument is impressive, coated in shiny gold. In fact, it has been recently recoated at an extremely high cost, but based on some media stories I read, some of the gold is mysteriously shedding. I read an article from 2014 where the experts were still trying to sort it out. I tried to give it my own personal inspection, but Uncle Billy sits too high off the ground to get a good look, at least with my old eyes.

The statue is supposed to be the most lifelike rendition of the general anywhere. He sat through eighteen different sessions for Saint-Gaudens to form the bust. I bet Sherman loved that! Saint-Gaudens took ten years to complete the work. There's another major statue of Sherman in DC, finished five months after the New York statue. Maybe there was some kind of race to finish these, but unlike Farragut, New York won this race. Due to this statue's location, I'd have to guess that it's the most photographed memorial to the War anywhere. Every time I pass it, dozens of people are gathered around Billy, gawking and taking pictures, and not just Civil War buffs, but tourists from everywhere in the world.

I took another cab up to Riverside Park, on the Hudson River in the Upper West Side, to the Soldiers' and Sailors' Monument dedicated in 1902 by the State of New York as a tribute to the Union Army during the American Civil War. It's a massive monument, a marble and granite conical structure, sixty feet wide, ninety-five feet tall, and cased with twelve columns that dominates the park. Teddy Roosevelt officiated the opening. The monument contains only one inscription: "To the memory of the brave soldiers and sailors who saved the Union."

Unfortunately, it's been decaying for decades, covered with painted-over graffiti and surrounded by crumbled steps and sidewalks. A fifty-foot-high rotunda of carved and ornamented marble sits behind the large vandalized bronze door, but due to the dangers of falling mortar or stone, it's closed to the public. The day I went, I only found one homeless person loitering on the monument, but the graffiti is everywhere. The city has been trying to raise or appropriate money for the monument's rehabilitation for the last ten years, but based on some news stories I read, it doesn't seem to be a priority.

The landscape north of the Mason–Dixon is dotted with these massive soldiers' and sailor's monuments or other regimental or state memorials. The Grand Army of the Republic, the forbearer to the Sons of Union Veterans of the Civil War, spent decades promoting and raising money for these. They're everywhere. Brooklyn has a huge arch at Prospect Park. It's eye-opening in its scale, the traffic weaving around it. A simple Internet search revealed more than a dozen more gargantuan soldiers' and sailor's monuments in northern cities, including one almost thirty stories tall in the center of Indianapolis. I hope the other cities have done more to preserve their monuments than New York. The War in the North, once so celebrated, looks like it's fallen to the back-burner of what's important in the twenty-first century.

We don't have these big memorials down south. We've got monuments, but nothing so grand that streets had to be relocated for their construction.

Soldiers' and Sailors' Monument, New York City

Of course, the decades after the War weren't triumphant, more a struggle to survive. I made a note to see these other monuments the next time I'm in these northern cities.

I made my last hike into the Civil War, not over southern hills or through haunted breastworks, but thirty-eight more blocks up Riverside Park, exactly 1.8 miles, to the War's symbolic terminus, the mammoth tomb of General Grant, 35,000 square feet and 150 feet tall. It's a nice hike, kids, parents, and senior citizens of all origins enjoying the green space. I just appreciated that insect repellent wasn't required, and I wouldn't have to later check for ticks. The entire hike from the War's beginning, Cooper Union, to here is about eight miles.

The sheer size of Mr. Grant's tomb overwhelmed me. I had read it was the largest tomb in the United States. It resembles a smaller version of the Lincoln Memorial. Of course, if not for Grant, there would be no Lincoln Memorial.

More than one and a half million people, the largest assembly at the time in America, attended Grant's funeral in a seven-mile-long parade through New York in 1885. Sherman, Sheridan, and Admiral Porter, along with Confederate generals Johnston and Buckner were pallbearers. Grant wasn't born in New York, but he lived and died here after the War.

Grant's Tomb, New York City

There are plenty of pictures around of Grant's funeral, the miles-long lines of ex-soldiers and citizens stretch farther than the camera's lens can see.

The tomb around Grant and his wife, Julia, was funded privately and constructed twelve years after his death. More than a million people attended the dedication. Grant's final burial site became a matter of debate, many suggesting Washington, DC, or other places more applicable with his service to the country. During the fundraising, an Indiana newspaper wrote: "We have not a cent for New York in the undertaking, and would advise that not a dollar of help be sent to the millionaire city from Indiana."

Imagine, the heartland and New York City at odds!

In 1958, the NPS took over the tomb. Sadly, by the 1990s, the tomb had fallen into disrepair, its steps and crevices playing host to drug dealers, the city's homeless, and graffiti artists. Local interest lobbied Congress, and hence, money was appropriated to restore the tomb, and the NPS's annual operating budget was tripled. By my inspection, my tax dollars were put to good use.

I toured the tomb on the 132nd anniversary of Grant's death. For this occasion, the Grant Monument Association that raised the money for the tomb and is still in existence laid a wreath at the tomb. I'd say about thirty

Wreath-laying ceremony at the 132nd anniversary of General Grant's death, Grant's Tomb, New York City

people attended the wreath laying. I visited with the association's president, Frank Scaturro, who led the efforts for the tomb's restoration while volunteering at the tomb during his days at Columbia University across the street. I could write an entire chapter on Frank and the association's long and courageous fight to save the monument.

Frank gave a tour before the wreath laying. The visitors center also has a great movie about the general.

As I left, I paused on the tomb's steps. There are dozens of postcards and pictures of the tomb in 1897. Then, the Hudson River, a few carriages, and a dozen or so nice homes surrounded the park. Today, it's utter madness, glass and steel reaching for the sky on both banks of the river, the roads and sidewalks full of cars and people, all enjoying the fruits of the world's most prosperous land.

The greenery of the park and columns of stone portray a serene, solemn atmosphere. All in complete contrast to Grant's service, clad in dirty, unkempt uniforms, facing death and ordering the waste of America's youth in faraway places that have become known to the world, Shiloh, Vicksburg, Chattanooga, and Petersburg.

Above the entry, engraved in stone, are four of Grant's most famous words: "Let us have Peace."

It was time for me to "strike the tent," go home, back to the little, slow-moving Southern towns where it all happened. Who knows where the story of the War is going. Even as I finished this book, more controversies and even violence erupted around its memorials, first in Charlottesville, and then it seemed like somewhere else daily. The War, or at least the Southern part of it, has gotten controversial in some quarters, but it happened. That can't be changed. It's part of us, whether we like it or not.

My journey of discovery, for now, was over, every bit of it a pleasure. It could have gone on and on and on, the interesting, lesser-known places everywhere, seemingly lost in time and place. There were a half dozen other places that my grandfathers fought that I didn't explore, and everywhere I went, somebody suggested some spot down the road where something big, and significant, occurred during the War.

With time, landscapes change, people forget, more wars and calamities befall us, the newest supposedly our greatest threat. America has only faced one real threat.

I quote Mr. Lincoln: "All the armies of Europe and Asia could not by force take a drink from the Ohio River or make a track on the Blue Ridge in the trial of a thousand years. No, if destruction be our lot, we must ourselves be its author and finisher. As a nation of free men we will live forever or die by suicide."

It's the Civil War that produced the America of the twentieth and twenty-first centuries. And it's that America that changed the world. Get out and find the War. It's everywhere around you, at least in the America that was around during the War. Every bit of it is a human drama on a scale few people today experience in their entire lives, and all as important as anything in our history.

I couldn't believe how much of it is still there to see.

General Grant National Memorial
W 122nd St. & Riverside Dr.
New York, NY 10027
(212) 666-1640
https://www.nps.gov/gegr/index.htm

INDEX